Religious Education, 1960–1993

D0082088

Recent Titles in
Bibliographies and Indexes in Religious Studies

Religious Education, 1960–1993

An Annotated Bibliography

Compiled by
D. Campbell Wyckoff
and
George Brown, Jr.

Bibliographies and Indexes in Religious Studies,
Number 33
G. E. Gorman, Advisory Editor

GREENWOOD PRESS
Westport, Connecticut • London

Library of Congress Cataloging-in-Publication Data

Wyckoff, D. Campbell.
    Religious education, 1960–1993 : an annotated bibliography /
compiled by D. Campbell Wyckoff and George Brown, Jr.
        p. cm.—(Bibliographies and indexes in religious studies,
ISSN 0742–6836 ; no. 33)
    Includes indexes.
    ISBN 0–313–28453–9 (alk. paper)
    1. Christian education—Bibliography. I. Brown, George, Jr.
II. Title. III. Series.
Z7849.W94   1995
[BV1471.2]
016.268–dc20   94–24125

British Library Cataloguing in Publication Data is available.

Library of Congress Catalog Card Number: 94–24125
ISBN: 0–313–28453–9
ISSN: 0742–6836

First published in 1995

Greenwood Press, 88 Post Road West, Westport, CT 06881
An imprint of Greenwood Publishing Group, Inc.

Printed in the United States of America

The paper used in this book complies with the
Permanent Paper Standard issued by the National
Information Standards Organization (Z39.48–1984).

10 9 8 7 6 5 4 3 2 1

Contents

Foreword

Christian education may be understood as the product of the creative interpretation of historical context, an active content, a personal process of growth, an educational science and art, and a working theology. It is practical, however, as a discipline with its own life.

Wayne R. Rood, *Understanding Christian Education*

Whether, from the perspective of our various religious traditions, we prefer to speak of "Christian education" or "religious education," "religious instruction" or "catechesis," the reality is the same. That is, we are dealing with a field which is multidisciplinary in its derivation and multifaceted in its intentions. Like the secular discipline with which it maintains significant links, religious education draws upon the theory and praxis of a host of other fields, including education, theology, sociology, psychology, and history. It is, in an academic sense, a complex field of study within the social sciences. This emerges with clarity in the essay, "Religious Education, 1960-1993," that opens the present volume. Here the key words spread across theology, philosophy, and history to behavioral sciences, administration, and curriculum; and the range of cited authors is equally multidisciplinary—Tillich, Whitehead, Freire, Cremin, Piaget, Maslow, and Mead are just a handful of the more prominent among them.

If its derivation is thus catholic and multidisciplinary, in its intention religious education is at least equally wide ranging. As Westerhoff reminds us, religious education (or "catechesis" in his schema) is a bipolar enterprise, drawing on the past (Christian heritage) and also on the present (living community of faith) in order to assist believers in their quest for a meaningful relationship with Ultimate Being. "Catechesis, understood as process, is best defined as deliberate, systematic, and sustained interpersonal helping relationships of acknowledged value which aid persons and their communities to know God intimately, to live in relationship to God, and to act with God in the world."[1] To know, to live, to act—such an inclusive purpose of necessity impinges on virtually all facets of life, both personal and corporate. Religious education or catechesis, then, arises from and incorporates "...a concern for every aspect of life, the political, the social, and the economic;...involvement of the entire person in all of that person's relationships with God, self, neighbor, and the natural world."[2]

To help understand and contain this plethora of responsibilities, writers on religious education have long sought to categorize the various components of the enterprise, with varying degrees of success. Russell, for example, speaks of the context of religious education as the witnessing community, the structure of religious education as dialogue, the method of religious education as participation, and the purpose of religious education as celebration.[3] From the practitioner's standpoint such categorization assists greatly in comprehending the vast array of ideas being generated in the literature about the intentions, methods, procedures, and outcomes of religious education. At the same time, religious education is not only the provenance of the practitioner but also of the scholar, and from the scholarly perspective, religious education has a strong theoretical base characterized by a variety of paradigms. These theoretical or scholarly approaches to religious education may be described in a number of ways, one of the most accessible being that proposed by Harold Burgess, who speaks of the traditional theological theoretical approach (exemplified by the works of Gaebelein and Jungmann), the social-cultural approach (Coe, Bower, and Chave), the contemporary theological approach (Crump, Miller, Sherrill, and Smart), the social science approach (the works of James Lee and others).[4]

In these few words, we have sought to highlight some of the key features of religious education as an academic enterprise and as part of the religious life. From an academic viewpoint, religious education draws on a wide range of cognate disciplines, which gives its literature an unusual breadth. Furthermore, within itself religious education manifests a complex network of theoretical frameworks that are not easily traced through the literature. From the practitioner viewpoint religious education has one eye on the past and one on the present, drawing substantially on a particular heritage to inform and direct action in the present. This aspect of the religious life focuses on people of all ages who are trying to live out a life of faith, and to maintain this focus religious educators utilize all appropriate means.

No one would deny that education is a significant component in the religious enterprise, whatever the particular tradition might be. But at the same time many of us are somewhat unaware of the fact that this religious education has such complex disciplinary origins and such wide-ranging impact on the lives and actions of the faithful. Furthermore, the substantial corpus of literature devoted to religious education will surprise all but the most accomplished scholars and practitioners. For these combined reasons it was deemed appropriate that we commission a volume specifically on religious education in the bibliographical series. Other volumes in the series have treated specific aspects of education; for example, Paul Soukup's *Christian Communication: A Bibliographical Survey* (Greenwood Press, 1989) and Samuel Southard's *Death and Dying: A Bibliographical Survey* (Greenwood Press, 1991) cover, respectively and in part, the media as an educational tool and education about death. Until now, however, there has not been a volume that covers the theory, administration, and practice of religious education in broad terms.

To shoulder the burden of compiling and annotating such a bibliography we have been fortunate in securing the services of two scholars well known in religious education circles, Dr. George Brown, Jr. (Dean of Faculty at Western Theological Seminary in Holland, Michigan) and Dr. D. Campbell Wyckoff (Professor Emeritus in Princeton Theological Seminary), both of whom are eminently suited to the task of preparing this detailed guide to the literature on religious education published during the last three decades. George Brown has been a minister of education in the Reformed Church in America and holds higher degrees in both Christian and adult education. Although retired for more than a decade, Campbell Wyckoff remains well known as former editor of the *Bibliography in Religious Education and Related Fields*, and as the author of numerous monographs on Christian education (including *Theory and Design of Christian Education Curriculum* and *How to Evaluate Your Christian Education Program*).

Religious Education: A Bibliographical Survey accomplished two tasks. Brown and Wyckoff first present a bibliographical essay on the theory and practice of religious education, highlighting and mapping the materials listed in the annotated bibliography which follows. The essay is an introduction to the various components of religious education: theological foundations, philosophy and history of education, behavioral studies, educational theory, administration and curriculum, etc. This discussion is replete with references to items in the bibliography, thereby leading readers from general discussion to specific entries. The second section of the work, in seven main sections, cites and annotates 1169 items which the authors believe represent the most important literature on the subject.

In this bibliographical study, Brown and Wyckoff present a record of the scholarship on religious education and offer a summary of the key literature as an aid to further study. In both regards the authors have more than met our expectations, providing a volume that offers at once a clear overview of the field and a detailed guide to appropriate published resources. In doing so they provide scholars and practitioners in education and religious education with a valuable compendium that will serve as a major resource for some time. Beyond doubt the themes and issues recorded here will continue to evolve in the coming years, and this volume will be a bibliographical benchmark in this evolution. Therefore, we are pleased to include this publication in Bibliographies and Indexes in Religious Studies as part of a continuing contribution to the bibliographical study of religious education, and we commend it as another substantial addition to the series.

The Rev. Dr. G. E. Gorman
Advisory Editor
Charles Sturt University - Riverina
June, 1994

[1] John H. Westerhoff III, "A Catechetical Way of Doing Theology," in *Religious Education and Theology* edited by Norma H. Thompson (Birmingham, AL: Religious Education Press, 1982).

[2] Westerhoff, pp. 220-221.

[3] Letty M. Russell, *Christian Education as Mission* (Philadelphia: Westminster Press, 1967).

[4] Harold Burgess, *An Invitation to Religious Education* (Birmingham, AL: Religious Education Press, 1975).

Preface and Acknowledgments

The compiling of this book actually began more than thirty years ago, in 1960, when D. Campbell Wyckoff began to provide theological libraries and religious education professionals with an annual religious education bibliography. These annotations provided librarians, professors, and other religious education professionals with a brief description of significant works in the field. The bibliography was a resource that helped librarians make informed choices about selections, assisted professors of religious education in keeping abreast of the growing body of literature in their field, and alerted professionals to new titles for the practice of ministry.

More recently, George Brown continued this work through a review of new books in the field of Christian religious education. These were circulated informally through *Readings* among religious education professionals and students within the Reformed Church in America and other Protestant denominations.

The present volume is a combined effort to provide a more permanent and workable resource for our colleagues in religious education. It consists of a selection of annotations from that previous work, reviewed and in many cases rewritten, plus annotations of a number of additional books, as well as articles in scholarly journals. While our bibliographical work has always aimed to be interfaith and international, a special effort has been made to expand the coverage in these areas. Dennis Williams, of Denver Seminary, and Clifford Payne, of the World Council of Churches, helped us in this effort.

While the book's arrangement is straightforward and self-explanatory, one note on using it is perhaps in order. It seemed to us most helpful to key the indexes of names and of titles to the annotation numbers, while the subject index is keyed to page numbers in the opening chapter. Readers looking for particular topics of interest can thus move more surely and, we hope, more efficiently to the most helpful titles.

We are grateful to those who have proposed books and articles to be included: Jerome W. Berryman, Christ Church Cathedral, Houston, Texas; Doris A. Borchert, Southern Baptist Theological Seminary, Louisville, Kentucky; Joy Bunyi, Asian Theological Seminary, Manila, Philippines; Eleanor Daniel, Cincinnati Bible College and Seminary, Cincinnati, Ohio; Charles R. Foster, Candler School of Theology, Atlanta, Georgia; Denham Grierson, Victorian Council of Christian Education, Caulfield, Victoria, Australia; Ron Habermas, Columbia Biblical Seminary, Columbia, South Carolina; Klaus Issler, Talbot School of Theology, La Mirada, California; William B. Kennedy, Union Theological Seminary, New York, New York; Ian Knox, Catholic Office of Religious Education, Toronto, Ontario, Canada; Mark A. Lamport, Gordon College, Wenham, Massachussetts; Randolph Crump Miller, Yale University, New Haven, Connecticut;

Gabriel Moran, Program in Religious Education, New York University, New York, New York; C. Ellis Nelson, Austin Presbyterian Theological Seminary, Austin, Texas; David Ng, San Francisco Theological Seminary, San Anselmo, California; Sharon Daloz Parks, Harvard University; Marv Roloff, Augsburg Fortress Publishers, Minneapolis, Minnesota; Mark H. Senter, III, Trinity Evangelical Divinity School, Deerfield, Illinois; W. Alan Smith, Florida Southern College, Lakeland, Florida; Les Steele, Seattle Pacific University, Seattle, Washington; Catherine Stonehouse, Asbury Theological Seminary, Wilmore, Kentucky; Gary Teja, CRC Publications, Grand Rapids, Michigan; Norma H. Thompson, Program in Religious Education, New York University, New York, New York; Suzanne C. Toton, Villanova University, Villanova, Pennsylvania; Michael Warren, St. John's University, Jamaica, New York; James C. Wilhoit, Wheaton College, Wheaton, Illinois; Barbara A. Wilkerson, Alliance Theological Seminary, Nyack, New York. In several cases they not only suggested items to be included but also provided the annotations. Gary Teja also wrote an annotation. These are acknowledged in the text and were most helpful to us in covering the field as broadly as possible.

The Rev. Dr. G.E. Gorman, of Charles Sturt University in Australia, the advisory editor of this series, first suggested this project to us. His careful scrutiny of our proposals has helped us expand their effectiveness and avoid a number of pitfalls.

Funding has been provided by the Lilly Endowment, Inc., whose vice-president for religion, Craig Dykstra, has maintained a keen interest in the progress of the project.

Western Theological Seminary provided a home for our work and technical assistance with research and preparation of the manuscript. We're grateful for the generous support of this community and its president, Marvin D. Hoff.

Special thanks are due Laurie Zwemer Baron, our editorial assistant, who saw the project through with great patience and skill.

D. Campbell Wyckoff and George Brown, Jr.

Religious Education,
1960–1993

Introduction

Religious education as a self-conscious discipline is a fairly recent development. Basic religious beliefs, values, and practices are passed from generation to generation in a fairly instinctual way. But this process is challenged in societies where different religions exist side by side, where individualism is valued over social conformity, and where the validity of religion itself is challenged by various political and scientific ideologies.

Under such conditions, those who are interested in religious education seek more sophisticated ways of accomplishing their ends and explaining and defending what they are trying to do. They discover a need for fundamental methodologies for understanding the tasks involved in teaching and learning and for determining and evaluating effective plans, processes, and strategies.

Developing a fundamental methodology is not a simple matter of choosing among existing options. It is rather a matter of sorting out the problems and questions involved in doing religious education, determining the sources of insight and guidance for solving the problems and answering the questions, and using those sources productively to develop a comprehensive set of principles—a theory—for the guidance of practice.

The way this volume is organized represents such a methodology. Materials related primarily to practice are gathered under the categories of "Administration of Religious Education" and "Program, Curriculum, and Method." Those related primarily to the sources of insight and guidance are gathered under the various foundations of religious education. Those related primarily to principles are gathered under the category of "Religious Education Theory" and, since religious education and education itself are so closely related, under the category of "Educational Theory." There is also a significant literature concerning two special settings where the relation of religion and education is under discussion—the school, both public and private, and higher education. A number of reference books span the categories.

Problems and questions are identified as education and religious education conduct their business. These questions are addressed to the "Foundations of Religious Education," those disciplines upon which religious education depends for guidance. The principles of religious education, the theory of religious education, emerge to be tested for their comprehensiveness and effectiveness again in practice. Thus, the discipline of religious education keeps developing and refining itself.

In the writings themselves, the categories are seldom as clear as this plan would seem to imply. For instance, youth work spans most of the categories. Where, then, should a particular book or article be placed? We have had to decide the main thrust of each and place it accordingly, not limiting the treatment of a particular category in the essay to the books and articles that appear under that category in the annotations.

Recent Religious Education: A Critical Survey

"Religious education," in the context of this essay and bibliography, requires a broad definition. When it is broadly defined, those of us who come at it from particular sectarian positions are enabled to adapt the definition to our particular purposes, and at the same time to identify the common ground that we have with other faiths.

There is a level of education at which we teach people how to do things, the level of technical education. There is a level at which we help people engage in critical inquiry and in the discovery and testing of values against the richest possible historical, cultural, and experimental background, the level of liberal and scientific education. Then there is a level of education at which views and appreciations of what is highest, best, and most valuable are brought to permeate thought and feeling and to guide and motivate human behavior, the level of religious education, a level of education involving deep and abiding commitments. That is religious education's common ground.

Many of the works in the bibliography have a Christian orientation. Christian education as a discipline is an inquiry into teaching and learning as modes and means of response to "God's self-disclosure and seeking love in Jesus Christ." Such a definition of the discipline of Christian education reveals it as a specific way of doing religious education, which as a discipline is an inquiry into teaching and learning as means and modes of commitment to value. Christian education is religious education guided by a particular set of assumptions as to truth and value.

The literature of religious education in the period between 1960 and 1993 is difficult to interpret and assess without taking several factors into consideration. First, religious education is not just a field of inquiry. It is primarily an art to be practiced. Second, religious education was an institutional reality long before it became an academic discipline, a fact that has greatly affected its development as a discipline. The tension between its integrity as a discipline and its service to the institutions through which it is practiced has yet to be resolved. Third, unlike most academic disciplines, and in spite of the fact that many religious educators would like to think of themselves as doing independent research, it is a derivative discipline, dependent on other academic disciplines and on the institutions it serves.

Religious education as an academic discipline emerged in the early twentieth century and took on both constructive and critical roles in relation to the institutions of the Sunday school and its satellite enterprises, the parochial school, state and public schools, and colleges and universities. Where religious education was a state function, the discipline was located in universities and in special training schools. Where religious education was a church function, the discipline was located in seminaries, church colleges, and teachers colleges.

A reaction occurred when the discipline was perceived to be growing distant from the concerns and needs of the churches and when theological developments, mainly neo-orthodoxy, challenged its hegemony. A period of educational and theological change and consolidation followed. In Protestant circles the consolidation took the form of new curriculum developments. In Roman Catholic circles it was introduced by the "new catechetics."

The period under consideration here, 1960-1993, has been quite different. It has been a period of proliferation, of innovative thinking, and to some extent of confusion. A wide and effective ecumenism has devleoped, and that has meant that a wide and very diverse set of assumptions and interests have had to be taken into account. Theological consensus has evaporated. The institutions of religious education, while still strong and effective, have felt themselves to be on the defensive. Professional training has grown markedly, as has the self-consciousness, the self-identity, and the status of the profession in the churches. The academic discipline of religious education has lapsed into a forum-like posture. All this is clearly reflected in the literature we are about to analyze.

Under such conditions it is very difficult to discern lines of development in the discipline. Contemporary religious educators are not often in conversation with one another about religious education itself. They are more likely to be in conversation about various theologies, scientific aspects of learning, pastoral concerns, or emergent social concerns. Rarely is there convergence on the specific educational implications of these matters resulting in general agreement as to their practical applications.

FOUNDATIONS OF RELIGIOUS EDUCATION

The foundations of religious education consist of those disciplines to which the problems and questions of religious education may productively be addressed. At one time the term meant a standard body of information derived from the disciplines and supporting a particular ideology of education. That definition no longer holds. Each foundation discipline is now treated with integrity. Differences in research results and differences in interpretation are recognized and honored. Inevitably, differences of opinion emerge among religious educators as they seek to understand and use these disciplines.

"Theological Foundations" and "Philosophy of Education," each with its own structures, deal with basic issues of life and belief. "History of Education" helps establish the universal concerns of religion and education, to sharpen developing educational issues, and to prevent tackling problems already solved. Questions like those of the processes of religious learning and faith development are put to "Behavioral Studies of Religion," chiefly those of the psychology and sociology of religion and education, but also to disciplines like social psychology and anthropology. In recent years many scholars doing research in religion and education have found it valuable to address their questions to several disciplines at the same time. Thus the category "Multidisciplinary Foundations" has been established.

Theological Foundations

At the beginning of the period under consideration, biblical theology, developed by followers of Karl Barth, was at its most influential in religious education (58, 66, 72, 703). There is still a lively interest in dealing with its themes (145), and there are echoes of its influence in more conservative circles (157).

A by-product of this era has been an interest in New Testament views of education (13, 259), Jesus' educational views and methods (95, 107, 125, 131), and Paul's views of the teaching church (6). The social relevance of biblical insights in religious education has also been explored (19, 41).

In Roman Catholic circles the interest in biblical theology (or "salvation history") gave rise to the "new catechetics" (kerygmatic catechetics), which placed chief emphasis on the learner's response to God's acts in history rather than on traditional dogma (57, 69, 585, 661, 687, 920). A new kind of catechism was needed (25, 62, 77, 967). Protestants joined Roman Catholics in exploring the possibilities (22, 227). This movement is now seen as a phase in the development of modern Roman Catholic education, which currently stresses nurture in the faith community (705).

Mary Boys has written a critique of these methods of biblical interpretation for religious education and has explored other options (14). Walter Brueggemann suggests canon criticism as an alternative (17, 18), while Walter Wink has built a system of biblical education on a combination of insights from sociology of knowledge and psychoanalysis (1041, 1042).

More recently, a number of theological movements have been examined for their implications for religious education:

narrative theology (5, 110, 670, 872);

liberation theology (7, 10, 116, 420, 710), with special attention to its most obvious educational outgrowth, the "base community," which combines worship and Bible study with local social action (10, 35, 870);

process theology (32, 82, 160, 678);

postliberalism (56);

evangelical renewal (38, 103, 105, 106, 517, 518);

phenomenology, which, while mainly a philosophical position and method, is a potent factor in contemporary theological thinking (81);

the "new theology," mainly a British proposal for coping with theological and cultural pluralism (61, 126).

There have also been a number of comparative studies in which various theological trends are examined in terms of their usefulness for religious education (65, 80, 118, 126).

At the same time there have been a number of studies of traditional theological themes, some going so far as to suggest that religious education thinking may be organized around a particular theme, but most mining the theme either because it is considered to have particular value for religious education, or because it has been believed to be misunderstood or neglected by religious educators. These studies involve the themes of redemption (7), justification by faith (50), the Holy Spirit (51, 135), eschatology (70), kerygma (88) and other biblical themes (76), transcendence (68), ecumenics (75, 84, 679), ethics (46, 47, 79, 132, 483) the creeds (78, 121), and the sacraments (3, 12, 16, 93, 100). In this last category, particular studies have appeared on religious education in relation to baptism (3, 15, 26, 36, 93), confirmation (9, 93, 491, 497), the Eucharist (93), the Rite for the Initiation of Adults (12), and reconciliation (100).

In this same connection, a German symposium has examined religious education in relation to a broader spectrum of belief systems—Christian, Jewish, and Marxist (8).

While it has been difficult to find studies of religious education in the world's various faiths, a study of Baha'i religious education has been included (109).

A number of theologians have addressed themselves specifically to education and religious education, and the thought of others has been analyzed by scholars for its implications in this field. During the years under consideration, important studies have appeared on John Calvin (31, 89), Søren Kierkegaard (168, 507), and Horace Bushnell (1, 20, 123, 124, 580, 704). Among recent and contemporary theologians there are Martin Buber (580), Nels Ferré (32), Abraham Heschel (580, 668), Bernard Lonergan (4, 129), Thomas Merton (614), Carl Michalson (133), Jürgen Moltmann (111), Richard Niebuhr, on whom James Fowler wrote his doctoral dissertation (34), Edith Stein (102), and Paul Tillich (73).

Theological approaches to the understanding of faith experience have enriched the literature upon which religious education may draw (28, 37, 48, 114, 128). J.S.K. Reid has developed a biblical theology of personality (101). Sharon Daloz Parks has examined the metaphors of pilgrimage and journey as characteristic of the Christian life and pleads for the restoration of such metaphors as home, homesteading, dwelling, and abiding (94). Of particular significance is Thomas Oden's study of the centrality of the experience of awareness (91).

Neill Q. Hamilton has, from a theologian's point of view, suggested an alternative to Fowler's way of looking at faith development (42). William L. Hendricks (54), Larry Richards (104), and Doris Blazer (877) have provided theological approaches to childhood and children's ministry. Hendricks has provided the same kind of study, focused on aging (53).

The experience of conversion is analyzed (3, 318, 341), as is personal renewal (49). Stanley Hauerwas deals with character in the Christian life (46). There have been in-depth treatments of spirituality (891), the practice of the presence of God (60), and spirituality and the religious educator (71).

In a broader treatment of the Christian life, Letty Russell has shown how theology may be reoriented to the concept of partnership (112, 113). Theologies of social action and social transformation are proposed by Dieter Hessel (55) and Allen Moore (677). Marianne Sawicki examines the impact of the "culture of consumption" on the Christian life (115).

Religious education is generally conceived as a subdiscipline of practical theology (98). There are specific analyses of schooling and religious education in this context (64, 85, 90, 111, 522). An interesting angle on the field is provided in David Duncombe's construction of a "behavioral theology" (24).

The study of the church as a functioning entity, one of whose functions is education, is a basic aspect of practical theology. Studies of the church stress renewal, including educational renewal. They also insist on treating the study of the church in a holistic way (86, 99, 108, 130, 528, 619, 636, 688, 788, 882). A promising spin-off from practical theology is an emphasis on theologies that are developed indigenously, whether in terms of local functions and needs (97) or in terms of prophetic vision (117). Evangelism and education are dealt with in the context of the church as a community of faith (43, 723), although in older treatments the emphasis tends more toward the individual (723). Theological education is beginning to be seen as a function of the congregation (29, 67, 695), with concern also for theology and curriculum (900, 1040).

The theology of ministry is also a concern of practical theology. During the years under consideration, greatest emphasis has been placed on developing the ministry of the laity, an enterprise with specific reference to education or training for lay ministry (21, 23, 33, 40, 44, 96, 261, 623). Some considerations of ministry deal with those set aside for ordained functions (2, 87, 92, 119, 122). There are special calls for mutual ministry (30) and for women in church vocations (45).

Specific educational functions are also dealt with theologically: learning (134, 724), communication (59, 63), and the use of language, myth, and symbols (39, 74, 962).

Philosophy of Education

Historically, the discipline of philosophy of education has probed questions that have linked it closely to religious concerns, especially metaphysical and axiological questions. In addition, its interest in questions of knowledge has resulted in fruitful inquiry into human nature and human learning. To be specific, philosophy of education has been especially productive in the guidance of curriculum and method, and this has spilled over into the guidance of curriculum and method in religious education.

The major philosophical options in the past have been idealism, realism, and naturalism, with religious education being most influenced by idealism and realism. Just prior to the period under consideration, existentialism entered strongly into the picture, since in its more conservative forms it clarified many of the dynamics of human experience, including religious experience. Interest in this approach to philosophy has not diminished but has been augmented by the rise of its kindred approach, phenomenology. Most recently, Marxist critique has entered the picture, but has made very little impression on religious education, except as it has appeared within the context of liberation theology.

Works in this section address aesthetics (202), axiology, epistemology, and ethics (181, 182). The books, articles, essays, and monographs reflect a broad range of philosophical schools or movements: existentialism (166), the Frankfurt School (199), British idealism (178), linguistic philosophy (163, 167, 173), Marxism (188), phenomenology (143, 144), process philosophy (141, 148), and realism (169).

Those seeking an introduction to the philosophical foundation of religious education will find several general and introductory works (156, 177, 185, 196, 200), including a textbook (164). Two books by Van Cleve Morris (one coauthored with Young Pai) offer especially helpful surveys of educational philosophy (175, 176).

Several writings in this section focus on the work of a particular philosopher. Among them are works on the Danish existentialist Søren Kierkegaard (168), Ortega y Gasset (170), Harold Rugg (142), Roman Catholic philosopher Romano Guardini (190), Georg Hegel (194), and Alfred North Whitehead (148).

Alfred North Whitehead, whose influence continues to be felt in education (141), is the subject of an introductory monograph (148) and an article that explores the implications of his thought for religious education (158), as well as a study which links Whitehead with William James in contrast both to logical positivism and to the thought of Edmund Husserl, Martin Heidegger, and Maurice Merleau-Ponty (149). Whitehead's influence on religious education can also be seen in other works, such as Mary Elizabeth Mullino Moore's examination of process theology in relation to educational method (82).

Philip H. Phenix is noted for his work in the area of curriculum. In this section, *Education and the Common Good* (183) and *Realms of Meaning* (184) relate philosophy to curriculum.

The liberation perspective reflected in the work of Brazilian educator Paulo Freire is one of the currently significant philosophical influences in religious education. Freire's influence began with the translation of *Pedagogy of the Oppressed* (152) into English in 1970 and has continued with the publication of numerous books and articles (150, 151) by him as well as through those works which have introduced or extended his thought, such as John Elias's *Conscientization and Deschooling* (541) and Ira Shor's *Empowering Education* (574).

While subjects like axiology, aesthetics, epistemology, and ethics continue to occupy the minds of those concerned with education and philosophy, *mathetics* is the term that MIT computer scientist and educational philosopher Seymour Papert (179) has advanced to help educators think about learning. He hopes that *mathetics* will do for learning what *pedagogy* has done for teaching.

Many of the works in this section apply some aspect of a particular philosopher's work, the contribution of a philosophical movement, or an arena of philosophical thought to the task of religious education. Jerome Berryman relates the insights of existentialist philosophers to religious education (139), Anton Grabner-Haider uses American and British as well as German sources in exploring the implications of linguistic analysis for religious education (153), Terry Hokenson analyzes the work of Freire and Henry Nelson Wieman in examining the contribution of process philosophy for religious education (160), Randolph Crump Miller presents the challenge of linguistic analysis for religious education (173), and Siegfried Vierzig relates ideological criticism to several theories of religious education (199).

While several writers are concerned with appropriating insights from philosophy to religious education, only one essay examines the implications of educational philosophy to a specific age group. Mary Ann Ankoviak applies the new hermeneutic to the religious education of adolescents (136).

History of Education

It is a well-known principle that when people ignore the lessons of history they condemn themselves to repeat its mistakes. Yet religious education has been characterized as a discipline without a memory. In the past there has been remarkably little interest in its history. Most of its historical studies have been superficial. Fortunately the same has not been true of the history of education itself, although religious educators have generally passed it off as not worth the trouble to master.

The more recent period has seen something of a surge in concern for the history of religious education. This has been fostered in part by a new approach on the part of historians of education, as they see education as a function of the whole community, including the church and the family, rather than limited to schooling. It has also been fostered by a new attitude on the part of religious educators in reaction to the "only innovation is valuable" approach. It is increasingly recognized that knowledge and assessment of the past may profitably guide the present, may help avoid repeating mistakes, and may prevent casting aside valuable ideas and practices.

The eighty books and articles included in this survey fall into several distinct categories. Some of the entries focus on education generally, while others have religious education as a specific focus. They can be organized into groupings according to country, religion or denomination, historical period, institution, or movement.

Australia (265), Great Britain (260), Germany (246, 267), Ethiopia (237), Indonesia (205), Ireland (204, 240), Israel (252), Kenya (277), and the United States (213, 221, 222, 223, 224, 236, 247, 250, 266) are among the countries covered by histories of education and religious education.

Adventist (241), American Baptist (275), Lutheran (207), Methodist (211, 270) and Presbyterian (219) denominations are the among the subjects of Protestant religious education histories. Roman Catholic religious education (208, 214, 215, 244, 264, 265) and Jewish religious education (229, 243) are also covered.

Among educational institutions and movements, the Sunday school (212, 220, 239, 242, 245, 248, 249, 251, 273) receives a great deal of attention. Some of that attention may be attributed to the celebration of the Sunday school movement's 200th anniversary during the latter part of this period. The Chautauqua Movement (230, 258) is the subject of two historical works in this bibliography. The history of the Presbyterian School of Christian Education (256) offers insight into the training of religious education professionals. Histories of the Society for the Propagation of the Gospel (216), the Religious Education Association (271), and the character education movement (283) are also among those works which focus on institutions and movements.

During the years covered by this bibliography, the late Lawrence A. Cremin, A.P. Barnard Professor of Education at Teachers College, Columbia University, wrote a massive three-volume history of American education (221, 222, 223). Cremin's broad understanding of education allowed him to attend to the contributions of religious thought, religious institutions, and religious leaders to American education. Significant contributions to a contextual understanding of the American Sunday school (251) have been made by Robert Wood Lynn, who served as professor of religious education at Union Theological Seminary (New York) until 1976 before becoming vice president for religion at Lilly Endowment, Inc. Lynn's interest in *paideia* is reflected in several of his writings (247, 248, 250).

Marianne Sawicki approaches the history of the teaching church (269) using cognitive development as an interpretive frame and then analyzing each major period through the ministries of Word, sacraments, and service. Like Mary Charles Bryce (214), Sawicki stands within the Roman Catholic tradition.

Several writings address methodological concerns and point in the direction of fruitful approaches for historians of education. Robert W. Lynn's and Stephen A. Schmidt's essays on the uses of history (250, 272) in relation to religious education are two examples. Jack L. Seymour underlines the value of history as a resource for policy-making (274).

Behavioral Studies of Religion

At one time there were fairly distinct behavioral sciences devoted to the study of religious phenomena, the psychology of religion and the sociology of religion in particular. Then other areas of study were carved out, derivative from disciplines that had once been segments of broader areas, or that combined distinctive aspects of the broader studies—anthropology, social psychology, ethnography, sociology of knowledge, and the like. As the angles on behavioral study of religion proliferated and combined, it became difficult to categorize particular works within segmented disciplines. Therefore, we have gathered them under the general heading, "Behavioral Studies of Religion."

A major question is how broadly religion is to be defined. There is no question about including religion as a personal experience and religion in its institutional forms, but recent treatments have been more inclusive, dealing with values and processes of valuing, for instance (290, 330, 346, 364). It has been fairly well agreed that moral development is also to be included (336).

Two works of historical interest have appeared during the period under study, biographies of Edwin Diller Starbuck, the first scholar to write in the field of the psychology of religion (291), and of G. Stanley Hall, who first distinguished the phenomenon of adolescence in a scientific way and included adolescent religion in his research (366).

Among the behavioral disciplines dealing with religion, the psychology of religion is acknowledged to be the parent, with William James's *Varieties of Religious Experience* as the prototype. There are recent and contemporary studies in this same vein (294, 317, 360, 369, 370, 382). Outstanding in the empirical investigation of religious experience has been the work of the Religious Experience Research Unit, Manchester College, Oxford (331, 363). Most such recent studies have been oriented to psychoanalytic theories (293, 305, 333, 361). Typically, areas of religion such as the following have been the subjects of research: religious conversion (318, 341), prayer (320), meditation (323), conscience (352), religious imagination (326), and ecstatic experience (325). There has been direct reference to psychological sources in books specifically intended for the religious educator (321, 362).

General sociology of religion (332) has been augmented by particular research on religious belonging (296), American piety (371), religious inculturation (354), and problems of cultural influence (384). Those working in the area of sociology of knowledge have been particularly interested in belief systems and their transmission and change, as well as the dynamics of religious groups (389, 344). Social psychological analyses are proving to be particularly fruitful (285, 286, 329).

Among behavioral scientists, more attention has been paid in recent years to human development than to most other areas of investigation. The most important names in this connection are Jean Piaget and Erik Erikson, who in turn have had a profound influence among religious educators. Erikson's work (303, 304) has been examined carefully for its religious implications (319). Piaget has been influential through Ronald Goldman and his research on stages of religious thinking in childhood and adolescence (322, 1067) and through Lawrence Kohlberg's subsequent work on stages of moral judgment (338, 339, 350, 368). Kohlberg in turn stimulated the work of James W. Fowler on faith development. Fowler's powerful work on stages of faith development (311, 312, 313, 314), in addition to its pervasive influence on American religious education (372), has been taken up in other parts of the world, particularly in Germany (355, 356), and has been subjected to careful scrutiny by other theorists (316, 621).

The work of Piaget and Kohlberg has also provoked thoughtful critique. Edward Robinson's research on the religion of childhood (363) provides an alternative to Piaget's vision. Carol Gilligan (427) presents a feminist critique of Kohlberg's work in moral development and Craig Dykstra offers an alternative view from the perspective of Christian education (620).

There have been other studies of religious development (334, 340, 390, 1169). Such studies have often concentrated on a particular age level: early childhood (337, 877), childhood (297, 298, 299, 300, 302, 345, 349, 380), youth (288, 308, 341, 365, 373, 376, 377, 381, 387, 389), handicapped youth (367), young adults (301, 357), adults (295, 307, 310, 343, 347, 374), and cross-generational studies (378). There is even a method suggested and illustrated for projecting the development of the person twenty-five years ahead (335).

Theory and research on religion and family life are represented by Edwin Friedman's work on family process in church and synagogue (315), Roy Fairchild and J.C. Wynn's investigation of Protestant families and the church (306), André Godin on the relation of parents' and children's conceptions of God (320), Armin Gram's study of a variety of religious concepts held by Lutheran parents and their children (324), Merton Strommen's determination of parents' major concerns regarding their relations with their children (379), and Antoine Vergote and Alvaro Tamayo's work on parental figures and the representation of God (383).

Psychological research has been addressed to the particular problems of religious education (388, 1153), exploring such questions as the nature of personality, learning theory, Christian approaches to learning, group processes, and the dynamics of religious maturing (328). Research has been done on youth ministry in black and white churches (351), and on the problem of resolving the cognitive conflicts between religious language and the language of contemporary experience (136).

On other problems the research has been spotty but still significant: assessment of Protestant education and the conditions for its effectiveness (287), assessment of the results of Catholic education (327) and the beliefs of Catholic young people (348), the verbal and graphic contents of the curriculum of religious education in the schools in Quebec (353), the influence of Lutheran schools on the beliefs, church loyalty, and church activities of their pupils (292), the ethos and program of a fundamentalist school (358), the experience of being a religious minority in a community where the religious majority is homogeneous and dominant (284), the religious education of handicapped persons (367, 385), and the challenge of alternative life-styles to the church (309).

Behavioral Studies of Education

At one time, religious education looked almost exclusively to educational psychology for its guidance on personality, learning, human development, and motivation. Later, with a broader grasp of the dynamics of human behavior, it expanded its field to include educational sociology. As is evident from the survey that follows, the present understanding is that none of the disciplines that deal with human behavior in any of its aspects may be ignored. This does not mean, however, that they may be adopted, used, and applied indiscriminately. The nature of religion and religious experience determines the criteria for the selection and use of behavioral findings and insights, ruling out for practical purposes those based upon deterministic and behavioristic assumptions. Other psychological positions also have to be carefully scrutinized for their underlying assumptions, and weighed accordingly.

Behavioral studies of education cover a wide range of topics. Specific age levels (adults, children, and youth), family and school, education and religious education, teachers and teaching, exceptional children, and disadvantaged minorities are among the subjects of behavioral studies. Anthropology (434, 446, 447), cognitive science (422, 425, 426), gerontology (468), educational psychology (397, 430), developmental psychology (427), social psychology (404), and personality theory (392) are among the disciplines used to study these subjects. Ethnographic (435), longitudinal (429), and intercultural behavioral studies of education (394) are to be found here as well.

John L. Elias (415) provides a useful introduction to psychology and religious education.

Anthropology guides several studies (434, 446, and 447). The influence of anthropology is to be seen in methodological concerns (402, 451) and in the study of aging (393).

Gordon W. Allport (392), Robert Coles (411), David Elkind (417), Erik H. Erikson (421), Robert M. Gagne (424), Howard Gardner (425, 426), Carol Gilligan (427), Abraham H. Maslow (444), Margaret Mead (446), and Jean Piaget (456, 457) are among those whose studies have been included in this section. Their range of interests includes personality theory, the moral life of children, the religious development of children, a psychosocial analysis of play, learning theory, cognitive science, women's development, "third force psychology," cultural evolution, and child psychology.

Adolescence has received a great deal of attention in behavioral studies of education (sixteen of the eighty-five annotations in this section). James S. Coleman (408, 409), John C. Coleman (410), Charles Glock, Robert Wuthnow, Jane Piliavin, and Metta

Spencer (428), Susan Littwin (438), Guy J. Manaster (440), Rolf E. Muuss (452), Muzafer and Carolyn W. Sherif (465, 466, 467), and Ernest A. Smith (469) are among those who have written studies of adolescence. *Growing Up in River City* (429), a longitudinal study of adolescents and young adults, and *Adolescent Coping* (449) both study midwestern adolescents. Joseph Kett's *Rites of Passage* (433) explores the concept of adolescence in America from the late eighteenth century to the 1970s. Daniel Erdman (420) proposes an action-reflection model of education for Indo-Hispanic youth of the American southwest. Middle adolescence is the focus of Robert E. Nixon's *The Art of Growing* (453).

The family also receives a good deal of attention (399, 406, 413, 431, 432, 473). The parent-child relationship is the focus of a study by Marianne Marschak (443).

By contrast, only two behavioral studies of education focus on old age. *Other Ways of Growing Old* (393) is an anthropological examination of aging in different cultures, and *Introduction to Educational Gerontology* (468) is a comprehensive collection of articles on education in the older years.

The Teaching Church (460) examines the findings of a major study of effective Christian education involving six Protestant denominations. This study, conducted by the Search Institute in Minneapolis, made use of both qualitative and quantitative research methods.

Some works in this section deal with the research methods employed in behavioral studies of education. Burt D. Braunius (402) discusses the strengths and vulnerabilities of ethnographic research for religious education, and Bill J. Mowry (451) critiques the positivistic research paradigm and suggests an alternative approach. Both authors represent the growing contribution evangelical religious educators are making to research.

Multidisciplinary Foundations

The very nature of religious education as a derivative discipline that strives for cohesion and integrity argues for multidisciplinary efforts. This section analyzes the disciplines that are lending themselves to multidisciplinary treatment, and the topics, problems, and questions that religious educators seek to address in multidisciplinary fashion.

Multidisciplinary foundations come into play when the problems religious educators are trying to solve and the questions they raise require information and guidance from several disciplinary sources. While many of the works in this category might be placed elsewhere, there are two reasons for grouping them here. First, it helps make clear the areas of investigation upon which religious education draws. Second, it indicates something of the variety of issues in religious education that can benefit from attention to more than one discipline.

The most prominent discipline represented here is, as might be expected, theology. Closer analysis reveals the aspects of theology that are called upon in religious education inquiry: systematic theology and doctrine, biblical theology, ethics, spirituality, liberation theology, feminist theology, and practical theology, where ministry, preaching, worship, pastoral care, and, of course, education are specified. In addition, scripture and biblical studies are present in the majority of cases.

One reference notes "science" as a foundation, which in the context means the physical sciences. But in all other cases science refers to the behavioral sciences, where psychology, sociology, and social psychology predominate. There are frequent references to research methodology. The approaches to psychological phenomena are cited as educational psychology, developmental psychology, depth psychology, and psychotherapy. Four aspects of educational psychology are mentioned: moral development, learning theory, personality theory, and motivation theory. Within sociology, sociology of religion and sociology of knowledge come to the fore. Cultural analysis and ethnic studies receive special mention. Social psychology seems increasingly fruitful as a source of insight, with special reference to communication theory, cybernetics, information theory, decision theory, language and psycholinguistics, and organization theory.

There is some mention of philosophy in this multidisciplinary context, along with ideology, phenomenology, and epistemology. Aesthetics is also gaining attention, with reference to affectivity, the various arts, symbolics, and sensory and motor processes. Other disciplines referred to are history, biography, anthropology, ecology, and economics.

The topics, problems, and questions that concern the religious educator fall into three major groups: the theoretical, bridges between theory and practice, and the very practical.

Theoretical concerns subjected to multidisciplinary scrutiny include a unified approach to the study of society (505), the study of religion in terms of sociology of knowledge (521), the process of human becoming (477), the person in social relationships (511), the modern identity (525), understanding personality and learning (492), and conscience as self-transcending subjectivity (483).

Theoretical questions with specific religious reference include a social-scientific theory of religion (512), a Christian psychology (503), Christian personality theory (506), religious understanding (498), moral and religious transformation (485, 513), the development of a Christian consciousness (526), Christian learning theory (484), religion and the unconscious (527), and a holistic and integrated concept of Christian education (517).

Bridges between the theoretical and the practical are concerns like these: renewing the vitality of religious education (516), Christian formation (522), spiritual development (496), moral development (482, 500), the moral and spiritual beliefs and practices of Christians (481), convictional experiences (508), creativity, conflict resolution, and Christian faith (507), and the transformation of life at the mid-century mark (478).

Multidisciplinary insight is sought on bridge questions involving religion and society: pervasive secularization vs. the universality of religious experience (493); the television culture (487, 524); personal and public faith (488); the renewal of public life (515); theology, justice, and peace (509); the communication of the Christian faith across cultures and languages (514); the church and the adolescent society (528); and cognitive development and ethnicity (523).

Insight is sought on bridge questions involving the humanities and the arts: Christian humanism in the traditional sense (489); Christian culture, literature, and the arts (490); the education of vision (502); and the emotions, play, and the arts (501).

Practical questions are also addressed to multidisciplinary sources: the character and work of the local church (524), church leadership (518), women and ministry (494), the helping professions (504), the training of counselors (479), the moral context of pastoral care (480), catechesis (524), inculturation in the Roman Catholic church (520), black church life-styles (510), the black family and the church (519), conversion (500), confirmation (491, 497), adult education (486, 487), and hindrances to adult learning (499).

EDUCATIONAL THEORY

Education is caught in the same theoretical tensions as religious education. It is an art to be practiced at the same time that it is an academic discipline. At the service of specific institutions, it strives toward independent thought. Even so, it is inevitably indebted to other disciplines from which it derives much of its most essential data. The chief task of educational theory is to resolve these tensions in ways that will maintain the integrity of educational thought and at the same time serve the best interests of its institutions. The secret is to be able to understand educational aims, processes, and institutions realistically enough to be able to bring appropriate foundational material to bear on its practice, and to assess and where necessary reenvision its institutions and practice.

Religious educators have in the past paid careful attention to developments in educational theory. The names Rousseau, Comenius, Pestalozzi, Froebel, Herbart, and Dewey appeared frequently in the discussion. This is accounted for, in part, by the fact that until recent years religious education was not only an accepted part of, but central to, the educational process in Western culture. Even Dewey was deeply concerned with religious education as he defined it.

Educational theory is still a source of guidance in the field, as indicated by religious educators' considerations of the import of various theories for their field (579, 580). This section reviews some of the major educational theories that have been attended to by religious educators, that have proven to be important and influential, or that might well prove to be important and influential.

Humanistic and affective educational theories (534, 537, 550, 557, 576) call for a socially responsible humanism (544) that at the same time fosters mature disciplines of thought and action that release the uniqueness of the self (553). Closely related are theories that seek to conserve and enhance children's natural learning styles, "learning-centered instruction," based on how the mind works when learning (548, 559). In such theories the role of the teacher is that of resource person for the learning subject (564). A step farther in this direction results in nonformal education (539, 558, 582) and alternative education (565).

Ivan Illich sees schools as an abstraction from the realities of life, and through his theory of "deschooling" seeks to link education to the natural dynamics of social life, involving free socialization and creativity (541, 549, 572). Deschooling and A.S. Neill's freeschooling have been carefully analyzed and critiqued (531).

As religious educators have sought to be responsible in relation to the religious disciplines, they have been attracted by theories that see education as guided by the structures of knowledge, utilizing the logical order of concepts in various fields of inquiry (536, 540). Applied to the training of leaders, teacher education likewise is to be adapted to the structure of the discipline of education (532).

Great interest has been shown in Paulo Freire's call for conscientization, or consciousness raising, as religious groups have become more alert to the mandate for social justice (541, 552, 574). Conscientization calls for the development of critical consciousness with regard to the powerful inherited structures that perpetuate injustice in education and society.

B.F. Skinner's behaviorism has led to an attempt to make education something of an exact science (575). With carefully chosen objectives and subject matter, the learner is placed in situations that lead to conditioning through positive and negative reinforcement. Precise evaluation of educational results is part of the picture. Without subscribing to the behavioristic assumptions of this theory, taxonomies of educational objectives have been developed for the cognitive, affective, and psychomotor fields, along with suggestions for testing for appropriate results (555). Religious educators have found close relationships between their aims and those incorporated in the taxonomy of the affective domain.

Teaching models and styles have been gathered, explained, and weighed in a comprehensive way (551). Deciding among them in particular situations is a matter of taking philosophical and educational orientations into account (566).

There have been critiques of American education and of current theories (560, 570). Along the way there have been vigorous proponents of classical theories of education (546), as well as advocacy of the simplest theory of all, "Do a good job, examine what you are doing, and you will have your principles" (554).

Other theoretical approaches have also received attention and might be of interest to religious educators. N.L. Gage, who has specialized in a scientific approach, holds that research-based teaching promises modest hope for improvement (545). In cognitive learning a promising approach is meaningful verbal learning through using advance organizers (567). The classroom use of deductive logic has been suggested, especially for precision in defining, explaining, and justifying ideas (542). Mortimer Adler's *Paideia Proposal* is a plan for single-track, concentrated public school education (529). The Waldorf Schools practice the educational philosophy of Rudolph Steiner, the anthroposophist (569).

Some educators would put almost exclusive emphasis on the individual (547). Carl Rogers has used his famous nondirective approach to counseling in formulating his educational ideas (573). Parker Palmer, critical of most contemporary educational institutions, proposes a "spirituality" of education, whose key is "to create a space in which obedience to truth is practiced" (568). There are feminist (556) and nonsexist (578) approaches to education. In 1964, Matthew Miles compiled descriptions and evaluations of innovations in education that were outstanding at that time and that still merit attention (563).

Theories focused on specific aspects of education have been produced: moral education (583), values education (561), education for wisdom in times of crisis (583, 611), multiethnic education (535), black education (584), and international and intercultural education (582).

Adult education presents particular problems, in that adults generally believe they are beyond schooling and systematic learning. However, participative adult learning is promising (538). There are approaches to adult learning that are transformative (562). A community education has been suggested, one that responds to real needs, empowers people, and builds human resources and networks (543). Open education is more inviting and less threatening to adults than some other approaches, because it allows learners to proceed at their own pace on subjects of their own choosing (577).

RELIGIOUS EDUCATION THEORY

Like educational theory, religious education theory attempts three major tasks. First, it analyzes the phenomena of religious education and thinks critically and constructively about the aims and processes involved in the formation of religious life and character. Second, it sifts the foundation disciplines for appropriate insight and guidance that may be brought to bear on religious education's thought and practice. Third, it serves its institutions critically and constructively, even to the point of suggesting ways in which they may be renewed and reinvented.

It is in the construction of theory that everything in the discipline of religious education comes together. Theory is structured in terms of the essential questions for which religious education must find answers:

What purposes does religious education seek to accomplish?
With what aspects of knowledge and experience is it concerned?

What processes of learning and human formation are appropriate to its nature and
purposes?
Where does it take place? What variety of situations and settings are appropriate?
Who are the partners to the educational transaction? What roles does each play?
What is the time factor?   When does religious education take place?   What
frequencies and sequences are involved? How long does it take?
What feeling tones are appropriate to the educational transaction?

The answers to questions like these emerge from individual and shared experience
and from being addressed selectively to the foundation disciplines. The answers take the
form of principles, guides, and directives for religious education practice and are used to
shape its administration, program, curriculum, and method.

A good and useful theory requires coverage of every aspect of religious education,
consistency and coherence, and practicality. As it is tested in practice and inadequacies
appear, it goes back to its roots in experience and its foundations for correctives. A good
theory in time becomes widely shared as a basis for program, curriculum, and method
by various religious groups.

One of theory's advantages for the religious educator is its flexibility. Theory
does not have the status of theology or philosophy but is much easier to change as
circumstances change and as new data and insights become available. Only a few
theorists are tenacious about their views, and those that are tend to be on the periphery
of the discipline.

Religious education theory in the fifties and early sixties was dominated by a
handful of Protestant religious educators and reflected in five seminal works: Iris V.
Cully's *The Dynamics of Christian Education* (1958), Randolph Crump Miller's *The Clue
to Christian Education* (1950), Lewis J. Sherrill's *The Gift of Power* (1955), James D.
Smart's *The Teaching Ministry of the Church* (1954), and D. Campbell Wyckoff's *The
Gospel and Christian Education* (1959).

A cursory survey of this section of the bibliography reflects several shifts. While
the contribution of Protestant writers is still evident in works by Iris V. Cully (605, 606,
607, 608), Randolph Crump Miller (672, 673, 674, 675), and C. Ellis Nelson (688, 689,
690), the writings of Roman Catholic religious educators like Mary C. Boys (596), Gloria
Durka, Joanmarie Smith, and Maria Harris (616, 617, 642), Thomas H. Groome (637,
638), Brennan Hill (644), James Michael Lee (659, 660, 661), Gabriel Moran (679, 680,
681, 682, 683, 684, 685), Padriac O'Hare (693, 694), Didier-Jacques Piveteau (699), and
Michael Warren (731, 732) have come to exert a major influence in the field. Groome's
Christian Religious Education (637), published in 1980, served as a widely used textbook,
shaping seminarians and sharpening the practice of religious education professionals for
more than a decade until the publication of his second book, *Sharing Faith* (638) in 1991.
Groome's shared-praxis approach has made a major impact on religious education.
Outstanding new Protestant voices include Susanne Johnson (651), Sara Little (664), Mary
Elizabeth Moore (677), Richard Osmer (695), Letty Russell (706, 707), and Malcolm
Warford (730). There have been specific critiques of some of these developments (666,
687).

Religious education theories reflect a diversity of sources, ranging from theology
(613, 615, 618, 634, 647, 675, 724), the Bible (703), and philosophy (624, 674) to the
arts (616), creativity (589, 593), psychology (652), and technology (588, 663). Some
works in religious education theory reflect a specific ecclesiastical orientation: Church of
the Brethren (643), Episcopal (609, 650), Lutheran (626, 632, 657, 702), Mennonite
(656), Orthodox (655), Roman Catholic (645, 716), Southern Baptist (604, 719, 722),
United Church of Christ (718), and United Methodist (701). Religious education theories
also reflect the Jewish tradition (698, 715, 727). Other works are distinguished as much

by geography as ecclesiology: Australian (636), British (646, 649, 665), Canadian (597), French (697), German (590, 592, 630, 640, 711, 725), and Latin American (709, 710, 728) perspectives are represented.

Religious education theories can also be arranged along the theological spectrum. Evangelicals have published a number of other works in the recent past. There have been general surveys of the field from an evangelical perspective (586, 603, 610, 631, 635, 639). Individual studies from an evangelical point of view include Le Bar (658) and Wilhoit (742). Robert Pazmiño's *Foundational Issues in Christian Education* (517) and *Principles and Practices of Christian Education* (696) are written from an evangelical Christian perspective. A fundamentalist orientation is reflected in H.W. Byrne's *A Christian Approach to Education* (601). Daniel Schipani's work (116, 708, 709, 710) reflects Latin American liberation theology. Randolph Crump Miller, who from the beginning saw theology as the clue to Christian education, drew on process theology to shape his approach (675). Liberation theology is found reflected in a number of works (625, 653, 654, 700).

James Michael Lee's massive trilogy on religious instruction (659, 660, 661) and Leon McKenzie's work on the religious education of adults (669) represent a theoretical approach grounded in social science rather than in theology. C. Ellis Nelson's religious enculturation approach, grounded in anthropology and sociology (689, 690) was made accessible to a wider audience of religious education practitioners by John H. Westerhoff III through books like *Values for Tomorrow's Children* (737) and *Will Our Children Have Faith?* (739) and numerous other writings (691, 733, 734, 735, 736, 738, 740).

Like theology and the social sciences, philosophy has also served as a useful foundation for religious education theorizing. Randolph C. Miller explored the implications of linguistic philosophy for religious education in *The Language Gap and God* (674), while Wolfgang G. Esser looked to existential phenomenology (624). J. Gordon Chamberlin, whose *Freedom and Faith* (602) examines the approaches of James D. Smart, Randolph C. Miller, and Lewis J. Sherrill, drew on phenomenology for his own approach (143, 144). An existentialist-phenomenological approach was used by Ross Snyder (720, 721).

Several theorists focus their attention on the faith community. The work of Nelson has already been mentioned (688). To his name should be added those of Craig Dykstra (619, 620), Charles Foster (629), and Donald E. Miller (670). Two studies by the World Council of Churches also belong in this category (622, 726).

A number of theoretical works focus on a specific age level, such as adults (669), adolescents (686, 692, 717), or children (587, 591, 676). Of these, Jerome Berryman's *Godly Play* (591) offers a fresh and promising approach for religious education with children.

Small groups (623); moral education (743) and ethical action (744); moral and religious development (599); faith development (621); evangelism and education (585, 723); ethnicity (628); futures (598, 617); teaching (594, 595); catechesis (612, 645, 662, 697, 705); pastoral concerns (611); a professional quality of teaching (627); women's issues (633); social justice (641); action-reflection (648); conscience (671); meaning, learning, and vocation (712); and education of the public (714) are among the interests covered in this section. There have also been studies of the educational implications of the thought of religious leaders Abraham Heschel (668) and Thomas Merton (614).

Those wishing a general introduction to religious education theory will find Mary C. Boys' *Educating in Faith* (596) a useful map of the field. Marlene Mayr's *Modern Masters of Religious Education* (667) introduces leading contemporary religious education theorists. Other useful introductions to religious education theory include *An Invitation* to *Religious Education*, by Harold William Burgess (600); *Understanding Christian Education*, by Wayne R. Rood (704); *Contemporary Approaches to Christian Education*, edited by Jack L. Seymour and Donald E. Miller (713), Marvin Taylor's survey (729), and R.E.Y. Wickett's discussion of models of adult religious education (741).

ADMINISTRATION OF RELIGIOUS EDUCATION

While the literature dealing with the administration of religious education is designed mainly to serve its institutions, it serves them best when it deals with them both constructively and critically.

Here the concerns are with planning institutions and enterprises for effecting religious education, and organizing, managing, and supervising them. Planning attempts to envision these institutions and enterprises in realistic and effective ways. Organization attempts to set them up to accomplish their tasks. Management is concerned with their day-to-day operations. Supervision involves fact-finding, developing and applying criteria for examining and evaluating their operations, improving leadership, and conducting appropriate research. Thus administration seeks both to support religious education's institutions and enterprises and to rethink and reinvent them when necessary.

These four subject areas—planning, organization, management, and supervision—are addressed in the works in this section. While not all the articles and books included fit neatly into one of these four areas, a number do and are considered here before the more general works.

Planning, an aspect of administration also treated in more general works, is the specific focus of John C. DeBoer's *Let's Plan* (761). Planned change is the focus of two other books (751, 858) and an article (771).

Administering Christian Education (754) is one of several general works that includes a discussion of planning and organizing.

While many general works on educational administration include management (754, 760, 827), Peter F. Drucker's *Managing the Non-Profit Organization* (765) addresses the subject specifically.

Leadership, a closely related subject, is the focus of a number of works in this section, including *Leadership Jazz* (763), *Competent to Lead* (774), *Servant Leadership* (779), "New Styles of Church Leadership" (810), and *Christian Leadership* (826). David E. Klopfenstein's article, "Research in Leadership" (796), reviews some of the significant literature on leadership.

Supervision is the theme of the 1992 yearbook (777) of the Association for Supervision and Curriculum Development (ASCD). *Supervision: The Reluctant Profession* (818) is one of the older works on the subject, while *Clinical Supervision* (778) is a 1980 revision of another standard work on supervision.

Locke E. Bowman, Jr., founder of the Arizona Project, which later became known as the National Teacher Education Project (NTEP), developed an instrument for observing teacher-learner interaction (755, 756). INSTROTEACH, widely used to improve the quality of volunteer teaching in church schools, is one practical tool developed for the training of volunteer teachers. Microteaching, another successful resource for teacher training, is the focus of another book (745).

The key role of the minister in the church's teaching ministry has long been recognized by religious educators. The minister's role as teacher or educator is the focus of several works (757, 768, 822, 835). The increasing awareness of the importance of the minister's educational role can be seen when one examines the copyright dates of these four books: almost a decade separates *The Pastor's Role in Educational Ministry* (822), a volume in a yearbook series published by the Lutheran church, and *The Pastor in a Teaching Church* (768), published in 1983. *The Pastor as Religious Educator* (757) and *The Pastor as Teacher* (835) were both published in 1989.

The role of the professional religious educator, variously identified as a "director of religious education" (D.R.E.) or "director of Christian education" (D.C.E.), is the subject of books in this section of the bibliography (767, 781, 782, 786, 805). Of these books, Timothy Arthur Lines's *Functional Images of the Religious Educator* (805) is the most recent and perhaps the most comprehensive.

As in other sections of the bibliography, some of the works on administration can be grouped by age level. Adult religious education (762, 770, 797, 811) and youth ministry (769, 773, 828, 841) are examples of this age-specific attention in the area of administration.

Architecture (750, 807, 852), camps and conferences (775, 808, 820, 850), change (751, 771, 858), church growth (748, 836, 845), conflict (753, 814), evaluation (856), libraries (837), research (784, 785), and volunteers (792, 854) also receive attention in this section.

PROGRAM, CURRICULUM, AND METHOD

The full impact of practice guided by theory is felt in the areas of program, curriculum, and method. It is here that teaching and learning meet; here changes in ideas, attitudes, commitments, and behavior take place; and here more experienced and less experienced people meet face-to-face in educational encounter.

It is here also that the period under consideration has been characterized by the most marked differences of opinion and has shown the greatest divergence of theoretical underpinnings. Yet it is here that religious educators as individuals, as groups of practitioners, and as religious groups have had to make the most difficult decisions and effect the most strategic compromises. For it is in the diurnal decisions on programming, curriculum, and method that theory has to be tested and adjusted in the interests of effective practice. It is here, too, that religious education and institutional reality meet head-on, for it is in program, curriculum, and method that institutional support, change, and renewal are most potently effected.

Works on program, curriculum, and method overlap to a considerable degree, which makes sorting them into clear categories difficult. It is necessary again to make judgments as to the major thrust of each work. Those that deal in an overall way with how various groups are to be served are classified as program. Those that deal with specific plans for carrying on the educational process are listed as curriculum. Those that concentrate on particular educational activities are clustered as method.

Program

The educational work of the parish as a whole (912) has been seen as the creation of a "wisdom community" (882), and best served when planning is done locally (990). Special attention has been given to the small membership church (915), to the enrichment of the parish's program (1004), and to the responsibility of the minister to use the pulpit as a focus for teaching (1009). The special needs of urban and inner city churches have been included (997, 974), as have those of the black church (958).

The bases for children's work (297, 877, 898, 979) include comparative child development (968). The practical aspects of planning are covered (957, 1050), with an emphasis on the orientation of new children (905). Several works treat the participation of children in public worship (985, 1012). The program is expanded to include the preschool (983).

During the years under consideration more attention has been paid to youth work than to any other aspect of religious education. Understanding youth culture has been a developing theme (686, 1014), as has adolescent spirituality (717). Major attention has been given to the programming of youth ministry (758, 769, 828, 867, 936, 952, 959, 984, 1031, 1032, 1049). Various aspects of youth ministry come in for special treatment: junior high work (288, 886, 930, 946), senior high work (795), black and white styles (351), peer ministry (817), wilderness camping (808), parents' concern with youth ministry (829), ministry with troubled youth (1016), youth leadership (773), and the work of the minister to youth (841).

Because of the ramifications of running a school program as well as a parish program, research and professional programming have been major emphases among Roman Catholics (308, 819, 902, 1030). The Jewish community has strengthened its school program (931). German religious educators have done a great deal of creative innovating with their nonschool programs (203, 834, 839, 874, 1006). An intensive retreat program for youth has been developed by the Taizé Community in France (896).

Adult religious education has been explored in a variety of ways (669, 680, 762, 770, 811, 861, 933, 934, 991, 1003, 1028, 1029, 1037, 1051). Some focus has been on young adult work (801, 976), on women (939, 942), on single adults (955), and on older persons (890). Base communities (870) and the lay academy (918) serve important adult needs in special situations. The empowering of adults as volunteers is seen as an important aspect of programming (956).

Parish sponsored programs of religious education include the church school (993) and its classroom (897, 987), the learning center (906), growth groups (986), retreats (995), and intergenerational religious education (1035).

General considerations of family ministry (789, 940, 948, 1007, 1047) are supplemented with suggestions for religious education in the home itself (971, 1002), family camps and conferences (775), and a cross-cultural family program (972).

During this period it has become evident that service to persons with special needs is a priority for religious education (876, 970, 978, 989, 1023, 1025, 1048). This is expanding to include the gifted (980).

Curriculum

Following the trends in general education may be more characteristic of religious education in curriculum than in other areas, and this tendency has come under scrutiny. Curriculum development in the churches has been examined analytically by Burt Braunius (881). Maria Harris has broken away from dependence on secular sources in her recent book on curriculum (941).

Religious educators have generally looked to secular curriculum theorists for a great deal of guidance in setting up their educational systems. General reviews of curriculum theory and practice have been used (932, 951). The "reconceptualists" advocate curriculum reform in ways that appeal to religious educators because of the dynamic approaches to learning implicit in their thought (992). Philip Phenix shows how, using a structure of knowledge approach, religious thought, dynamics, and issues are involved in the general curriculum (184). Elliot Eisner emphasizes the play of imagination in curriculum theory and practice (909, 910). There are age-level treatments that provide useful guidance (911). With its problem of religious education in the schools of an increasingly secular society, Germany provides valuable guidance on the relation of religious education to general curriculum theory (1034).

Early in the period under consideration a long build-up of interest in curriculum theory came to its climax at the same time that the particular curriculums were published. Consequently, it seemed useful to accompany the curriculums with explanations of the theory undergirding them. The overall theory (1046) was published within a year or two of the books on the Lutheran curriculum (632), the Episcopal curriculum (650), the curriculum of the United Church of Christ (718), and a theory of biblical education (608).

A few years later the work of the Cooperative Curriculum Project (889, 900, 1015, 1020) dominated the scene. More recent reviews (894, 1018) cover a number of later curriculum projects, including those that are specific to particular cultures. A project that carried particular challenge was the "New Life in Christ" curriculum, designed to introduce the Christian faith to preliterate people in South America (1024).

Descriptions of other curriculum enterprises are: Roman Catholic (920), Jewish (1010), ecumenical and socially aware (866), the Union College Character Research Project (1039), Methodist (211, 885), Presbyterian (219), Southern Baptist, including descriptions of other curriculum projects (892), family curriculum (953), and theological education (916).

Curriculum work often focuses on particular topics that are to be included in the curriculum: Bible (703), church history (954), spiritual growth (913), stewardship (999), religious language (949), symbols (962), parenting (1008), mission (871), world religions (901), citizenship and discipleship (879), peace and justice (693, 973, 1043), world hunger (1022), nonviolence (960), divorce (860), alcohol and drugs (919).

Method

Some valuable considerations of method and teaching come from general education (545, 551, 554, 564, 569). Others are specific to the field of religious education (458, 591, 594, 595, 660, 664, 875, 998). Some are as specific as to deal with the skills of lesson planning (917). There are treatments of method for the age levels: children (944, 967), youth (914, 943, 964, 981, 1011), and adults (865, 883, 895, 924, 975, 988).

As one would expect, much is available on methods of Bible study. Some are general guides (969, 1038). Heavy emphasis is placed on using the Bible with the various age levels: children (921, 922, 923, 927, 1026), youth (928), and adults (945, 1041, 1042). Experimental methods are proposed (1033). A conservative approach is explained and defended (996).

A number of works center on worship (606, 691, 929, 947, 1013, 1017, 1027), prayer (963), meditation (961, 1000, 1005), ritual (982), and spirituality (891).

Creative methods are strongly advocated (425, 436, 642, 863, 903, 966) with specific reference to the arts (490, 616, 642, 859, 878), including music (1021, 1045) literature (935), painting (1044), drama (908), dance (899, 1019), creative movement (977), recreation and play (501, 864, 869, 887), storytelling (872, 873, 907, 1036), autobiography and journal writing (880, 1000), and doing your own theology (1040).

Some methods make use of other interpersonal resources: discussion (888); conversation with children (950); group conversation among persons of varied ethnic and social backgrounds, centered on their early experiences of holiday festivals (904); "faithcare," life-long ministry to persons' needs (862); helping persons in meeting life crises (611, 995); and maintaining discipline (848).

There are methods that enrich the educational process by making it more vivid: the use of audiovisuals (925, 937, 938, 1001), the use of case studies (965), and the use of simulation games (926).

Methods that broaden social horizons and sensitivities include ethnic studies (868), consciousness raising (708), and the powerful dynamics of action-reflection (648).

RELIGION AND THE SCHOOL

In situations where religious education is a function of the state, there have been two major developments.   First, there have been vigorous discussions and experimentations occasioned by the rapid emergence of multiculturalism. Where formerly there was general agreement on the bases and character of religious instruction, the schools now face such a variety of faiths that accommodation has become necessary. The general solution has been to deal with world religions, with values, and with morality and ethics. Second, because the schools are no longer able to maintain a particular sectarian stance, the churches and other religious groups have been awakened to their own responsibility for the propagation of the faith.

In situations where the churches and other religious groups shoulder primary responsibility for religious education, the schools have still felt the necessity to deal with religion, primarily as an aspect of culture.   Thus there has been experimentation with literary approaches to the Bible, to instruction in values and morality, concern for character education, and the study of religion and religions as an aspect of the social sciences. Interestingly, there has been little change in approaches to religious content in the study of literature, music, and the other arts.

Schools conducted under church auspices have faced some of the same problems of adjustment. Protestant-sponsored schools have ranged from those newly organized to maintain a certain sectarian character to those that are almost indistinguishable from public schools. Roman Catholic and Jewish schools have been less affected by the need for such adjustments.

During this period the problem of religion in American education has become more critical. There have been careful reviews of the ways in which the relationship has developed in the past (236, 248, 1071), and analyses of the factors in the present situation (1085, 1106, 1108).   The legal issues have been delineated (1064), including the controversial issue of prayer in the schools (1079).

The close relationship of religion to personal and social concerns that cannot be ignored by the schools has prompted curricular projects in character education (283) and in values education (561, 571). During these years the interest in released time waned, but shared time, where certain elements in the curriculum were to be shared with the religious institutions, was proposed (1100). The question of the personal faith of the public school teacher was explored (1072).

It has been pointed out that religious subject matter cannot be neglected in public education, and the arts and social studies have been singled out as particularly appropriate curricular areas in this regard (1091). However, the major constructive project of recent years has been Indiana University's project on teaching the Bible as literature (1052, 1053, 1055, 1068, 1069, 1078, 1103).

A number of educational and religious education theorists have made proposals as to the role of religion in education (184, 490, 681, 1090, 1092).

The role of religion in private schools has been examined (1060, 1066, 1083), and the educational concerns and enterprises of religious bodies in America have been described (262, 263, 1059). Particular attention has been given to Roman Catholic schooling (244, 262, 266, 327, 348, 1058, 1081, 1088, 1095, 1101). Other systems have also been analyzed: Christian schools (358, 1080, 1107), Jewish schools (698, 830), and Lutheran schools (207, 292, 1082).

Outside of the United States, religious education is usually an accepted element in public educational systems. Among the most thoroughly developed are those of Great Britain and Germany. In Great Britain the debate has centered around the problems of secularism in society, theological orientation, and biblical interpretation (260, 487, 649, 1063, 1067, 1073, 1074, 1075, 1096, 1099). In Germany the same factors have dominated the debate, but with a great concern for professional teacher training and for understanding learners and meeting their particular needs (246, 725, 855, 1056, 1065, 1070, 1076, 1077, 1084, 1087, 1089, 1097).

State systems of religious education in other areas have been analyzed: Australia (265, 1094), Canada (1061, 1093, 1102, 1105), Ethiopia (237), Europe at large (697), Ireland (204, 240), Kenya (277, 1062), Melanesia (1109), New Zealand (1086), Nigeria (1054), Poland (1057), and Sweden (1098).

RELIGION AND HIGHER EDUCATION

While much of higher education has stemmed from concern by the churches and other religious bodies for the education of their young people in an atmosphere permeated by their faith, various pressures have greatly changed the situation. Those pressures have been to a great extent economic, but they have also included problems of staffing, accreditation, a growing diversity in student bodies, and a pervasive cultural secularization.

In publicly supported colleges and universities, however, demands for cultural comprehensiveness and a growing market for doctoral candidates in religion have resulted in the strengthening of existing departments of religion and the establishment of new ones. These departments of religion have been, in the main, culturally and religiously inclusive, and have approached the study of religion with the assumptions of the social sciences.

The major challenge to religion in higher education in America is the growing secularization of school and society (1129). Campus and church have very little understanding of each other (1114), yet congregations have a vital ministry to the members of the university community (1118). While ministry on the campus presents serious problems (1120), it remains a feasible approach (1112).

The secular college and university are challenged to recover a religious quality (1143) and to deal with ultimate questions (1145). Concern is felt for the spiritual development of students (1133), for education in values (1130), for appropriate commitments (1110), and for exploration of the relation of religion and public life (1138).

Questions are raised about the place of religious studies in higher education (1137, 1142), the place of theological education in the church and university (1117, 1119, 1127), and the meaning of Christian scholarship (1141). There are proposals for differential treatment of religion at the various levels of higher education (1132). The Bible is seen as important for the study of world literature and for the sociological understanding of religious groups and their beliefs (1111).

Religiously affiliated higher education (1139, 1140) and its history (264, 1144) have been studied. Among Protestants, the basis for evangelical higher education has been looked at (1113), along with its concern for moral education (1126); mainline higher education has been reexamined (1116); and curriculum studies in the liberal arts and sciences have led to reform (1115, 1122, 1125). Among Roman Catholics there has been research and appraisal (1121, 1131, 1147), as well as careful examination of the role and mission of the university (1123). There have also been studies of higher education in the Lutheran church (1135) and the Reformed church (1146).

Theological education has also come in for reappraisal, with examinations of its character (1128), its task of moral formation (1136), and the contemporary challenges that it faces (1149).

REFERENCE WORKS

The nature of reference works makes the task of analysis difficult. The books encompass a diverse range of genres, from dictionaries (1157) and encyclopedias (1153) to handbooks (1158) and bibliographies (1161). There are single-volume (1150) and multiple-volume (1155) works. They cover a wide variety of subjects. Some have religion or religious education as their specific interest (1162, 1169), while others have a more secular focus (1151, 1154, 1159). A few are compendiums of empirical research in a particular area.

Research on Religious Development (1169), a project of the Religious Education Association, represents an organization's effort to provide a comprehensive collection of research on religious development. While there are other handbooks with a focus on some aspect of human development or one of the human sciences, such as psychology, they are primarily the work of an individual editor and publisher.

Among individuals noted for their contributions is Kendig Cully, who edited a dictionary (1157) and, with his wife, Iris, an encyclopedia (1156). Donald Ratcliff, who has served as an editor or coeditor for four handbooks published by Religious Education Press, is another prominent editor. British religious educator, Jeff Astley, is a well-known compiler of collections of readings, like *Christian Perspectives on Faith Development* (1152).

Starting with the publication of the *Handbook of Moral Development* (1168) in 1973, Religious Education Press has published a variety of handbooks, ranging from topical guides such as the *Handbook of Faith* (1162) and *The Complete Guide to Religious Education Volunteers* (1167) to age-level handbooks on adulthood (770), adolescence (1166), and childhood (1164, 1165).

Some handbooks which might be considered reference works appear in other sections, such as "Behavioral Studies of Religion" (334), "Administration" (817, 825, 827, and 849) and "Program, Curriculum, and Method" (937, 974).

The publication of *The Christian Educator's Handbook on Adult Education* (1160) signals an important shift among evangelical Christian educators. The contributors to this volume have drawn on the work of more secular scholars and researchers in the field of adult education, in contrast to earlier works in which such dependence was not evident. Recognition of the contribution adult education can make to the ministry of evangelical Christian educators opens possibilities for fruitful conversation.

CONCERNS FOR THE FUTURE

The literature clearly reveals the present condition of religious education, as far as its foundations, theory, and practice are concerned. What questions does it raise for future consideration?

Religious education during the period under consideration has used an appropriate variety of foundation disciplines and will continue to do so in the future, but several concerns arise. First, have religious educators really assessed the adequacy of the data available? An agenda item for the future may well be the development of a more vigorous posture in respect to the foundation disciplines, a posture in which religious educators take the initiative in seeking data on questions they need to have answered, thus asking the foundation disciplines to design and generate research to meet their particular needs.

Second, the present state of theology creates confusion for religious education, especially when religious educators see their task as being guided by particular theological fashions. The varieties of approaches are bewildering. Single-issue theologies steer religious education into by-paths. New cores of consensus are needed, new consolidations of views, new schools of thought that synthesize data in educational terms, and around which effective practice may be designed and used.

The significance of philosophy of education for religious education is waning and will continue to wane as long as education continues to become ever more secular. Yet there is likely to be a reaction in which it may become more useful, as issues of belief, character, ethics, and morality press for attention. There are no purely secular solutions to these issues.

Present approaches in history of education are more promising, as a broad social and cultural context for research is used in place of the narrower context that limited historical research to schooling. Yet it is religious education's responsibility to make clear which historical matters most need research attention.

The same applies to behavioral studies, both of religion and of education. In addition to sifting and receiving useful information, religious educators need to decide what they most need to know and to insist that research be conducted in those areas. Furthermore, religious education must be critical about the assumptions behind the research that it uses. An uncritical attitude has resulted in unresolved debates about such matters as systems for understanding human and faith development, and in the adoption of such inappropriate devices as behavioral objectives.

As promising as multidisciplinary approaches are, they have their dangers, especially when they attempt to integrate disciplines with diverse methodologies. One eminent scientist, asked about the integration of the disciplines, responded, "I know nothing more corrupt!" Religious educators must be extremely cautious in dealing with disciplines whose methodologies they do not understand, and they must be especially careful not to mix incompatibles.

Religious education has always leaned to some extent on educational theory, a situation that becomes increasingly problematic as educational theory becomes more secular. This makes it imperative that religious education clarify the methodologies that it uses in the construction of theory. The forum needs to be replaced by the clearinghouse, in which consensus is sought and consolidation of views takes place. To be useful, individualism in the construction of theory must yield, not to some monolithic position, but to cores of consensus around which religious education practice may be designed and put into effect. The clearinghouse may thus be used for the resolution of the tensions between religious education as a discipline and religious education as a practical art that requires institutions that have a functional degree of stability and continuity.

Those institutions must be served, but they must also be carefully renewed, a task that again requires cooperation between theorists and practitioners. On occasion institutions need more than renewal. Reform and the creation of new institutions may be called for. This applies to schools and institutions of higher learning as much as it does to congregational educational institutions.

But religious education is a field in which such change has always come slowly, and when it has been effective it has come deliberately. Practitioners require a degree of stability and continuity to accomplish their tasks. Thus administration and program become matters of balancing creativity and responsibility. So does the curriculum, where at present its nature and context are under fruitful discussion.

Of the various aspects of practice, method has received the least theoretical attention. Yet the heart of educational practice is the astute matching of objectives and the means for their realization. Intuitive approaches have reigned where research and experimentation are required. As in curriculum, which has perhaps leaned too heavily on secular sources, method has either been determined by guesswork, habit, or personal preference. Clarification of curriculum theory and religious education methodologies are key agenda items for the future.

Foundations of Religious Education

THEOLOGICAL FOUNDATIONS

1 Adamson, William R. *Bushnell Reconsidered*. Philadelphia: United Church Press, 1966.

> A vigorous treatment of Horace Bushnell's thought and its development, chiefly centering on his contributions to religious education. Brief but meaty, the book serves well as an introduction to Bushnell for students of religious education, since it is set up to point directly to sources and critical materials. Takes religious education writers severely to task for dealing with Bushnell superficially.

2 Anderson, Ray S., ed. *Theological Foundations for Ministry*. Grand Rapids, MI: William B. Eerdmans Publishing Company, 1979.

> Twenty-eight basic documents selected to define and explicate a neo-Reformation view of the church and of ministry. Religious educators are left to extrapolate a corresponding definition of their task (an exacting task for them), but a clear foundation is here on which to build.

3 Baillie, John. *Baptism and Conversion*. New York: Charles Scribner's Sons, 1963.

> Deals with divergent views of baptism and conversion, the question of where the Christian life begins. Takes primarily historical and evangelistic perspectives, but handles them in such a way that nurture and the life-long educational responsibility of the church are freed from the ambiguities that such perspectives often occasion. See also 12, 15, 16, 26, and 36.

4 Barden, Garrett, and Philip McShane. *Toward Self-Meaning*. New York: Herder and Herder, 1969.

> An invitation to engage in the quest for meaning and self-understanding that is the pursuit of wisdom. Written by two students of Bernard Lonergan, the book is an attempt at self-education in philosophy and religion. The object is to become

intelligently self-conscious about how our minds operate—how we think, believe, and decide.

5   Barth, Markus. "The Cowboy in the Sunday School." *Religious Education* 57 (1962):39-46, 80, 120-27.

A spirited theological and historical appeal for the use of stories in religious education, maintaining that revelation comes mainly in the form of event, and is available to us chiefly in the form of narration of revelatory event. Calls for discriminating use of Bible stories, avoiding moralism and dealing realistically with human tragedy and hope.

6   Bartlett, David L. *Paul's Vision for the Teaching Church.* Valley Forge, PA: Judson Press, 1977.

Acknowledging that Paul's writings are not the most promising direct source of guidance on Christian education, the author, a New Testament scholar and pastor, analyzes Paul categorically for insight into the answers to such questions as, "What is the context for Christian education?" "Who really does the teaching?" "How does the church teach?" and "What does the church teach?" A whole church, as the community of the new age, teaches, and does so through tradition, proclamation, exhortation, and initiation. What is taught is faith and love.

7   Bitter, Gottfried. *Erlösung.* Munich: Kösel-Verlag, 1976.

A study of the treatment of redemption in religious education, raising the critical question of liberation or redemption. The investigation is pursued in philosophical, psychological, and theological perspectives, centering on the question of meaning as the point at which the educational and theological problems converge for religious education. A large section of the text is an analysis and evaluation of the handling of the theme in German religious education texts between 1955 and 1974.

8   Bloch, Ernst, *et al.*, eds. *Bildung und Konfessionalität.* Frankfurt: Verlag Moritz Diesterweg, 1967.

A symposium on the fundamental question of the relation of education and religious belief. The contributors represent a variety of points of view--Christian, Jewish, and Marxist. Ernst Bloch has provided the chapter, "Hoping and Believing."

9   Bloesch, Donald. *The Reform of the Church.* Grand Rapids, MI: William B. Eerdmans Publishing Company, 1970.

A quietly stated book, but one of urgent concern, dealing with key areas of needed change in the church. This, for the educator, provides a context for a number of opportunities for reexamining the church's educational work. One chapter, "A New Kind of Confirmation," does this directly, pointing out that confirmation is a means of grace that strengthens one for service in the Kingdom and equips one for apostolic vocation in the world. Practical standards and procedures are suggested for this and other aspects of the church's educational task.

10 Boff, Leonardo. *Ecclesiogenesis: The Base Communities Reinvent the Church.* Maryknoll, NY: Orbis Books, 1986.

> Many see the "base community" as a contemporary rebirth of the primitive church as well as the most basic form of worship-study-action group. Boff knows these communities well and here interprets them theologically. In addition, he raises pertinent questions regarding laity and women in the leadership of the church as it is found in the base community. See also 35 and 870.

11 Boff, Leonardo. *Liberating Grace.* Maryknoll, NY: Orbis Books, 1979.

> A theology of grace as power and corrective for personal and social freedom. This book could be used as a basis for a theory of religious education, with special attention to two of its four parts: "Experiencing Grace" and "God and Humankind as Revealed in the Grace Experience."

12 Bourgeois, Henri. *On Becoming Christian: Christian Initiation and Its Sacraments.* Mystic, CT: Twenty-Third Publications, 1985.

> The Rite for the Initiation of Adults and the Rite for the Baptism of Infants make urgent a reconsideration of the unity of the sacraments of baptism, confirmation, and the Eucharist, plus other related aspects of the Christian life. This book seeks to show how all these interrelate in the life journey of the Christian.

13 Bowman, Locke E., Jr. "Teaching and Learning—Toward a New Testament View." *Nexus* (a Presbyterian Church (U.S.A) publication), Fall 1964.

> A profound study of Paul (who worked and taught from the realization of being "in Christ") and Jesus (whose teaching was marked by pointedness, clarity, and urgency), but with the necessary warning that Christian learning is not to be thought of as complete at any point. Teaching from a New Testament standpoint sends us away to learn more, because the teacher teaches from a personal knowledge that is never complete.

14 Boys, Mary C. *Biblical Interpretation in Religious Education.* Birmingham, AL: Religious Education Press, 1980.

> An exemplary study in biblical research (centering on the rise and fall of *Heilsgeschichte* as a hermeneutical principle), church history (dealing with recent Roman Catholicism), and religious education (as the specific arena of concern). Provides a good base from which to reexamine the place of the Bible in religious education.

15 Bromiley, Geoffrey W. *Children of Promise: The Case for Baptizing Infants.* Grand Rapids, MI: William B. Eerdmans Publishing Company, 1979.

> For churches in the Reformed tradition, infant baptism is a firm sacramental and theological base for religious education. While this book does not deal with the educational implications of infant baptism, it discusses the subject so thoroughly that the informed religious educator is able to use it in theological and theoretical work on the matter. See also 3, 12, 16, 26, and 36.

16 Browning, Robert L., and Roy A. Reed. *The Sacraments in Religious Education and Liturgy*. Birmingham, AL: Religious Education Press, 1985.

> A multidisciplinary study, ecumenical in scope, of sacramental theology as it relates to religious education and worship, and of religious education and worship as they relate to each other in that context. A broad conception of the sacraments (baptism, Eucharist, confirmation, marriage, vocation, penance, and new sacraments) is used to inform a model of sacramental life. Sacramental dimensions of faith development are explored, and many examples useful to religious education are provided.

17 Brueggemann, Walter. *The Creative Word: Canon as a Model for Biblical Education*. Philadelphia: Fortress Press, 1982.

> Canon criticism is developed for insights pertinent to religious education. The three aspects of the Old Testament canon—Torah, prophets, and wisdom—are examined both as to the process of their formation and the shape of their message. A final chapter on the Psalms personalizes the divine-human relationship with its reminder of the centrality of the pronoun "Thou." Richly interspersed with hints for religious education.

18 Brueggemann, Walter. "Passion and Perspective: Two Dimensions of Education in the Bible." *Theology Today* 42 (1985-1986):172-80.

> Basing his argument on Old Testament texts, Brueggemann calls for a church education in which the younger generation appropriates the concrete passion of the faith with zeal and imagination, and at the same time for one with perspective that "permits one to function in public places and to make sense of general human interaction without recourse to obscurantist or sectarian claims." Thus, he maintains, "we shall have men and women in public life who have a passion for justice and a perspective of mystery, awe, and amazement."

19 Brueggemann, Walter, Sharon Parks, and Thomas H. Groome. *To Act Justly, Love Tenderly, Walk Humbly: An Agenda for Ministers*. New York: Paulist Press, 1986.

> With focus on Micah 6:8, the three authors develop an agenda for religious educators in which the emphases are on social responsibility, personal relationships, and a "holistic understanding of faith—a lived activity of knowing, doing, and trusting God's will."

20 Bushnell, Horace. *Christian Nurture*. Grand Rapids, MI: Baker Book House, 1979.

> A reprint of the 1861 edition (the most complete of the several editions of the classic). John Mulder provides a new introduction that puts the book in historical and theological context and reviews the critical response it elicited.

21 Come, Arnold. *Agents of Reconciliation*. Philadelphia: Westminster Press, 1964.

> A revised and enlarged edition of the 1960 book, adding a review of the swift developments (critical and constructive) connected with the concept of the laity and its ministry. Provides a theological platform for creative, flexible, and serious

educational program planning, but stops short of the development of such implications.

22 *The Common Catechism: A Book of Christian Faith*. New York: Seabury Press, 1975.

Signaled a significant set of changes in catechetics. Although unofficial so far as ecclesiastical bodies are concerned, it was the responsible joint product of Protestant and Roman Catholic scholars. At 690 pages, a catechism is obviously no longer something for children to memorize. Furthermore, it is anything but a set of answers; rather, it indicates what the questions are and how theology attempts to answer them.

23 Doohan, Leonard. *The Lay-Centered Church: Theology and Spirituality*. Minneapolis: Winston Press, 1984.

An assessment of developments in the ministry of the laity in the Roman Catholic church since Vatican II, and a constructive theology of the laity, seeing the church as a family living a family spirituality that encompasses all of the baptized. Addresses the variety of approaches (ecclesial, incarnational, service-oriented, and liberational) characteristic of the contemporary church. See also 33, 96, 854, and 956.

24 Duncombe, David C. *The Shape of the Christian Life*. Nashville: Abingdon Press, 1969.

A successful attempt at "behavioral theology," prompted by the author's perplexity as minister, educator, and counselor in knowing what distinguishes a Christian life from any other. Thesis: Christians have a security that makes them free, know themselves, are capable of honest expression, perceive things accurately, and do what the situation demands.

25 Dyer, George J., ed. *An American Catholic Catechism*. New York: Seabury Press, 1975.

A large (308 pages) but handy compendium of Catholic faith and practice. A sacramental theology of Christian education can be read into the chapter on grace and expanded in part 2 on the Christian sacraments. Parts 3 and 4, "Principles of Morality," and "Living the Christian Life," are quite specific on the bases for Christian education, and in part 5, "Moral Education," the directions and dilemmas of religious education itself are dealt with in concrete fashion.

26 Eastman, A. Theodore. *The Baptizing Community: Christian Initiation and the Local Congregation*. New York: Seabury Press, 1982.

An exposition of the sacrament of baptism as embodied in the new rite of the Episcopal church. The emphasis is on full preparation for and intense participation in the sacrament. Implications for education (and "continuing education and spiritual formation") are cited. See also 3, 12, 15, 16, and 36.

27 Edge, Findley B. *The Greening of the Church*. Waco, TX: Word Books, 1971.

> Reinterprets the life of the local congregation, including its educational work, in terms of renewal, stressing mission, evangelism, and social responsibility. Implications for grouping (small groups), administration, program, and "the local congregation as a miniature theological seminary."

28 Edwards, Denis. *Human Experience of God*. New York: Paulist Press, 1983.

> Foundational for religious educators as they seek to understand the meanings of faith experience and the relationship between experiencing God's reality, presence, and work and the communication of the faith. Systematically explores the realms of mystery and grace, Jesus as object of faith, contemplative experience, and faith experience as basic to mission.

29 Farley, Edward. "Can Church Education Be Theological Education?" *Theology Today* 42 (1985-1986):158-71.

> Faith faces reality, with the result that theology (ordered learning) is required, and ordered learning has been present throughout the church's history. But why has it been limited to the clergy, so that we have an educated clergy and an uneducated laity? Unfortunately, this problem is built into the church's overgeneralized understanding of education. A step in the right direction would be to see the educator on the church staff as a theologian-teacher, rather than an administrator.

30 Fenhagen, James G. *Mutual Ministry*. New York: Seabury Press, 1977.

> Focusing on the local church, this book explores in depth a theology of ministry to each other, applicable to clergy, professional church workers, and lay people alike. It is a book about which one may say, "Read it, and you will be led to new insight in what your ministry can be, insight that will lead to new ways of ministering to one another and together."

31 Fennema, Jack. *Nurturing Children in the Lord*. Phillipsburg, NJ: Presbyterian and Reformed Publishing Company, 1977.

> An intricate Calvinist analysis of the nature of the child, with implications for discipline, instruction, "chastening," and counseling. Biblical instruction is "preventive discipline" and is both formal and informal. The author shows considerable resourcefulness and imagination in distinguishing between the two and in analyzing their dynamics.

32 Ferré, Nels F.S. *A Theology for Christian Education*. Philadelphia: Westminster Press, 1967.

> Sees Christian education in relation to the spectrum of foundation disciplines, defines theology's role in the process of undertaking and conducting the educational enterprise, and in a searching way "does theology" in educational terms within a context of God's nature and role as educator.

33 Finn, Virginia S. *Pilgrim in the Parish: A Spirituality for Lay Ministries*. New York: Paulist Press, 1986.

> Rich resources for undergirding the ministries of the laity. The heart of the matter is prayer, together with biblical and theological study and reflection, and deep involvement in the life and work of the church. On the side of practical training, the author uses the figure of growth and nurture, tracing the process from "readying the soil for ministry" through harvesting.

34 Fowler, James W. *To See the Kingdom: The Theological Vision of H. Richard Niebuhr*. Nashville: Abingdon Press, 1974.

> A study of H. Richard Niebuhr "from the inside." In Niebuhr's concepts of the evolution of religious consciousness, the ethics of response, and the dynamics of faith there are basic materials for building a theology of religious education.

35 Galdamez, Pablo. *Faith of a People: The Life of a Basic Christian Community in El Salvador*. Maryknoll, NY: Orbis Books, 1986.

> A view of the base community from the inside, under the most difficult circumstances—the El Salvador of recent years. The actuality of the redemptive community emerging among the poor in the slums in a situation of national turmoil and violence becomes startlingly vivid. One sees a type of fundamental religious education at work, in the training, for instance, of those called "acolytes"—those who are learning in action the most basic servant ministry. See also 10 and 870.

36 Ganoczy, Alexander. *Becoming Christian: A Theology of Baptism as the Sacrament of Human History*. New York: Paulist Press, 1976.

> It is possible to build a theology of Christian education on the foundation of the sacrament of baptism, and this book provides a number of clues for the enterprise. "Christian life is a pilgrimage in freedom. In moving from the past through the present to create the future, the baptized enter into solidarity with Jesus, sharing his destiny and espousing his life as their own. Their lives marked by the cross and the resurrection, Christians live in hope, straining to go beyond what is to what will be." See also 3, 12, 15, 16, and 26.

37 Gelpi, Donald L. *Experiencing God: A Theology of Human Experience*. New York: Paulist Press, 1978.

> A personal and scholarly account of the development of a theology that is integrally charismatic. The last half of the book (chapters 5-8) is of specific interest to religious educators, since it deals theologically with themes related to intellectual, affective, moral, and spiritual development and education. A succinct statement of principles for American Catholic education is found on pages 253-255.

38 Getz, Gene A. *Sharpening the Focus of the Church*. Chicago: Moody Press, 1974.

   This fine product of the renewal movement in evangelical circles presents a model
   of methodology for determining the church's ministry and uses that method to set
   up a theology of ministry that encompasses evangelism, edification, leadership,
   organization and administration, and communication. The "lenses" used to
   develop a philosophy of ministry and its contemporary strategy are scripture,
   history, and culture. So germane to religious education that it amounts in effect
   to a theory of educational ministry.

39 Goodenough, Erwin R., and Evelyn W. Goodenough. "Myths and Symbols for
Children." *Religious Education* 57 (1962):172-77, 236-37.

   "The value of [myths and symbols] lies in their concreteness, and every religion
   that uses them presents them to children long before they have any notion of an
   abstract reference for their potency." Myths are stories that broaden and enlarge
   life. Symbols are concrete forms, acts, or experiences "that themselves embody
   and convey broad conceptions, or deep emotional terrors or gratifications." Thus
   myths and symbols are not to be withheld from children but given to them in their
   concreteness so that children may grow with them into maturity.

40 Grimes, Howard. *The Rebirth of the Laity*. Nashville: Abingdon Press, 1962.

   Describes and explains developments in lay adult education in this country and
   abroad, setting the discussion in the context of the ministry of the laity and the
   doctrine of the church.

41 Groome, Thomas H. "The Critical Principle in Christian Education and the Task of
Prophecy." *Religious Education* 72 (1977):262-72.

   Granting the educational power of socialization, Groome goes on to stress the
   importance of modifying its use by the use of "the critical principle," akin to the
   biblical element of prophecy. He warns, however, that "our prophecy must be a
   'being with' rather than a 'being over' others."

42 Hamilton, Neill Q. *Maturing in the Christian Life*. Philadelphia: Geneva Press, 1984.

   Taking account of psychologically oriented stages of faith development, the author
   suggests that theological data be given more serious consideration in determining
   the "stages" to be used in the achievement of Christian maturity. His alternative
   stages are discipleship, a shift in locus to the Spirit, and maturing in the Christian
   community and mission. To him, the pastor's basic criterion for the church's
   work is the attainment of Christian maturity in these terms.

43 Häring, Bernard. *Evangelization Today*. Slough, England: St. Paul Publications,
1974.

   Essential reading for a contemporary approach to evangelism, and for an
   understanding of the role of education in evangelism. The church is an
   evangelizing community, evangelizing for Christian community. Religious

educators will benefit from the treatments of pre-evangelization, the pedagogy of faith, and education towards reconciliation.

44 Harkness, Georgia. *The Church and Its Laity*. Nashville: Abingdon Press, 1962.

A simple and thorough exposition of the ministry of the laity set in historical, cultural, theological, and educational perspectives. Indicates the place of Christian education among the functions of the church's ministry and details the then current movements in creative adult Christian education.

45 Harkness, Georgia. *Women in Church and Society*. Nashville: Abingdon Press, 1972.

A historical, biblical, and theological review of the role of women in the church and in society in general, prompted by the women's movement. Some reference is made to women and church vocations, including vocations in religious education.

46 Hauerwas, Stanley. *Character and the Christian Life: A Study in Theological Ethics*. San Antonio, TX: Trinity University Press, 1975.

If the focus is not so much on right and wrong or on freedom and responsibility, but on virtue and character, the way is open to new insights into moral formation. The implication, not developed in the book, is that religious education may become in this sense appropriately oriented as a theological, ethical enterprise directed toward intentionally acting self-agents.

47 Hauerwas, Stanley, *et al. Truthfulness and Tragedy*. Notre Dame, IN: University of Notre Dame Press, 1977.

If religious education were to be reoriented as a branch of Christian ethics, Hauerwas, with his rehabilitation of the concept of character and his bringing together of specific ethical concerns, personal story, and biblical story, might well be its primary resource. "I am trying to do theology in a manner appropriate to the way Christian convictions operate, or should operate, to form and direct lives."

48 Haughton, Rosemary. *The Theology of Experience*. Paramus, NJ: Newman Press, 1972.

An exploration of the experiential sources of religious life and thought in community, ministry, family, sexuality, and spirit.

49 Haughton, Rosemary. *The Transformation of Man*. Springfield, IL: Templegate, 1967.

This remarkable book "attempts to show the elements of the human theological crisis in which our whole culture is involved and to interpret them in terms of the processes of formation and transformation." It thus takes the essence of Catholic education (formation) and the Reformed tradition (transformation) and suggests a theological approach to the renewal of persons in contemporary culture.

50   Henderlite, Rachel. *Forgiveness and Hope: A Theological Basis for Christian Education*. Richmond, VA: John Knox, 1961.

A short and meaty book proposing the doctrine of justification by faith as an appropriate organizing principle for a theology of Christian education and considering four problems in light of this doctrine: the meaning of faith, the nature of the human, the nature of new life, and the meaning of history.

51 Henderlite, Rachel. *The Holy Spirit in Christian Education*. Philadelphia: Westminster Press, 1964.

The work of the educator in light of the work of the Holy Spirit. General education and Christian education are sharply contrasted as to aim, content, and method. Christian educators teach the data of the faith but do not teach faith. They teach the Word of God non-literalistically and not on their own authority, so that the testimony to its validity may be the Spirit's. They make the heritage available, educate for mission, and subject all aspects of the life of the church to the Holy Spirit to be used for the nurture of the members. The church "only has to put itself and its means at the disposal of the Holy Spirit, whose enterprise it is."

52 Hendrick, John R. *Opening the Door of Faith*. Atlanta: John Knox Press, 1977.

A well-conceived book on evangelism, with a tremendous amount of input from clergy, laity, and ordinary citizens. Faith as both a personal and relational act is viewed developmentally as well. Three concluding chapters are quite specific on the functions the congregation can perform in conducting a penetrating evangelistic emphasis. There is an unusual sensitivity to the relation of evangelism to education.

53 Hendricks, William S. *A Theology for Aging*. Nashville: Broadman Press, 1986.

Rooted in a conservative theology that stresses conversion, this book sees in the experience of aging adults the possibility of fresh and revelatory theological insight.

54 Hendricks, William L. *A Theology for Children*. Nashville: Broadman Press, 1980.

A book for adults, to help them grasp and guide the theological experience and understanding of children. The heart of the matter is set forth in appendix A: how to correlate the insights of developmental psychology and the demands of a biblical conversionist stance.   The author has tried to go deep, to be comprehensive, and the same time to come through simply, clearly, and helpfully.

55 Hessel, Dieter T. *Reconciliation and Conflict*. Philadelphia: Westminster Press, 1969.

The church's imperative to social action has now become so much a part of its life and operations that it may be analyzed and assessed in a mature way. This book does this, the result being an overview that serves as a guide to policy and practice. As religious educators try to use an action base for learning, they will find this book especially helpful.

56 Higgins, Gregory C. "The Significance of Postliberalism for Religious Education." *Religious Education* 84 (1989):77-89.

> Recognizing the link between theological foundations and teaching methodologies, Higgins explores the implications of postliberalism for religious education. He relates the three basic approaches to the study of religion described by George Lindbeck (propositionalist; experiential-expressivism; cultural linguistic or postliberal) to corresponding contemporary teaching methodologies (catechism and experiential approaches). Higgins concludes with a discussion of postliberalism and what it might mean for religious education.

57 Hofinger, Johannes, and Frances J. Buckley. *The Good News and Its Proclamation*. Notre Dame, IN: University of Notre Dame Press, 1968.

> This "post-Vatican II edition of *The Art of Teaching Christian Doctrine*" spells out the basis of the position that was embodied in "the new catechetics." Hofinger was the acknowledged leader of these new developments in Roman Catholic religious education, and this is his major work.

58 Howe, Reuel L. *Herein Is Love*. Philadelphia: Judson Press, 1961.

> Subtitled, "A Study of the Biblical Doctrine of Love in its Bearing on Personality, Parenthood, Teaching, and All Other Human Relationships," this book distills the practical wisdom of other of the church's outstanding authorities on interpersonal relationships.

59 Howe, Reuel L. *The Miracle of Dialogue*. New York: Seabury Press, 1963.

> Explores the field of interpersonal and divine-human communication in an attempt to show how dialogue may unlock the powers of persons in relation.

60 Huebner, Dwayne. "Religious Education: Practicing the Presence of God." *Religious Education* 82 (1987):569-77.

> "Our agenda for religious education...is one of scrutinizing the fabrics of relationships that we have, those of intimacy and those of community, and of asking how God is present or absent in those relationships. And then, with the help of our religious traditions, imagining how we can practice the presence of God in these relationships of intimacy and community. From that act of imagination, informed by the resources of our religious traditions, we need to transform our present relationships to include God's presence."

61 Hull, John M. "What Is Theology of Education?" *Scottish Journal of Theology* 30 (1977):3-39.

> Arguing that educators' theological premises are to be particularized, even though this means varieties of points of view in the field, focus is on the religious consciousness as religiously involved in education. To guide and facilitate the process of development of theologies of education, a "taxonomy of problems in the theology of education" is outlined, indicating in detail the questions to be dealt with.

62   Hurley, Mark J. *Declaration on Christian Education of Vatican Council II*. New York: Paulist Press, 1966.

> Contains the declaration itself, together with an analytical commentary on various aspects of its preparation, content, and prospects. Other useful data, such as the "interventions" of certain bishops, are included.

63 Hutchinson, John A. *Language and Faith*. Philadelphia: Westminster Press, 1966.

> Although only passing reference is made to education as such, the argument of this book is of the utmost importance for religious education theory, because of its analysis of religious communication. Categories of communication are listed and defined. Religion is then defined as "total or comprehensive life orientation," and religious statements as "orientation statements." Consideration of the varieties of cognitive experience leads to differentiation between science, art, and philosophy as "languages," and between "religious" statements (images, faith language) and "theological" statements (concepts, explanations). Promise is seen here for clarification of biblical faith and pursuit of interfaith conversation. See also 136, 153, 163, 173, and 674.

64 Illich, Ivan D. *Celebration of Awareness: A Call for Institutional Revolution*. New York: Doubleday, 1970.

> Illich has a keen mind that sees the "taken for granted" in fresh ways and talks about them with unusual candor. Among the things he discusses is schooling, and the religious educator will gain from the discussion a new insight into its limitations and possibilities in local and worldwide contexts.

65   Jarvis, Peter, and Nicholas Walters, eds. *Adult Education and Theological Interpretations*. Malabar, FL: Krieger Publishing Company, 1993.

> These essays amount to a debate about various theological interpretations of adult education. Michael Welton writes about Christian conversion and conscientisation; Reg Wickett about contract learning and covenant; Mechthild Hart and Deborah Horton about spirituality and adult education; and Peter Willis about catechism, preaching, and indoctrination. Essays focus on faith and knowledge (part 2), learning (part 3), the individual (part 4), community (part 5) and society (part 6). Nicola Slee writes the concluding reflection.

66 Joyce, J. Daniel. "The Biblical Basis of the Teaching Ministry." *Encounter* 23 (Spring 1962):170-80.

> The Old Testament assumption that we are born in a covenant and growing up in it, taught by family, sages, and priests, is contrasted with the New Testament idea that the goal of the teaching ministry is "personal decision and dedication followed by stimulated and guided growth....In general, teaching addresses itself to those who are not in rebellion but in repentance and who seek to know the will of God, as well as children who have the openness toward the Word of God because of parents or others who have created it."

67 Kennedy, William Bean. "Learning in, with, and for the Church: The Theological Education of the People of God." *Union Seminary Quarterly Review* 36 (1981 suppl.):27-38.

> Calls for a religious education that goes beyond socialization to the point of skilled use of critical consciousness through corporate service and action by the members of particular communities of faith. Such action is to be coupled with theological reflection in order to gain perspective and develop meaning and significance. Furthermore, religious education achieves ecumenical character "when Christians from diverse circumstances engage seriously with each other, when something is at stake."

68 Knox, Ian P. *Above or Within? The Supernatural in Religious Education.* Mishawaka, IN: Religious Education Press, 1976.

> Some religious educators orient their position to a God of transcendence; others think of God as immanent. After examining both positions and what each means for religious education, the author proposes a view that holds the natural and the supernatural in equilibrium. But this view is not insisted upon. Rather, the emphasis is on showing how, when analyzed in terms of aim, content, teacher, student, environment, and evaluation, a theorist's view of God does make a difference in the religious education proposed.

69 Laforest, Jacques. *Introduction à la Catéchèse.* Quebec: Les Presses de l'Université, 1966.

> A theology of Christian education from the Catechetical Institute of Laval University, in which a major reorientation of catechetics specifically toward "la foi vécu" (living faith) is proposed and developed historically and theologically, with stress on personal encounter and liturgical participation in the context of salvation history.

70 Langford, Norman F. "Eschatology and Christian Education." *Nexus* (a Presbyterian Church (U.S.A.) publication), Winter 1961.

> Noting that eschatology, one of the most prominent elements in the Bible, has been neglected in discussions of religious education, Langford calls for attention to specific eschatological passages in order to counter false interpretations of history, in order to be able to face the future realistically, and in order to maintain a balance between insecurity and hope.

71 Lee, James Michael, ed. *The Spirituality of the Religious Educator.* Birmingham, AL: Religious Education Press, 1985.

> The religious educator's own spirituality as a religious educator is viewed by religious educators from four perspectives (life-work, developmental, process, and ecumenical spirituality) and by four specialists in the field of spirituality itself (western contemplative, Jesuit, Orthodox, and eastern).

72 Little, Sara. *The Role of the Bible in Contemporary Christian Education*. Richmond, VA: John Knox Press, 1961.

> One of the most significant studies in the attempt to articulate basic religious education theory, this book pinpoints areas of consensus and divergence among theologians and Christian educators on the meaning of revelation, the nature of the biblical witness, the relevance of the Bible, and the appropriation of the biblical message. See also 206 and 219.

73   Lo, Samuel E. *Tillichian Theology and Educational Philosophy*. New York: Philosophical Library, 1970.

> A doctoral dissertation that does a carefully discriminating job of analyzing Tillich and weighing his views for their educational implications. The study of religious education that is included would serve to orient the Protestant student of religious education to then prevailing trends in the field.

74 Lohff, Wenzel. *Glaubenslehre und Erziehung*. Göttingen: Vanderhoeck und Ruprecht, 1974.

> An attempt to reinterpret the basic symbols of the Christian faith so that they may function faithfully in the context of religious education when the aim is liberation rather than authoritarian indoctrination. The educational implications of key symbols are developed: revelation, creation (creation as experience; the image of God; motivation, sexuality, and marriage; property; power), sin as alienation, reconciliation as the overcoming of alienation, and eschatology as Christian hope. A final chapter deals with using the symbols of the faith with children.

75 Mackay, John A. *Ecumenics: The Science of the Church Universal*. Englewood Cliffs, NJ: Prentice-Hall, 1964.

> A definition and exposition of the science of ecumenics--"the worldwide Christian community studied in its essential character as a missionary reality, together with all that is involved when this ecumenical society is true to its nature and fulfills its destiny." In this single discipline are caught up questions of the church's essence, mission, unity, and relations with the world. Involves a reassessment of theological and other forms of education. Studded with brilliant insights that are the product of Mackay's far-ranging interests and mature wisdom.

76 Marino, Joseph S., ed. *Biblical Themes in Religious Education*. Birmingham, AL: Religious Education Press, 1983.

> James Michael Lee provides a sharp and insightful set of seven principles for dealing with the Bible in religious education. Marino reverses the process by an analysis from "a biblicist's view." In this context scholars provide seven chapters opening the basic biblical themes for religious education: the discovery of God, faith, commitment and discipleship in the New Testament, prayer, justice, sin, and reconciliation.

77 Marthaler, Berard. *Catechetics in Context*. Huntington, IN: Our Sunday Visitor, 1973.

A detailed interpretation of and commentary on the *General Catechetical Directory*. The commentary suggests directions and resources that "flesh out" the items in the directory for American Catholics.

78 Marthaler, Berard. *The Creed*. Mystic, CT: Twenty-Third Publications, 1987.

Drawing on biblical, liturgical, historical, and theological studies, the author develops an interpretation of the Nicene Creed as a basis for common confession of the apostolic faith. Developed as a course at the Catholic University in Washington, it seeks to meet the need for an interpretation that takes into account how various social and cultural factors gave rise to the development of creedal authority.

79 May, William E. *Becoming Human: An Invitation to Christian Ethics*. Dayton, OH: Pflaum Publishing, 1975.

Some books do not intend to be about religious education but are actually basic to it. This is such a book. Ethical decision-making is "the endeavor to discover what it takes to make and keep life human," with emphasis on the dimensions of growth and becoming. Such an invitation to Christian ethics might easily become a model for Christian education.

80 McConnell, Theodore. "The Scope of Recent Theology: New Foundations for Religious Education." *Religious Education* 63 (1968):339-49.

McConnell calls detailed attention to the work of the theologians of the 1960s in order to help religious educators understand them and to discover their implications for religious education theory and practice. The categories that he uses are "Radical Theology and the Idea of God," "Science and Religion," "Theology and Culture," "The Nature of Belief," and "Philosophy and Theology."

81 Moore, Allen J. "Religious Education as Living Theology: Some Reflections on the Contributions of Ross Snyder." *Religious Education* 73 (1978):541-50.

Ross Snyder combines in religious education the elements of John Dewey, George Herbert Mead, social existentialism, and phenomenology. For him, religious education is a theological discipline, with theology reconstructed as an empirical inquiry into the hidden and ultimate meanings that human life incarnates. Theological reflection is the "exegesis of human experience." The church is a people who both have a culture and who, through the educational enterprise, are building a culture.

82 Moore, Mary Elizabeth Mullino. *Teaching from the Heart: Theology and Educational Method*. Minneapolis: Fortress Press, 1991.

Moore takes an interactive approach in relating process theology to five educational methods: case study ("Midwife Teaching"), gestalt ("Integrative Teaching"), phenomenological ("Incarnational Teaching"), and conscientization

("Liberative Teaching"). Her concern for holistic education leads her beyond process theology as the content of teaching (Miller), a philosophy of education (Whitehead), or source of educational principles (Cobb) to a transformative dialogue with both process theology and educational method. See also 141, 148, 158, and 675.

83 Moran, Gabriel. *Catechetics of Revelation*. New York: Herder and Herder, 1966.

Faced with a "somewhat frightening collapse of tightly organized systems of religious teaching...the new bases of unity and organization must emerge from the experience of teachers together with an understanding provided by a solid scriptural-theological knowledge." God's revelation is taking place now in the students' lives. "All depends upon their eventual realization that Jesus Christ is a living person, that God spoke to him, and that in the glorifying act of raising him God continues to speak the word of his love."

84 Moran, Gabriel. *Religious Body: Design for a New Reformation*. New York: Seabury Press, 1974.

An analytical consideration of the reconstitution of the church as "a valid religious body...where education and community join to reveal the religious expressions of human life." Religious education is a matter of "the whole religious community educat(ing) the whole religious community to make free and intelligent decisions vis-a-vis the whole world."

85 Mudge, Lewis S., and James N. Poling, eds. *Formation and Reflection: The Promise of Practical Theology*. Philadelphia: Fortress Press, 1987.

Eight theologians propose substantial methods for approaching problems of ministry and of human existence. The authors propose that the problems themselves, theological insights on them, and insights from other disciplines be brought into dynamic and reflective interplay to the end of more principled approaches to the tasks of ministry. The methods they suggest vary and have not been reconciled with one another. That task is left to practical theologians themselves. Note particularly the chapter by Don S. Browning, "Practical Theology and Religious Education," in which he argues that the failure to anchor Christian religious education in the discipline of practical theology, and in its subdiscipline of theological ethics, has resulted in confusion about its proper goal. After reviewing how Westerhoff, Fowler, and Groome place Christian religious education within the context of practical theology, Browning sets out to offer an ethical refinement of Groome's five movements. In making a theological ethic more explicit, he relates his own theory of five levels of moral thinking to Groome's shared praxis method and concludes by outlining a five-level action-reflection model.

86 Muller, Alois. *Orientations Pedagogiques Vers L'Eglise Nouvelle*. Mulhouse, France: Editions Salvator, 1967.

Develops the educational implications of four aspects of the new view of the church: religion and faith, the church, the Christian life, and the world and Christian values.

87 Neuhaus, Richard John. *Freedom for Ministry*. San Francisco: Harper and Row, 1979.

> Neuhaus holds a high view of the ministry and of the ordained minister. This detailed and very practical study explores situations and relationships of ministry and demonstrates how the minister in full humanity is at the same time a very special person. Applies equally well to professional religious educators.

88 Niederstrasser, Heinz. *Kerygma und Paideia*. Stuttgart: Evangelisches Verlagswerk, 1967.

> A massive theology of education, exploring basically the proclamation-education problem and the possibility of a grace-oriented education. Practical theology done in light of biblical and historical theology and intended to illuminate theory and practice in religious education.

89 Nixon, Leroy. *John Calvin's Teachings on Human Reason*. New York: Exposition Press, 1963.

> Useful to religious educators particularly because of part 2, "Implications for Theory of Reformed Protestant Christian Education," in which the author states four fundamental principles: Christian education's mystical orientation, use of regenerate reason, central emphasis on the family, and focus on adults as the beginning point for the educational program.

90 Oden, Thomas C. *Pastoral Theology: Essentials of Ministry*. San Francisco: Harper and Row, 1983.

> A searching analysis of the pastoral ministry, based on exhaustive historical and contemporary scholarship and on intimate and detailed knowledge of the authority and tasks of the minister. Teaching is given its integral place among clergy functions. A book for the minister and religious educator to live with and around which to order life and work.

91 Oden, Thomas C. *The Structure of Awareness*. Nashville: Abingdon Press, 1969.

> The objective of religious education centers on "awareness." The scope of religious education is "the whole field of relationships—God, the human, nature, and history—in light of the gospel." This volume, a humanistic and theological study, could be taken as a direct exposition of these concepts. "To be aware is to be awake to reality, to recognize the situation in which one stands." The bulk of the book deals with "time-awareness" (past, future, present)—what religious education means by "history." Then, more briefly, the categories of God, self, neighbor, and nature are explored.

92 O'Meara, Thomas Franklin. *Theology of Ministry*. New York: Paulist Press, 1983.

> While it does not deal with the educational ministry in any explicit way, this book will be of great help to religious educators in establishing a theological context for their work and their relationships to Christ, the church, and those engaged in other forms of ministry.

93 Osborne, Kenan B. *The Christian Sacraments of Initiation*. New York: Paulist Press, 1987.

From a Roman Catholic base, the author develops an ecumenical analysis of baptism, confirmation, and the Eucharist as constituting a unified movement of incorporation into the community of faith. Provides much of the material out of which a sacramental theology of Christian education might be formed.

94 Parks, Sharon Daloz. "Home and Pilgrimage: Companion Metaphors for Personal and Social Transformation." *The Drew Gateway* 60 (1990):22-41.

The author critiques the metaphors of pilgrimage and journey, observing that they have become the dominant metaphors for development to the exclusion of the companion metaphors of home, homesteading, and dwelling. Parks argues, "...we will not find the wholeness we seek until the imagery of home, homesteading, dwelling, and abiding is restored to a place of centrality in the contemporary imagination."

95 Patte, Daniel, ed. *Kingdom and Children: Aphorism, Chreia, Structure*. Chico, CA: Scholars Press, 1983.

The outgrowth of a seminar on the exegesis of Jesus' views of children, childhood, and the Kingdom. Patte provides a structural analysis, and Vernon K. Robbins a rhetorical approach, while John Dominic Crossan studies the aphoristic tradition. Other scholars provide critical responses.

96 Peck, George, and John S. Hoffman, eds. *The Laity in Ministry: The Whole People of God for the Whole World*. Valley Forge, PA: Judson Press, 1984.

A product of the faculty of Andover Newton Theological School, this reexamination of the idea and practice of the ministry of the laity explores the reasons why its acceptance has lagged, cites particular cases of such ministry, reworks its theological base, and suggests promising lines of action. A chapter by Richard R. Broholm deals with the education of the laity for ministry.

97 Perry, David W., ed. *Making Sense of Things: Towards a Theology of Homegrown Christian Education*. New York: Seabury Press, 1981.

Little snippets of theological thinking by practicing religious educators, mostly regional religious education coordinators in the Episcopal church. The book is intended to stimulate other religious educators to formulate and share their own theological thinking. It is interesting to note how Tom Groome and John Westerhoff are major influences throughout.

98 Poling, James N., and Donald E. Miller. *Foundations for a Practical Theology of Ministry*. Nashville: Abingdon Press, 1985.

The method proposed has six sequential elements: description of lived experience, critical awareness of perspectives and interests, correlation of perspectives from culture and Christian tradition, interpretation of meaning and value, critique of interpretation, guidelines and specific plans for a particular community.

99 Powell, Oliver. *Household of Power*. Boston: Pilgrim Press, 1962.

An exciting book in practical theology, defining religious education as a vital aspect of the life and mission of the church as the community of faith and showing clearly the roles of small group experience, mission, social action, worship, and the shared ministry of laity and clergy in relation to the educational task.

100 Prieur, Michael R. *The Sacrament of Reconciliation Today*. Bethlehem, PA: Catechetical Communications, 1973.

A reconsideration of the sacrament of penance in its theological and practical aspects. Important because of the changes in interpretation and practice of the sacrament in relation to children. Some attention is paid to the psychology of the child, the child's religious understanding and experience, and the nexus of human relationships (family and church) in which the sacrament is experienced meaningfully or not by the child.

101 Reid, J.K.S. *Our Life in Christ*. Philadelphia: Westminster Press, 1963.

Provides the religious educator with a competently constructed biblical theology of personality: critical, comparative, and constructive.

102 Reifenrath, Bruno H. *Erziehung im Licht des Ewigen: Die Pädagogik Edith Steins*. Frankfurt: Verlag Moritz Diesterweg, 1985.

A unique study in the theology of education, based on the thought of Edith Stein—convert, Carmelite, and martyr under the Nazis. With strong roots in Catholicism and in existential phenomenology, Stein provided the basis from which the author has developed a systematic view of her educational thought, including the education of women. Basically, "the horizon of the eternal" is given priority in determining educational aims, thus overcoming difficulties in theories rooted in culture and values.

103 Richards, Lawrence O. *A New Face for the Church*. Grand Rapids, MI: Zondervan Publishing House, 1970.

A pivotal book in the development of Richards's work in Christian education and in church renewal. Chronicles his experience and research in reworking his concept of the church truly responsive to its faith and its day. Implications are drawn for congregational life, Christian education, evangelism, and social concern.

104 Richards, Lawrence O. *A Theology of Children's Ministry*. Grand Rapids, MI: Zondervan Publishing House, 1983.

Ever since he instituted the curriculum "Sunday School Plus," it has been evident that Richards's concern for Christian education includes the whole life span. Here he gives us in intricate detail his thinking (and his sifting of others' thought) on children's ministry. To be rooted in a theology of integral participation in the life and worship of the Christian community and in developmental understandings (Piagetian), the institutions of

children's nurture are (in order) the home, the church, and the school.
The dynamics of each are explored, with attention to the Christian school
and to the enriched use of the Bible in curriculum and teaching.

105 Richards, Lawrence O. *A Theology of Christian Education*. Grand Rapids, MI:
Zondervan Publishing House, 1975.

A huge and challenging volume that leads the reader to engage in
self-directed theological inquiry into the theology of Christian education.
A theology of the church is carefully integrated with its implications for
Christian education. Administrative, organizational, and methodological
considerations follow. Each chapter includes "probes" to help the reader
think the matter through and draw personal conclusions.

106 Richards, Lawrence O., and Gib Martin. *A Theology of Personal Ministry*. Grand
Rapids, MI: Zondervan Publishing House, 1981.

Richards and Martin work essentially from a covenant concept of the
church to an identification of particular gifts in ministry, conceiving
ministry as a basically lay function in which clergy share. Theological and
biblical analyses and imperatives undergird the argument, and "probes"
provide illustrative material and enable the readers to arrive at their own
particular implications.

107 Robbins, Vernon K. *Jesus the Teacher: A Socio-Rhetorical Interpretation of Mark*.
Philadelphia: Fortress Press, 1984.

Robbins's thesis is that the Gospel of Mark was intended to present Jesus
as combining the prophet (as in Jewish tradition) and the
philosopher-teacher (as in the Greco-Roman tradition), thus aiming at Jew
and non-Jew alike. An emphasis for religious educators is the intricate
analysis of "the teacher/disciple cycle," consisting of three phases: initial,
intermediate, and final. A major contribution of biblical scholarship to the
understanding of Jesus as a "disciple-gathering prophet-teacher."

108 Rose, Stephen C. *The Grass Roots Church*. New York: Holt, Rinehart and Winston,
1966.

This is a first instance of those concerned with church renewal turning
their attention to specific new structures. Three functions of the renewed
church are developed: chaplaincy (worship, pastoral care, and preaching),
teaching (interpreted as a full-time job), and abandonment (giving up
everything peripheral to the other two ministries, and "giving up one's life
for another"). There is a short, pointed section on teaching (pp. 105-109),
but the main significance for religious education is the insistence upon
responsible indigenous educational planning for training for meaningful and
effective ministry.

109 Rost, H.T.D. *The Brilliant Stars: The Baha'i Faith and the Education of Children.* Oxford: George Ronald, 1979.

Baha'i, as a universal and uniting faith, has had some influence in the western world. Its ideals of peace and world unification are reflected in its educational stance, which is developed and argued in this volume. At the time of writing the author was a professor at Kenyatta University College, Nairobi.

110 Roth, Robert P. *Story and Reality.* Grand Rapids, MI: William B. Eerdmans Publishing Company, 1973.

The theme of communication of the faith through the medium of the story runs through theology and education. Primarily biblical and theological, this interpretation of "story truth" can serve as foundational material for religious education theory.

111 Runyon, Theodore, ed. *Hope for the Church: Moltmann in Dialogue with Practical Theology.* Nashville: Abingdon Press, 1979.

Moltmann lectured on practical theology at Candler School of Theology in 1978 and then engaged in dialogue with faculty members in the field. The book presents their lectures (together with that of one visitor). The result is a rich presentation of Moltmann's own views on the subject (including Christian education), plus the reflections of persons like James Fowler, who represented Christian education in the dialogue.

112 Russell, Letty M. *The Future of Partnership.* Philadelphia: Westminster Press, 1979.

An attempt to reorient both method and substance in theology. Within the argument the author makes a brief but significant statement on "Partnership in Learning."

113 Russell, Letty M. *Growth in Partnership.* Philadelphia: Westminster Press, 1981.

Russell here deals with the specific theme of educational ministry, developed around the concept of partnership. There is a developing community of learning that aims toward both "building the Body" and "growth toward maturity," through partnership. This is tied to liberation themes as "education as exodus" and "pedagogy for oppressors" are explored. A pervasive concern is a new approach to theological education.

114 Sauer, Ralph. *Religiöse Erziehung auf dem Weg zum Glauben.* Düsseldorf: Patmos Verlag, 1976.

As theology is challenged from many sources (hermeneutic, analytical, scientific, and other), many questions are raised for religious education. The author sees these challenges and questions as opportunities for the religious educator and shows how religious education can start from the questions of the analyst, skeptic, or inquirer and accomplish its task of

leading to the life of faith.   Specific examples for various levels of
religious teaching are given.

115 Sawicki, Marianne. "Teaching as a Gift of Peace." *Theology Today* 47 (1990-
1991):377-87.

Sawicki views the cultural ethos of consumption as a virus and the Christian
message as the immune system of humanity.   Four key elements of Christian
teaching and lifestyle—resurrection, covenant, commitment, and reconciliation—
strengthen the immune system against the attack of the damaging virus.   For
Sawicki, Christian education is a way of giving peace to the world through the
church.   She writes: "Christian education is a kind of portraiture, that is, a
copying of the face of Jesus, seen in the New Testament, into new media."

116   Schipani, Daniel S. *Theologia del Ministerio Educatavio: Perspectivas
Latinamericanas*. Buenos Aires and Grand Rapids: Nueva Creacion and Wm. B.
Eerdmans Publishing Company, 1993.

Schipani's newest book attempts to answer some basic questions facing Christian
educators today: Does our theology influence or determine the decisions we make
regarding the content of religious education?   In what ways does our theology
affect methodology, objectives, curriculum, and administration in religious
education?   What is the exact relationship between theology and Christian
education? Schipani believes that theology (specifically liberation theology) and
Christian education need to dialogue for mutual enrichment, and that religious
education mediates between theology and ministry.   Each chapter focuses on a
particular liberationist concept.

117 Schreiter, Robert J. *Constructing Local Theologies*. Maryknoll, NY: Orbis Books,
1985.

Working from the insight that "the great Christian tradition" consists of a
series of "local theologies," the author provides a study of the ways in
which the gospel, which is given in a societal and cultural context, may be
allowed to speak the language of an entirely different culture.   A
fundamental resource for those concerned with cross-cultural and
multicultural religious education.

118 Seymour, Jack L., and Donald Miller, eds. *Theological Approaches to Christian
Education*. Nashville: Abingdon Press, 1990.

Concerned with the relationship between education and theology, the book is a
sequel to the editors' previous collection of essays, *Contemporary Approaches to
Christian Education* (1982). Essays in the present volume are organized around
five categories: tradition, church, person, mission, and method. Mariane Sawicki,
Charles Foster, Fumitaka Matsuoka, Choan-Seng Song, and Robert O'Gorman are
among the contributors.

119   Shelp, Earl E., and Ronald Sunderland, eds. *Biblical Basis for Ministry.* Philadelphia: Westminster Press, 1981.

An attempt at conversation between biblical studies and "ministry" as a focal theme in practical theology. The religious educator is not directly addressed, but any religious educator who sees the task as an aspect of ministry will be enriched both by the substance and by the method of the book.

120 Sloyan, Gerard, *et al.* "Symposium: Kerygmatic Catechetics." *Religious Education* 57 (1962):329-62.

When this symposium was published, "kerygmatic catechetics" had come to a point of maturity from which it could be surveyed critically. Sloyan considers its use of Scripture its unique feature, so far as substance is concerned. Mariko M. Isomura reviews it historically, and finds it worthy as a way of linking past and present. Franz Schreibmayr views it as a way of dealing with doctrine. William J. Reedy develops an elaborate taxonomy of the questions involved in the approach. Lloyd E. Sheneman provides a Protestant response.

121 Smart, James D. *The Creed in Christian Teaching.* Philadelphia: Westminster Press, 1962.

Undertaken both as a personal discipline and as an extension of the author's *The Teaching Ministry of the Church,* this book defines the relationship between theology and Christian education and uses the creed both as a focus for Christian teaching and as a source of insights for Christian education.

122 Smart, James D. *The Rebirth of Ministry.* Philadelphia: Westminster Press, 1960.

A theology of ministry, based upon biblical sources, which characterizes the teaching ministry as a ministry of the Word in the context of all the tasks involved in carrying out the church's basic mandate.

123 Smith, David L. *Symbolism and Growth: The Religious Thought of Horace Bushnell.* Chico, CA: Scholars Press, 1981.

Bushnell's thought is "modeled on a theory of the power of symbolic expressions, linguistic and otherwise, to facilitate human moral growth." Bushnell's writings are reviewed, with an especially pertinent treatment of the theologian as educator, finding that "Bushnell believed that theology, properly conceived, could play a role in restoring human receptivity to God's self-communication."

124 Smith, H. Shelton, ed. *Horace Bushnell.* New York: Oxford University Press, 1965.

Consists chiefly of selections from Bushnell's writings, showing his theological method and his reconstruction of theological thought. Mainly valuable to religious educators for its delineation of the historical background and theological controversies that provide the context for *Christian Nurture*. Includes an introduction to and excerpts from that work.

125   Stein, Robert H. *The Method and Message of Jesus' Teachings*. Philadelphia: Westminster Press, 1978.

Religious educators are interested in differentiating the biblical traditions of sage and prophet. Stein examines them as they pertain to Jesus. He also examines Jesus' teaching (with special attention to the parables) and its content in the categories of the kingdom of God, the fatherhood of God, the ethics of the Kingdom, and Christology.

126 Strawson, William. *Teachers and the New Theology*. London: Epworth Press, 1969.

Written for British religious educators, this book deals with the content of religious teaching in light of then contemporary theological developments. It seeks "to narrow the gap between theologians and teachers....There is urgent necessity for teachers to base their approach on a tenable theological position, and not on views which can only be accepted by doing violence to their intellectual integrity."

127 Thompson, Norma H., ed. *Religious Education and Theology*. Birmingham, AL: Religious Education Press, 1982.

Norma Thompson and Randolph Crump Miller provide a historical review of the theologies that have influenced religious education since the turn of the century. Most religious educators will find themselves at home with Miller, Lawrence O. Richards, or John Westerhoff. But the greatest intellectual challenges are presented by Gabriel Moran, who distinguishes a generic religious education, and James Michael Lee, who takes a social science approach. A moral challenge is encountered in Olivia Stokes's presentation of black theology.

128   Thornton, Edward E. *Being Transformed: An Inner Way of Spiritual Growth*. Philadelphia: Westminster Press, 1984.

A significantly autobiographical study of the processes and dynamics by which the self becomes aware of the spiritual life. A revitalized Bible study, meditation, prayer, personal relationships, and social responsibility are all involved.

129   Tracy, David. *The Achievement of Bernard Lonergan*. New York: Herder and Herder, 1970.

Lonergan marks a major reorientation of theology toward the phenomenological, and this volume provides an overall interpretation of his views. While he does not deal directly with education, his concepts of insight, conversion, and meaning can be extremely important for religious education theory.

130 Webber, George W. *Today's Church: A Community of Exiles and Pilgrims.* Nashville: Abingdon Press, 1979.

> Within the context of the church as a pilgrim community in the city, Webber provides, in a chapter entitled "Life in Exile: A Nurturing Community," a critique of religious education, together with specific guidelines for the character of appropriate Christian nurture of adults and children.

131 Weber, Hans-Ruedi. *Jesus and the Children.* Geneva: World Council of Churches, 1979.

> The biblical texts on Jesus and children are examined for their uses in education and preaching. In the process, a theology of the child in the church emerges. Appendices provide additional valuable technical material and study helps.

132 Westley, Dick. *Morality and Its Beyond.* Mystic, CT: Twenty-Third Publications, 1984.

> Resituates the church in relation to personal and social morality, enables us to see ourselves as part of a movement for love and understanding (rather than for moral conduct) in the world, and helps us experience that build-up of love and understanding personally. The touchiest questions are handled in this light.

133 Wynne, Edward J., Jr. *The Implications of Carl Michalson's Theological Method for Christian Education.* Edited by Henry O. Thompson. Washington, DC: University Press of America, 1983.

> A publication of the Carl Michalson Society. Christian education is taken here as the content of the curriculum, and the aim is to give guidance toward a theology of Christian education. After exposition of Michalson's "theology as history," detailed comparisons are made between him and the categories of the curriculum as seen by the Cooperative Curriculum Project. Many specific implications that would infuse Michalson's theology into those categories are sharply drawn. "Theology as history" is a meaning-making and meaning-transforming process, shared but deeply personal, penetrated by an eschatological reality already present in Jesus Christ.

134 Ziegler, Jesse H. "Christian Education: A Constructive Theological Approach." *Encounter* 23 (Spring 1962):137-69.

> Biblical and theological insight are brought to bear upon the central questions of Christian education: Who is the teacher? Who is to be taught? What is the curriculum? How shall teaching and learning take place? Concludes that "the real teacher is God in his own self-disclosure....The best we can do is to so break up and disturb the ground that the Holy Spirit may do his own work."

135 Zuck, Roy B. *Spiritual Power in Your Teaching*. Chicago: Moody Press, 1972.

Constitutes a critical and constructive theology of Christian education in evangelical perspective. The doctrine of the Holy Spirit is developed biblically and historically in its significance for the human teacher, the use of the Bible, and the teaching-learning process. "In the final sense, God the Holy Spirit is the teacher."

PHILOSOPHY OF EDUCATION

136 Ankoviak, Mary Ann. "The New Hermeneutic, Language and the Religious Education of the Adolescent." *Religious Education* 69 (1974):40-52.

Deals in an extraordinarily well-informed way with the problems raised by the new hermeneutic, with its roots in existentialism and phenomenology, and "God-talk," with its roots in linguistic analysis. The question for the religious educator is: "How can the Word of God which once took the form of human speech in a given time and place be understood and translated without abridgement of power and meaning into a different time and place?" Ankoviak holds that with adolescents "a deep personal bond must be established through which [they know that they are] accepted. It is by reaching out to the young persons, not merely on the intellectual level, but at the level of the depth of our common being where the point of religious evolution can be reached." See also 63, 153, 163, 173, and 674.

137 Becker, Ernest. *Beyond Alienation*. New York: George Braziller, 1967.

A brilliantly written book that argues (from the behavioral sciences and from theology) that the "human spirit is defeated not from within, but is constricted and baffled from without, from the range of habits that make up our ponderous social fictions." Education is the exploration of "those evils which could be ameliorated by human effort."

138 Bernier, Normand R., and Jack E. Williams. *Beyond Beliefs*. Englewood Cliffs, NJ: Prentice-Hall, 1973.

The intent here is to get at some fundamental understandings of American education by identifying, describing, analyzing, and assessing certain influential ideologies (scientism, romanticism, puritanism, materialism, progressivism, and educationalism). There is a fine companion book of readings edited by the same men: *Education for Liberation*. Englewood Cliffs, NJ: Prentice-Hall, 1973.

139 Berryman, Jerome W. "Teaching as Presence and the Existential Curriculum." *Religious Education* 85 (1990):509-34.

This seminal article on teaching draws on the insights of existentialist philosophers. Death, freedom, aloneness, and meaninglessness are the existential limits Berryman identifies.

140 Brent, Allen. *Philosophical Foundations for the Curriculum*. Boston: George Allen and Unwin, 1978.

> The question is whether an objective basis for curriculum judgments can be found. Takes seriously the challenge of sociology of knowledge to both older and contemporary proposals for such an objective basis (from Plato to the present), but goes beyond sociology of knowledge finally to conclude that religion should be taught because "the religious form of awareness [is] an inseparable part of the normative psychology of the balanced seeker after truth and knowledge in all its forms."

141 Brumbaugh, Robert S. *Whitehead, Process Philosophy, and Education*. Albany, NY: State University of New York Press, 1982.

> Extends Whitehead's insights into education. Emphasizes the identity of the learner within culture, society, and civilization; the aesthetic quality of concrete encounter (as opposed to intellectual abstraction); and the recognition of the irreversible stages of learning: encounter, readjustment that is unstable, and final stabilization. Finally, "an educational curriculum and theory that is truly realistic must end in and include a vision of our place and our importance in cosmology." See also 82, 148, 158, and 675.

142 Carbone, Peter F., Jr. *The Social and Educational Thought of Harold Rugg*. Durham, NC: Duke University Press, 1977.

> Many years ago, Harold Rugg's leadership in education for reconstruction was accepted by a number of religious educators, but it was only in the 1970s that his emphasis on creativity became influential in the field (mainly through his posthumous book, *Imagination*). Carbone's book summarizes Rugg's life and development and explains and assesses both aspects of his position.

143 Chamberlin, J. Gordon. *The Educating Act: A Phenomenological View*. Washington, DC: University Press of America, 1981.

> The author's studies of education from a phenomenological point of view have led him to an analysis of: the educational act as intervention, expecting help, developing aims for oneself, the educational occasion as integral life experience, and helping-learning as an intersubjective relationship. He sees educational outcomes in terms of resolving conflicting authority claims, engaging in the full range of experiences in coming-to-understand, and undertaking appropriate action.

144 Chamberlin, J. Gordon. *Toward a Phenomenology of Education*. Philadelphia: Westminster Press, 1969.

> The author's interests have broadened from Christian education to educational theory itself, and on a sojourn in Latin America he encountered the educational use of the philosophy of phenomenology. The book is a kind of initial exploration of the meaning of phenomenology for American education. Not fully developed, but a landmark.

145 Conrad, Robert L. "A Hermeneutic for Christian Education." *Religious Education* 81 (1986):392-400.

> Faces the question of "linking faith statements from the past to the lives of people in the present." Basing his argument on the assumption that "biblical texts are a record of God's action, both in judgment and in grace, in relation to conflicts in human existence," the author shows how learners bring these conflicts in human existence to the text. "A consciousness of the anxieties, conflicts and guilt involved in the structures of human existence...the dark underside of life makes possible the acceptance of the Gospel, the Good News of what God has done about the conflicts of life. For it is the Christian educator's responsibility, not only to bring to consciousness the conflicts of life, but also to make present the grace of God in the resolution of those conflicts."

146 Denton, David E., ed. *Existentialism and Phenomenology in Education*. New York: Teachers College Press, 1974.

> Concerned that existentialism and phenomenology have been neglected by educational theorists, a number of educators and philosophers have contributed essays that explore the setting for these points of view in the American educational scene, their educational significance and implications, and possibilities for productive research.

147 Duck, Lloyd. *Teaching with Charisma*. Boston: Allyn and Bacon, 1981.

> A delightful introduction to the philosophy of education, pinpointing the key issues in essentialism, experimentalism, reconstructionism, existentialism, and perennialism in terms that intrigue and involve the reader. Assumption: "An intimate knowledge of one's philosophy of teaching can and does produce the inspirational quality we sometimes describe as 'charismatic.'"

148 Dunkel, Harold B. *Whitehead on Education*. Columbus, OH: Ohio State University Press, 1965.

> Unlike Dewey, Whitehead has not been readily accessible to the student of education. This monograph makes Whitehead available by presenting a comprehensive review and evaluation of his educational thought. Serves the purpose of guiding the reader more easily to the sources themselves. See also 82, 158, and 675.

149 Eisendrath, Craig R. *The Unifying Moment: The Psychological Philosophy of William James and Alfred North Whitehead*. Cambridge, MA: Harvard University Press, 1971.

> A basic source in philosophy of education. The author sees James and Whitehead together offering "a philosophy which represents an alternative line to that of Husserl, Heidegger, and Merleau-Ponty on the one side and the logical positivists on the other."

150 Freire, Paulo. *Education for Critical Consciousness*. New York: Seabury Press, 1973.

> In this volume we are able to "catch up" on two major documents of Paulo Freire's that were written before *Pedagogy of the Oppressed*. Included are "Education as the Practice of Freedom" and "Extension or Communication."

151 Freire, Paulo. *Pedagogy of the City*. Trans. by Donald Macedo. New York: Continuum, 1993.

> A collection of interviews with Paulo Freire during his tenure as secretary of education for the city of São Paulo in Brazil (1989-1991). The interviews by various publications and individuals portray Freire's progressive vision for and democratic approach to renewing an urban public school system. He sought to build public schools that were "serious, fair, joyous, and curious—a school system that transforms the space where children, rich or poor, are able to learn, to create, to take risks, to question, and to grow."

152 Freire, Paulo. *Pedagogy of the Oppressed*. New York: Herder and Herder, 1970.

> Out of practical experience as well as theoretical reflection, the author develops a dialogic philosophy of education that qualifies as a theology of education. (He is speaking of all education, not a specialized religious education, yet his approach is functionally theological.) The key is the creativity that emerges from the discovery that one is a "subject who acts upon and transforms his world, and in so doing moves toward ever new possibilities of fuller and richer life." See also 401, 541, 708, 710.

153 Grabner-Haider, Anton. *Sprachanalyse und Religionspädagogik*. Zürich: Benziger, 1973.

> Explores the significance and implications of linguistic analysis for religious education. British, American, and German sources are used. Introduces the idea of a "generative" grammar and semantics and the "disclosure situation" as a paradigm for religious education. Suggests implications for both cognitive and affective learning and sets forth educational examples. See also 63, 136, 163, 173, and 674.

154 Green, Thomas F. *The Activities of Teaching*. New York: McGraw-Hill Book Company, 1971.

> Uses conceptual analysis of such activities as thinking, learning, knowing, believing, teaching, wondering, explaining, etc., as an invitation to "do philosophy of education." Assists in raising to critical consciousness the philosophical processes and methods that are used, as encouragement to readers to do it for themselves.

155 Gribble, James. *Introduction to Philosophy of Education*. Boston: Allyn and Bacon, 1969.

> Philosophy of education came through a period in which the emphasis was on the analysis of basic terms. Gribble's book brought this to a mature level in his choice of issues and his careful tying together of the sequential logic of educational theory. The discussion of moral education (chap. 5) is of particular interest.

156 Gruber, Frederick C. *Foundations for a Philosophy of Education*. New York: Thomas Y. Crowell Company, 1961.

> A superb introduction to the philosophy and history of education, especially valuable to religious educators because of the author's sensitivity to religious issues and values. Introduces philosophy and its various positions; reviews the history of educational thought; and discusses the issues of nature and nurture, society's role in education, and education for value. Especially helpful charts and other aids.

157 Harper, Norman E. *Making Disciples: The Challenge of Christian Education at the End of the 20th Century*. Memphis, TN: Christian Studies Center, 1981.

> Tackling the question of education from a Reformed point of view, Harper develops a Christian philosophy of education as "a comprehensive approach to all aspects of the teaching-learning process, including agencies of education, according to the principles set forth in the Word of God." His concern for the education of "covenant children" leads to his interest in the Christian school, and his concern for the Sunday school leads to a more comprehensive concept of church education.

158 Hill, Brennan. "Alfred North Whitehead's Approach to Education: Its Value for Religious Education." *Religious Education* 85 (1990):92-104.

> While the author claims to have an educational rather than theological or philosophical concern, this article examines Whitehead's understanding of the mind, the limitations of knowledge, and the stages of learning. This examination leads to the identification of six values of Whitehead's thought for religious education. See also 82, 141, and 675.

159 Hirst, P.H., and R.S. Peters. *The Logic of Education*. New York: Humanities Press, 1970.

> Careful studies, from the analytic philosophical point of view, of the concepts of education, development, the curriculum, and teaching, with additional treatments of teaching and personal relationships in educational institutions. Contains valuable critical material on Kohlberg and Piaget. See also 338, 350, 356, 368, 386, 504, and 620.

160   Hokenson, Terry. "A Process Pedagogy for Christian Education." *Religious Education* 68 (1973):595-607.

> Deals with Henry Nelson Wieman and with Paulo Freire, "whose pedagogy fits well indeed into a process framework." Wieman and Freire are analyzed in some detail. Suggests that "the teacher's guiding concern for his or her comments and interventions must be...a constant vision and feeling for the process of creative interchange or dialogical commitment in the classroom between each of the students and his or her own social and private universe, and within the Biblical and ecclesial witness." Concludes with a "process view of God" and its implications for dealing with biblical and doctrinal matters. See also 150, 152, 401, 708, 710, 728.

161   Horton, Myles, and Paulo Freire. *We Make the Road by Walking: Conversations on Education and Social Change.* Brenda Bell, John Gaventa, and John Peters, eds. Philadelphia: Temple University Press, 1990.

> Conversations between Horton and Freire held at Highlander Folk School in December of 1987 were recorded and transcribed to produce this book. The relationship between education and social change was the focus of their conversation. Both educators stress the importance of starting with the experience learners bring to the educational process. See also 235.

162   Hullfish, H. Gordon, and Philip G. Smith. *Reflective Thinking: The Method of Education.* New York: Dodd, Mead, 1961.

> An unusual and thought-provoking treatment of philosophy of education from the point of view that "the method of thinking, of reflective activity, is the method of learning." Becomes particularly relevant in dealing with "believing—a willingness to act," "warranted beliefs," and "the classroom as reflective continuity."

163   Kneller, George F. *Logic and Language of Education.* New York: John Wiley and Sons, 1966.

> A good introductory overview of the role of logic (including problem-solving inquiry and linguistic analysis) in education. May serve as a guide to more penetrating study and comparison of the sources cited. A "first" in the field, in terms of its comprehensive definition of the scope of logic. See also 63, 136, 153, 173, and 674.

164   Knight, George B. *Philosophy and Education: An Introduction in Christian Perspective.* Berrien Springs, MI: Andrews University Press, 1980.

> A textbook of interest to all religious educators. Leading the reader through the problems of philosophy that bear on education and reviewing the options (traditional and modern philosophies, contemporary educational theories, and a special section on analytical philosophy), the book provides a method and guidelines for formulating a personal philosophy of religious education.

165   Langford, Glenn, and D.J. O'Connor, eds. *New Essays in the Philosophy of Education*. Boston: Routledge and Kegan Paul, 1973.

> A symposium that explores the main spheres of education—moral, religious, mathematical, and scientific. An entire section deals with education and values, and there is a perceptive chapter by W.D. Hudson, "Is Religious Education Possible?"

166   Lesnoff-Caravaglia, Gari. *Education as Existential Possibility*. New York: Philosophical Library, 1972.

> Explores the educational implications of the thought of the Italian existentialist, Nicola Abbagnano, in contrast to the existentialism of Sartre and Heidegger. The emphasis is on a pedagogy of freedom, choice, and responsibility, set within a context of hope rather than despair.

167 Lindquist, John T. "The Grammar of Religious Education." *Religious Education* 67 (1972):98-106.

> Maintains that religious education is the conceptual activity through which we are made aware of what is at stake in religious language and thus enabled to integrate its truth such that our own lives may manifest a living as well as reflective relationship to God. "The religious language it employs must manifest not only the Reality of God, but the reality of the individual as well." Uses two cases, the ontological argument and prayer, to reveal the nature of religious education.

168   Manheimer, Ronald J. *Kierkegaard as Educator*. Berkeley, CA: University of California Press, 1977.

> Interprets Kierkegaard's writings as a rather consistent attempt consciously to engage in self-education. "Kierkegaard regarded his authorship as his own education." The emphases are on interpretations of the Socratic educator ("the authorship, taken as Kierkegaard's dialectic of education, remains poised at the threshold where the Socratic and Christian meet"), either/or as a drama of education, and education as the communication of possibility. A foundational book of permanent value for the serious religious educator.

169 Martin, William Oliver. *Realism in Education*. New York: Harper and Row, 1969.

> An inquiry into final, material, formal, and efficient causation in the structure of the teaching-learning activity. In the process, purposes, pupil-teacher relations, knowledge, and the curriculum are subjected to intense linguistic analysis.

170 McClintock, Robert. *Man and His Circumstances: Ortega as Educator*. New York: Teachers College Press, 1971.

> In a critical biography, both personal and literary, Ortega y Gasset is interpreted with reference to his own term, "the civic pedagogue." The book is a mammoth study and important for philosophy of education in its search for education's functional and critical roots.

171 Meagher, Robert E. *Cave Notes: First Reflections on Sense and Spirit*. Philadelphia: Fortress Press, 1975.

> Refreshing and stimulating, this book stands in the tradition of education as finding oneself and one's way of life. The wisdoms probed are those of wonder, the fear of the Lord, and radical doubt. The probing is done through "imaging, decoding, resisting, seeing, hearing, touching." The play of sense and spirit is the underlying theme.

172 Merkert, Rainald, and Werner Simon. *Didaktik und Fachdidaktik Religion*. Zürich-Köln: Benziger Verlag, 1979.

> Basically a roundup of epistemological positions for religious educators, with expositions of the models that each epistemological position implies, and an estimate of the reception and use of each position in actual practice. The first chapter summarizes relevant educational theory up to 1970. The bulk of the book deals with education theory in the 1970s.

173 Miller, Randolph Crump. "Linguistic Philosophy and Religious Education." *Religious Education* 65 (1970):309-17.

> There is an integrity in the language that we use in our life and work. There is also an integrity in the language of the gospels. The fact that they do not match is what Miller means by "the language gap." The religious educator's challenge is to bridge the gap. After reviewing various schemes for the use and interpretation of language and providing many examples, the article concludes that the stress is to be "on evoking disclosure followed by commitment so that the language of response is a genuine performative." See also 63, 136, 153, 163, and 674.

174 Moran, Gabriel. "Interest in Philosophy: Three Themes for Religious Education." *Religious Education* 82 (1987):424-45.

> An article of major significance for religious education thought. Moran selects from current philosophical thought the three themes of meaning (hermeneutics), liberation (praxis), and relation (process). In the search for meaning, revelation of the divine requires a setting of mutual exchange in which "a precise and reverent use of speech must be combined with pregnant silence." For liberation, "the way out of ideological domination requires listening to other people and exploring the ambiguity of one's own statements," as well as development that is sophisticated about ends and means. Relation, in today's world, requires reconciliation within a context that is realistically and inclusively pluralistic and ecumenical.

175   Morris, Van Cleve. *Modern Movements in Educational Philosophy*. Boston: Houghton Mifflin Company, 1969.

A reluctant anthology (Morris discusses his reasons for adopting this device hesitatingly) in which a variety of philosophical points of view (scientific philosophy; philosophy as "the prevailing persuasion"; and philosophical anthropology, analytic philosophy, and existential philosophy as "modern movements") are presented in themselves and also for their educational implications.   Morris no longer believes in presenting philosophy of education via idealism, realism, and pragmatism.   He believes in letting protagonists for various points of view present their own cases.

176 Morris, Van Cleve, and Young Pai. *Philosophy and the American School*. Boston: Houghton Mifflin Company, 1976.

A reworking of one of the best books in philosophy of education. After setting the task for philosophy in education, the problems of metaphysics, epistemology, and axiology are systematically and comparatively explored in relation to education.   Three educational models (technological, humanistic, and social) are then assessed philosophically.

177 Nash, Paul. *Authority and Freedom in Education: An Introduction to the Philosophy of Education*. New York: John Wiley and Sons, 1966.

The exploration of one major theme in education, authority and freedom, using methods of philosophical analysis, in order to provide a model for the student in exploring other comparable themes.   "The concepts of authority and freedom are the principal concepts, for the person concerned with education today, that need clarification and in terms of which personal commitment must be worked out; furthermore, this is a study of the relationship between authority and freedom because...there are some fruitful consequences of the dialectical approach to educational problems." The author uses British sources, as well as American, extensively.

178 Norton, David L. *Personal Destinies: A Philosophy of Ethical Individualism*. Princeton, NJ: Princeton University Press, 1975.

In light of religious education's interest in various aspects of "self-actualization," a thoroughgoing philosophy of ethical individualism is welcome both as a corrective and as a guide.   The concept is traced briefly through the history of philosophy, with emphasis on British idealism and upon existentialism.   Most helpful is a long chapter on self-actualization at the various stages of life, doing for philosophical understanding what Erikson has done for psychology.   Implications for growth in knowledge of others, in friendship and love, and in society at large are drawn.

179 Papert, Seymour. *The Children's Machine: Rethinking School in the Age of the Computer*. New York: Basic Books, 1993.

> Papert offers a critique of public education and a constructive proposal for change rooted in his extensive work with children and computers (cf. *Mindstorms*, 1980). He proposes *mathetics* as a word for learning (comparable to *pedagogy* as the term for teaching) to help educators take a fresh look at schools and schooling. He argues that "The competitive ability is the ability to learn."

180 Perelman, Ch., and L. Olbrechts-Tyteca. *The New Rhetoric*. Notre Dame, IN: University of Notre Dame Press, 1969.

> In an era of dialogue, this book sets out systematically to restate a theory of argumentation. Science moves in the realm of the self-evident, but human decisions are more often in the realm of the credible, the plausible, and the probable. How, then, does one proceed to influence persons and to secure adherence in this realm?

181 Peters, Richard S. *Ethics and Education*. Glenview, IL: Scott, Foresman and Company, 1967.

> An examination of the meaning of education and an analysis of the fundamental ethical issues in education: equality, the worth of various activities, the consideration of interests, freedom, respect for persons, authority, punishment and discipline, and democracy. An American abridgement of the British edition.

182 Peters, Richard S. *Reason and Compassion*. London: Routledge and Kegan Paul, 1973.

> The well-known philosopher of education, R.S. Peters, who has also written extensively on ethics and education, here provides us with a series of lectures on ethics, moral development, moral education, and religion. In a modified relativist perspective, he helps us see the forms of ethical decision making and moral growth, thus allowing for a shape or structure to moral education, but without absolutist principle.

183 Phenix, Philip H. *Education and the Common Good: A Moral Philosophy of Curriculum*. New York: Harpers, 1961.

> A philosophy of education viewed as a moral enterprise guided by a concept of value as devotion to worth rather than to satisfaction of desire. The ideal of democracy is seen as the social expression of basic moral commitment. Within this context, education centers in the development of intelligence, creativity, conscience, and reverence.

184 Phenix, Philip H. *Realms of Meaning: A Philosophy of the Curriculum for General Education*. New York: McGraw-Hill Book Company, 1964.

> One of the most important treatments of curriculum. The task of the curriculum for general education is to foster meaning in a world threatened with meaninglessness. There are six realms of meaning, each a discipline of knowing, all to be represented in the curriculum: symbolics (language and mathematics), empirics (the sciences), esthetics (music, literature, and the arts), synnoetics (I-Thou), ethics, and synoptics (history, religion, and philosophy). In light of this position, solutions to the technical problems of curriculum (scope, sequence, etc.) are suggested. See also 219, 885, 889, 892, 932, 941, 951, 1010, 1020, 1034, and 1046.

185 Reid, Louis Arnoud. *Philosophy and Education: An Introduction*. New York: Random House, 1965.

> A British contribution to philosophy of education, axiological in orientation and personalistic in tone. The discipline consists of philosophical reflection upon educational problems, not deduction of educational directives from philosophical systems. The author has a keen interest in religious education.

186 Rugg, Harold. *Imagination*. New York: Harper and Row, 1963.

> Rugg's philosophy of education, edited after his death by Kenneth D. Benne, beginning with the question: "What is the nature of the act of thought when, in one brilliant moment, there is a sudden veering of attention, a consequent grasp of new dimensions, and a new idea is born?" Ends with a summary of imperatives for educational theory derived from his analysis of the creative imagination.

187 Saiyidain, K.G. *The Humanist Tradition in Modern Indian Educational Thought*. Madison, WI: Dembar Educational Research Services, 1967.

> The educational positions of six Indian leaders: Tagore, Iqbal, Gandhi, Azad, Radhakrishnan, and Husain. In each case, new insights in religious education are made available.

188 Sarup, Madan. *Marxism and Education*. Boston: Routledge and Kegan Paul, 1978.

> The commitment is to educational change. In developing a Marxist approach to a sociology of education, the author considers two other sociological approaches: positivism and phenomenology. Positivism is rejected. The phenomenological approach is criticized as "encouraging people to seek change through the way they think, instead of providing them with means by which they can change what they or others are doing." A Marxist approach, on the other hand, provides a basis for "a practical de-reification—an actual overthrow of social relations through praxis." Provides perspective on other philosophers of education.

189 Scheffler, Israel. *The Language of Education.* Springfield, IL: Thomas Books, 1960.

A philosophical analysis of forms of educational discourse (definitions in education, educational slogans, and educational metaphors) together with a study of the concept of teaching. An attempt at philosophical inquiry by proposing strategies of logical appraisal and applying them to these forms of educational discourse. The task of educational philosophy is seen as that of contributing to general perspective through study of the root ideas and assumptions of education. The concept "teaching" is subjected to such philosophical analysis, as an example of the mode of such inquiry.

190 Schmidt, Paul. *Die pädagogische Relevanz einer anthropologischen Ethik.* Düsseldorf: Patmos Verlag, 1972.

A contribution to the approach to education through phenomenology. In Germany, one of the theorists who is looked to for guidance in this is the Roman Catholic philosopher, Romano Guardini. This book summarizes and reviews his work.

191 Smith, B. Othanel, and Robert H. Ennis, eds. *Language and Concepts in Education.* Chicago: Rand McNally, 1961.

Essays that examine some of the more central and pervasive concepts in educational thought (learning by experience, needs, subject matter, the theory-practice dichotomy, mastery, teaching, neutrality, language and its operations in the classroom, equality of opportunity, the logical-psychological distinction, assumption-finding, explanation, and the logic of slogans) in an attempt to "take intellectual stock" in reordering education in the face of the demands of the "age of automation, atomics, and space." The purpose is not to solve educational problems or to set forth a program of action, but to show how educational words are used and to subject these uses to critical examination.

192 Smith, B. Othanel, and Milton O. Meux. *A Study of the Logic of Teaching.* Urbana, IL: University of Illinois Press, 1970.

What actually goes on in classroom discourse? The authors report research in which episodes of classroom discourse are identified, classified (thirteen major classifications, each with numerous subdivisions), and analyzed.

193 Smith, Huston. *Condemned to Meaning.* New York: Harper and Row, 1965.

A study of existential meaning, with implications for education. "Students need to see the facts they learn as invested with meaning derived from the theory to which the facts relate. They need to see the import of the theory as deriving from the basic purposes and methods of the discipline that produced it. They need to understand the meaning of the discipline as deriving from its place in human life: Why was such a venture launched; what role does it serve in life? Underlying all, students need to sense significance in life itself. If the current of meaning is broken at any point, learning declines and slows toward a stop."

194 Taylor, Mark C. *Journeys to Selfhood*. Berkeley, CA: University of California Press, 1980.

An extremely suggestive volume on personal development in religion and the life of the spirit. "Kierkegaard's notion of realized spirit is finally inadequate. Hegel's dialectical vision offers a more satisfactory perspective from which to comprehend the nature of the self and the dynamics of personal and corporate history."

195 Taylor, Richard. *Action and Purpose*. Englewood Cliffs, NJ: Prentice-Hall, 1966.

A philosophical study of human nature, radically critical of reductionist presuppositions in the behavioral sciences. Uses the teleological idea of explaining behavior in terms of reasons rather than causes, thus stressing "purposeful agency." A book for philosophers of education to grapple with long and seriously.

196 Ulich, Robert. *Philosophy of Education*. New York: American Book Company, 1961.

A strong answer to positivism on behalf of education that has "the courage of transcendence and disciplined imagination." The key concept is a broad and ethically stern "cosmic reverence," by which Ulich is able to come to philosophic terms both with religion and education.

197 Vandenberg, Donald. *Being and Education: An Essay in Existential Phenomenology*. Englewood Cliffs, NJ: Prentice-Hall, 1971.

Examines the whole field afresh and introduces major European phenomenologists (Guardini, Langeveld, and Bollnow) to the American reader. The religious educator will especially welcome the keenly critical treatment of character and moral education.

198 Vandenberg, Donald. "Life-Phases and Values." *Educational Forum*, March 1968 (n.pg.).

A spritely and illuminating analysis of the thought of Romano Guardini on human development. Certain "decisive events" characterize the "life-phases": conception (prenatal life), birth (childhood), pubescence (youth), practical experience (young adulthood), limitations (maturity), retirement (old age), helplessness (senility), and death. Concludes that "the phases of life in which pupils find themselves have to be lived fully, authentically, for them to become authentically human later on." The strongest influence in education is "the personal existence of the teacher."

199 Vierzig, Siegfried. *Ideologiekritik und Religionsunterricht*. Zürich: Benziger Verlag, 1975.

A careful study of the meaning of ideological criticism (Marx, Mannheim, and the Frankfurt School) and the response of religious education to it. The object is a religious education for intelligent and informed social criticism and for responsible social action. Various religious education theories (Kittel, Nipkow, Halbfas, Otto, etc.) are examined in this light.

200 Ward, Leo. *Philosophy of Education*. Chicago: Henry Regnery, 1963.

More of a commentary and polished essay on the meaning of philosophy and education than the usual textbookish treatment of the field. The author is experienced, well-read, wise, and irenic. His book tackles the central questions and the pertinent problems, and the readers join with the author in considering them, deliberating, going back to the sources, and making up their minds.

201 Wilson, John. *Fantasy and Common Sense in Education*. New York: John Wiley and Sons, 1979.

A philosopher of education identifies two corrupting "fantasies" in education and shows their injurious effects on educational practice: the relativist fantasy, "characterized by a desire for equality which causes a blurring of differences and a rejection of examination, competition, grading, streaming, and authority"; and the behaviorist fantasy, which "argues that educational issues can be handled in a mechanistic fashion."

202 Wolterstorff, Nicholas. *Art in Action*. Grand Rapids, MI: William B. Eerdmans Publishing Company, 1980.

The growing literature on art and religion finds a valuable addition in this book on aesthetic theory by a Christian philosopher. "Works of art are objects and instruments of action. They are all inextricably embedded in the fabric of human intention. They are objects and instruments of action whereby we carry out our intentions with respect to the world, our fellows, ourselves, and our gods." Some rather specific clues for Christian education are found in the final section, "Participation." See also 425, 490, 495, 859, 878, and 967.

HISTORY OF EDUCATION

203 Affolderbach, Martin, ed. *Grundsatztexte zur evangelischen Jugendarbeit*. Gelnhausen: Burckhardthaus-Laetare Verlag, 1982.

As a basis for discussion and decision-making in German youth work, the Evangelical Church and the Comenius Institute here made available the documents, papers, and critiques published or produced since 1933 that are important in determining the direction of work with young people. The arrangement of the material shows what the issues are, and the material itself provides the grist for intelligent policy and program decisions.

204   Akenson, Donald H. *The Irish Education Experiment*. Toronto: University of Toronto Press, 1970.

> The remarkable story of the Irish national educational system, from 1931 on, presents many facets of the relationship of religion and education. It was conceived and run by ecclesiastical authorities, Protestant and Catholic; its aims included religious education; and it developed from a nondenominational to a denominational enterprise.

205   Aritonang, Jan S. *Sejarah Pendidikan Kristen di Tanah Batak* (*A History of Christian Education in the Batak Lands*). Djakarta: BPK Gunung Mulia, 1988.

> Main sections trace the history of the German Rhenish missions' educational endeavor among the Batak people of North Sumatra, Indonesia, 1861-1940. Schools were begun as evangelistic tools for the formation of a people's church. Until the beginning of World War II, the Batak mission was the major supplier of education among the Bataks, beginning with elementary schools, vocational high schools, teacher training high schools, and finally regular high schools. The Batak mission made a serious attempt to evangelize while yet attempting to build a church that would remain rooted in Batak culture. (Robert R. Boehlke)

206   Barr, David L., and Nicholas Piediscalzi, eds. *The Bible in American Education*. Philadelphia: Fortress Press, 1982.

> A symposium, organized generally in terms of historical periods, that explores in detail both the use of the Bible in American education and the ups and downs of the Bible's educational influence and authority. Looks at public education, private schools, the changes effected by higher criticism, the curriculum situation in the churches, and the possibilities of teaching about religion in the public schools today. See also 72.

207   Beck, Walter H. *Lutheran Elementary Schools in the United States*. St. Louis, MO: Concordia Publishing House, 1965.

> A reissue of the 1939 "history of the development of parochial schools and synodical educational policies and programs" in the various branches of American Lutheranism. A long chapter on "development and status since 1940" has been added in this edition.

208   Betz, George, ed. *Dokumente der katholischen Kirche zur Bildungsdiskussion*. München: Kösel-Verlag, 1983.

> A record of official actions of the Catholic church in Germany on adult education, together with responses and reactions to them. The period covered begins in 1960. The editor provides a running interpretation.

209 Boehlke, Robert R. *A History of the Development of Christian Religious Education Thought and Practice, from Plato to Loyola*. Djakarta: PT BPK Gunung Mulia, 1991.

Surveys the history of Christian education from its roots in the Greco-Roman-Judeo cultures through the Reformation and the Counter-Reformation. Includes the educational practices of the New Testament, ancient, medieval, Reformation, and Counter-Reformation churches and the educational thought of Clement, Origen, Jerome, Chrysostom, Augustine, Charlemagne, Alfred the Great, Marus, Abelard, Thomas Aquinas, Gerson, Erasmus, Luther, Calvin, and Loyola. Major chapters are devoted to each of the final four. RRB

210 Bonino, José Miguez, "The Teaching Ministry in Historical Perspective." *Religious Education* 58 (1963):12-20.

Taking Smart's, "We teach so that through our teaching God may work in the hearts of those whom we teach," as the definition of Christian education, the author traces the degree of faithfulness exhibited by the church in its educational enterprise through the years, concluding that "the goal of all this tremendous effort of instruction is that every church member should gain a true knowledge of God's Word and thus become a conscious and committed confessant, a true member of the church of Christ...." A critique of the "Religious Education Movement" is included.

211 Bowen, Cawthon A. *Child and Church: A History of Methodist Church-School Curriculum*. Nashville: Abingdon Press, 1960.

A detailed, documented history of Christian education and curriculum development in the Methodist church, written by the former editor of church school publications.

212 Boylan, Anne M. *Sunday School: The Formation of an American Institution 1790-1880*. New Haven, CT: Yale University Press, 1988.

Unlike *The Big Little School* (Lynn and Wright, 1971), Boylan's focus is institutional rather than historical. She contrasts the American Sunday school with its English counterpart, noting the evangelical and voluntarist character of the American version. In America, for example, the Sunday school was an important source of new church members. See also 220, 239, 242, 251, 760, and 857.

213 Brauner, Charles J. *American Educational Theory*. Englewood Cliffs, NJ: Prentice-Hall, 1964.

Explores the historical traditions of American instruction (monitorial method, object method, Herbartianism, child study, and experimentalism, with some attention to the then current academic emphasis) to "see if some basic ground for distinguishing sense from nonsense in education can be found." Educational theory has consisted of advocacy of certain general methods and general disciplines. Schemes are proposed for classifying such general methods and disciplines as a basis for evaluating them and as a pattern for development of education as a discipline of theory and practice.

214 Bryce, Mary Charles. *Pride of Place: The Role of the Bishops in the Development of Catechesis in the United States*. Washington, DC: Catholic University of America Press, 1984.

> Mary Charles Bryce is the recognized authority on the history of catechesis in the United States. Here she gives a very detailed account of the relationship of the development of the catechetical function to the nation throughout the major phases of its development, emphasizing the role of the bishops in the process. What emerges is a fascinating analysis of a distinctive and difficult kind of Americanization of what would at first appear to be an undifferentiated universal teaching function of the church.

215 Buetow, Harold A. *Of Singular Benefit: The Story of U.S. Catholic Education*. New York: Macmillan Company, 1970.

> A voluminous chronological history of Catholic schooling in America, from its Spanish, French, and English beginnings. Foundations were laid prior to 1828, and a school system developed by 1884. It grew and matured from then until 1957. The book candidly assesses the confused situation that followed and takes on the critics of parochial education in point-by-point argumentation.

216 Calam, John. *Parsons and Pedagogues: The S.P.G. Adventure in American Education*. New York: Columbia University Press, 1971.

> Written in the context of the "new history of education," which looks not only at schooling but at all the influences in cultural transmission, this book tells the story of the work of the Society for the Propagation of the Gospel in Foreign Parts, so far as it relates to America, 1702-1783. Reaches the conclusion that S.P.G. efforts largely failed in relation to their stated and assumed objectives.

217 Castle, E.B. *Educating the Good Man: Moral Education in Christian Times*. New York: Collier Books, 1962.

> Approaching religious education as moral education and assuming a joint church-state responsibility for its fulfillment, this volume surveys developing thought and practice from early Christian times, giving special attention to Great Britain and the United States.

218 Chandler, Daniel R. "Sophia Lyon Fahs." *Religious Education* 84 (1989):538-52.

> Chandler offers a sympathetic account of the life and work of this influential religious educator. The universal, humanistic, and transracial perspectives of Fahs's writings receive attention in this article.

219 Coalter, Milton J., John M. Mulder, and Louis B. Weeks, eds. *The Pluralistic Vision: Presbyterians and Mainstream Protestant Education and Leadership*. Louisville, KY: Westminster/John Knox Press, 1992.

> Particular attention is called to two chapters. In "A Brief History of the Genre Problem: Presbyterian Educational Resource Materials," Craig Dykstra and J. Bradley Wigger identify four major periods (1838-1873; 1873-1947; 1947-1975;

and 1976 to the present) in the changing shape of denominationally produced curricular materials for congregational use. Despite three major curricular efforts by Presbyterians in the third period, the basic pattern set by the Uniform Lessons in the second period was not changed. They note a shift from helping teachers understand lesson content to providing teachers with step-by-step instructions for teaching. Dykstra and Wigger call curriculum designers to address the challenge of form before launching a new curricular effort. In "The Use of the Bible in Presbyterian Curricula, 1932-1985," David C. Hester traces the use of the Bible in the Westminster Graded Lessons, the Christian Faith and Life curriculum, Covenant Life, Christian Faith and Action, Christian Education: Shared Approaches, and the current Presbyterian Reformed Educational Ministries materials. Changes in expectations growing out of increasing specialization in biblical scholarship, education, and psychology were reflected in curriculum development over this period. In spite of these efforts, the author notes that biblical illiteracy is still prevalent among Presbyterians. See also 184, 885, 889, 892, 932, 941, 951, 1010, 1020, 1034, and 1046.

220 Cram, Ronald H. "The Origins and Purposes of the Philadelphia Sunday and Adult School Union," *Christian Education Journal* 10 no. 3 (Spring 1990):47-55.

Focusing on the rise of the Philadelphia Sunday and Adult School from 1817-1824, Cram highlights how the original purpose of the Sunday school shifted. At first, the American version of Robert Raike's English Sunday school was characterized by paid teachers, poor children students, free literacy education, and the absence of denominational affiliation. Literacy education was the primary purpose. By 1824, voluntary teachers were teaching primarily nonpoor children in Sunday schools that were usually connected to a denomination. Conversion and biblical literacy had become the primary purposes. The article shows the value of a narrowly focused historical study for understanding the dynamics of a broader movement. See also 212, 239, 242, 251, 760, and 857.

221 Cremin, Lawrence A. *American Education: The Colonial Experience, 1607-1783*. San Francisco: Harper and Row, 1970.

The first volume of Cremin's vast three-volume history of American education. His approach is broad and dynamic. It is broad in the sense that he sees education as involving the efforts of many institutions (not just schools). The church and the family are foremost in this regard. It is dynamic in that he traces the transformation of the aims, institutions, and processes of education from those inherited from Europe to those that served the gradually emerging independent nation. Outstanding is the analysis of the forces and persons effecting this transformation.

222 Cremin, Lawrence A. *American Education: The Metropolitan Experience 1876-1980*. New York: Harper and Row, 1988.

The concluding volume in a trilogy on the history of American education, a project that has spanned more than two decades. Cremin's approach includes religious leaders and institutions and their influence on American education. Education is broadly understood as "the deliberate, systematic, and sustained effort to transmit, evoke, or acquire knowledge, values, attitudes, skills, and sensibilities, as well as any learning that results from that effort, direct or indirect, intended or unintended."

223 Cremin, Lawrence A. *American Education: The National Experience, 1783-1876.* San Francisco: Harper and Row, 1980.

The second volume of Cremin's trilogy, dealing generally with developments characteristic of the nineteenth century. One reviewer notes that "the churches continued to have a decisive impact upon the educational process and helped to bring into existence the common school, parochial schools, and numerous institutions of higher education, and provided the nation's schools, largely through the influence of the dominant Protestant majority, the unity of a public religion, which in turn gave the educational process some of its coherence."

224 Cremin, Lawrence A. *Public Education.* New York: Basic Books, 1976.

Distinguishing carefully between public schooling and public education, Cremin develops an "ecology of education" that sees intentional education taking place in an interplay of families, churches, workplaces, publishing houses, television stations, and schools, within functioning communities. Here a concept that developed as a new focus for the study of the history of education is taken seriously as an organizing principle for contemporary education (including religious education).

225 Cully, Kendig Brubaker. *The Search for a Christian Education—Since 1940.* Philadelphia: Westminster Press, 1965.

A plea for historical dimensions in the study of Christian education, together with a critical historical review of Christian education theory since Elliott and Smith. Summaries of the theories of leading thinkers (including seldom consulted Roman Catholic and British writers) form the body of the book, with critical commentary providing the continuum.

226 Dawson, Christopher. *The Crisis of Western Education.* Garden City, NY: Image Books, 1963.

Contemporary world culture needs "a principle of spiritual co-ordination and a principle of unity—and it is in the field of education that this need and its solution can be brought together." This involves "a radical reform of Christian education: an intellectual revolution which will restore the internal unity of Christian culture." The essentials are recovery of the idea of "Christian people" as a true world society, and recovery of the traditional Christian conception of history. Historical and functional analysis supports this view, which is then discussed in terms of curricular implementation.

227 Edwards, O.C., Jr., and John H. Westerhoff, III, eds. *A Faithful Church: Issues in the History of Catechesis.* Wilton, CT: Morehouse-Barlow Company, 1981.

A substantive contribution to the history of catechesis (from the New Testament church to the present, and looking to the future), built on the thesis that the "school model" is a recent comer and inadequate to the task that catechesis undertakes. The present scene is canvassed by Westerhoff and made specific in articles from the perspectives of Roman Catholicism, Eastern Orthodoxy, and the American church. Westerhoff projects the future.

228 Furnish, Dorothy Jean. *DRE/DCE—The History of a Profession*. Nashville: Christian Educators Fellowship, The United Methodist Church, 1976.

A solid contribution to the history of Christian education. Traces the profession of director of religious (Christian) education from its beginnings in 1906 to the 1960s. Analyzes the functions and relationships involved. Assesses the profession's future. Particularly significant documents are reprinted as appendices. (One appendix, a list of known directors in 1920, I checked carefully, to find that I knew six of them personally. The 1926 list yielded twenty-one, two of whom I am still in touch with! —DCW)

229 Gartner, Lloyd P., ed. *Jewish Education in the United States: A Documentary History*. New York: Teachers College Press, 1969.

Thirty-nine historical documents in American Jewish education, dating from 1760 to 1960. The aim of the volume is to illuminate the dual relationship of American Jewish education to the development of American Judaism on the one hand and to general American culture on the other.

230 Gould, Joseph E. *The Chautauqua Movement*. Albany, NY: State University of New York Press, 1961.

The Chautauqua movement was a significant episode in the history of the Sunday school, leadership training, adult religious education, and adult education in general. Its story is told here in a lively way, indicating the roles played by Miller and Vincent and showing how Harper used his Chautauqua experience in designing the University of Chicago.

231 Grassi, Joseph A. *The Teacher in the Primitive Church and the Teacher Today*. Santa Clara, CA: University of Santa Clara Press, 1973.

Develops the idea of the early Christian teacher as the active person of faith, whose influence was mainly that of example and nurture, leading to learning as imitative participation. Furthermore, in the New Testament and the early church, Jesus and the Spirit were the teachers, encouraging spontaneity and creativity. Implications for today's Christian teaching are drawn, with a section devoted to the place of women in today's educational ministry.

232 Greaves, Richard L. *The Puritan Revolution and Educational Thought*. New Brunswick, NJ: Rutgers University Press, 1969.

Between the Renaissance, with its emphasis on an educated elite, and the modern period of universal public education, stands the Puritan and sectarian period in which education of the entire laity was seen as essential for broad social and religious reform. From primary sources not widely used before, the author traces this period in detail.

233 Henderson, Robert W. *The Teaching Office in the Reformed Tradition: A History of the Doctoral Ministry*. Philadelphia: Westminster Press, 1962.

Ways in which the teaching office (in parish, school, higher education, and theological education) has been defined and used in churches of the Reformed tradition from Calvin to the American scene are traced and analyzed. The author is convinced that the office needs rehabilitation but indicates that the history of the office cannot give much help in this task beyond showing its necessity and significance.

234 Holder, Arthur G. "Saint Basil The Great on Secular Education and Christian Virtue." *Religious Education* 87 (1992):395-415.

This research essay employs the tools of rhetorical criticism to analyze St. Basil's *Address to the Young* and uses his study to indicate the appropriate relationship of (Christian) religious teaching to secular (cultural) teaching. Holder finds in St. Basil's *Address* helpful guidelines for the Christian reading of pagan (secular or cultural) writings and appropriates these in outlining a six-point Christian cultural critique.

235 Horton, Myles, Judith Kohl, and Herbert Kohl. *The Long Haul: An Autobiography*. New York: Doubleday, 1990.

Written with the help of Judith and Herbert Kohl, this is the story of Myles Horton, an adult educator and founder of the Highlander Folk School in Monteagle, Tennessee. His work with rural poor, blacks, and labor movements utilized an action-reflection approach to adult education. See also 152 and 161.

236 Kaestle, Carl F. *Pillars of the Republic: Common Schools and American Society, 1780-1860*. New York: Hill and Wang, 1983.

Histories of schooling were not in style after the reorientation of the history of education to a broader concept of the field. This book comes back to schooling itself, but in its broad social context. Its detailed analysis covers the times from the American Revolution to the Civil War. Church and school, religion and education are intertwined throughout the period, their relationships clearly delineated.

237 Kalewold, Alaka Imbakom. *Traditional Ethiopian Church Education*. Trans. by Menghestu Lemma. New York: Teachers College Press, 1970.

A brief but substantive contribution to comparative religious education, exploring the history and functions of education under church auspices in Ethiopia.

238 Kathan, Boardman W., ed. *Pioneers of Religious Education in the 20th Century*. New Haven, CT: Religious Education Association, 1978.

A symposium that adds significantly to the data for the study of the history of religious education in North America. Five essays deal with the "progressive era," with perceptive studies of such figures as Harper, Cope, Coe, and Elliott, plus a study of Roman Catholic innovators. The "era of theological reconstruction" looks at Miller, Koulomzin, the catechetical movement, and pioneer Jewish educators. Fifty years of research are surveyed. There are special essays on Fahs, six Protestant pioneers, and Wornom.

239 Kennedy, William Bean. *The Shaping of Protestant Education*. New York: Association Press, 1966.

A critical history of the development of the Sunday school (1789-1860) in relation to the rise of the common school in America. Extremely valuable historical bibliographical resources are cited. See also 212, 220, 242, 251, 760, and 857.

240 King, J.D. *Religious Education in Ireland*. Dublin: Fallons, 1970.

A solid study of the history and status of religious education in the schools of Ireland. The first part deals with the situation up to 1963, and the second with later developments. The author anticipated renewal and sought to undergird it by such historical study.

241 Knight, George R., ed. *Early Adventist Educators*. Berrien Springs, MI: Andrews University Press, 1983.

A key contribution to the history of religious education through the stories of eleven major Seventh-Day Adventist educators. The vast denominational system of schools did not emerge early, but when it did, embodying a struggle between "academics" and "reformists" (akin to the later "progressives"), the results were solid and permanent. Described as "well in advance of the educational mentality of their day," they were "in touch with the issues of their culture and sought to create an educational system that would meet the needs of that culture, while, at the same time, being faithful to their Christian convictions."

242 Knoff, Gerald E. *The World Sunday School Movement: The Story of a Broadening Mission*. New York: Seabury Press, 1979.

A great addition to the history of religious education. The records of the World Sunday School Conventions, the World Sunday School Association, and the World Council of Christian Education are analyzed with great skill and understanding, and the movement's story (1889-1971) told with careful documentation and fascinating detail. The author brings his critical insight to bear on the events and records with illuminating organization and interpretation of the material. See also 212, 220, 239, 251, 760, and 857.

243 Kurzweil, Zvi E. *Modern Trends in Jewish Education*. New York: Thomas Yoseleff, 1964.

Illuminating vignettes of personalities and movements in Jewish education in Europe and Israel in the nineteenth and twentieth centuries, together with an estimate of the state of religious consciousness in Israeli education.

244 Lannie, Vincent P. *Public Money and Parochial Education.* Cleveland, OH: The Press of Case Western Reserve University, 1968.

A history of the conflict, beginning in 1840, over the character of the New York City schools where Roman Catholic children were concerned. Traces the efforts of church and state to come to terms with one another, culminating in failure and in Bishop Hughes's decision to develop a parochial school system, the prototype of parochial education in America.

245 Laqueur, Thomas Walter. *Religion and Respectability: Sunday Schools and Working Class Culture, 1780-1850.* New Haven, CT: Yale University Press, 1976.

The finest study of the Sunday school. Sees it as an indigenous institution growing out of and serving the working-class community and combining aspects of secular education, the new attitude toward children, and the renewal of evangelical Christianity. The author makes a convincing case for the independent and lay character of the movement.

246 Larsson, Rune. *Religion zwischen Kirche und Schule.* Göttingen: Vandenhoek und Ruprecht, 1980.

An important historical study (originally a dissertation at Lund, in Sweden) of trends in West German religious education from 1945 on. Secularization and democratization are the trends most marked—an integration of religious education into the total school curriculum, diminishing its use of sacral language and its confessional aims.

247 Lynn, Robert Wood. "Civil Catechetics in Mid-Victorian America: Some Notes About American Civil Religion, Past and Present." *Religious Education* 68 (1973):5-27.

Seeking to understand the decline of civil religion in the United States, Lynn turns to a study of the work of William Holmes McGuffey, whose "Readers" helped to shape the moral and civic consciousness of several generations of Americans. There he finds a three-fold idea: a public bound together by a memory, a common story; a public celebrating its past, present, and future by means of a cultus; and a public being recalled to its vocation. Since such a public does not exist at present, it is with considerable hesitation that Lynn suggests that it may be rediscovered in some contemporary form.

248 Lynn, Robert Wood. *Protestant Strategies in Education.* New York: Association Press, 1965.

A historical analysis of American Protestant education in relation to total schooling, culminating in a rejection of current attempts to create a theologically oriented church education and challenging the church to reopen vital communication with the national educational enterprise.

249 Lynn, Robert Wood. "Sometimes on Sunday: Reflections on Images of the Future in American Education." *Andover Newton Quarterly* 12, no. 3 (January 1972):130-39.

> Spurred on by "futurology," concerned with the counterculture, and using historical reflection to try to envision a future for religious education, Lynn sees a possibility in mutuality with the young person. "His speech, his actions, his concerns are as much a judgment on your dogmas and ways as your dogmas and ways are a judgment on him. In a spirit of mutual judgment, the future emerges through reconciliation."

250 Lynn, Robert Wood. "The Uses of History: An Inquiry into the History of American Religious Education." *Religious Education* 67 (1972):83-97.

> One of Lynn's most illuminating pieces, deft and detailed in its handling of the history of ideas in American religious education. In part 1, three historical perspectives are examined: the interpretation of religious education as a series of movements (the Sunday school movement is the example used), the use of history to establish a discipline or a profession (the Yale Studies are cited in this connection), and history in the service of a theology (like H. Shelton Smith's neo-orthodox challenge to Coe and liberal religious education). Part 2 suggests possible lines of historical inquiry: the dynamics of religious education within the complex American educational system, and a more sophisticated understanding of secularization and its challenges to religious education. See also 272.

251 Lynn, Robert Wood, and Elliott Wright. *The Big Little School.* New York: Harper and Row, 1971.

> A sparkling and refreshing history of the American Sunday school from its British beginnings to the time of its 200th anniversary. Carefully analyzes and assesses the growth of the movement and the influences that have been brought to bear on it: evangelicalism, professional education, neo-orthodoxy, and the like. (A revised and enlarged edition, with a new and substantive foreword by J. Blaine Fister, was published by the Religious Education Press in 1980.) See also 212, 220, 239, 242, 760, and 857.

252 Mar'i, Sami Khalil. *Arab Education in Israel.* Syracuse, NY: Syracuse University Press, 1978.

> A straightforward description and assessment of education of the Arab population in the State of Israel. The author is an Arab trained at Hebrew University and at the University of Wisconsin, teaching at the University of Haifa. Concentrating on majority-minority relations, conclusions for the education of minorities are drawn.

253 Marrou, H.I. *A History of Education in Antiquity.* New York: Mentor Books, 1964.

> A basic work in religious education by the professor of early Christian history at the Sorbonne. Stresses the rise, character, and enduring qualities of classical education from Homeric times to the medieval period. "The history of ancient education reflects the progressive transition from a 'noble warrior' culture to a 'scribe' culture."

254 Martin, Dennis D. "Trahere in Affectum: Praxis-Centered Theological Education in the Fifteenth Century." *Religious Education* 85 (1990):604-16.

This article describes fifteenth-century efforts in Vienna and Paris to reinject praxis into theological education. While noting the influence of Jean Gerson at the University of Paris, primary attention is given to the work of Nicholas Kempf, a Carthusian monk. It was Kempf's belief that the heart as well as the mind is involved in theological education; the learner must move from "cognitive appropriation to affective internalization of the material learned."

255 Matsagouras, Elias. *The Early Church Fathers as Educators.* Minneapolis: Light and Life Publishing Company, 1977.

A simple introduction to the methods, materials, curriculum, teachers, and schools involved in Christian education during the patristic period. Includes an intriguing chapter on teaching methods and discipline in monastic education.

256 McComb, Louise. *The First 70 Years: A History of the Presbyterian School of Christian Education, Richmond, Virginia.* Richmond: Presbyterian School of Christian Education, 1985.

PSCE started as a "training school" for women in church occupations and has developed into a professional graduate school. Its history, here delightfully detailed, indicates the way in which such an institution has grown in response to a changing field, changing expectations on the part of the church, and a new concept of men's and women's roles in the church's educational leadership.

257 McKinney, Larry J. "The Fundamentalist Bible School as an Outgrowth of the Changing Patterns of Protestant Revivalism 1882-1920." *Religious Education* 84 (1989):589-605.

Attempts to redress the lack of attention given to Bible colleges in histories of education by examining the relationship of late nineteenth and early twentieth century Protestant revivalism to early fundamentalist Bible schools. Along with evangelists like Dwight L. Moody and Billy Sunday, the Bible conference, and polemical literature, the Bible college or institute was an important means used by revivalists to challenge the moral and spiritual decline that followed the Civil War. The author pays particular attention to how Bible colleges met the need for lay leadership training.

258 Morrison, Theodore. *Chautauqua: A Center for Education, Religion, and the Arts in America.* Chicago: University of Chicago Press, 1974.

There is little detailed material in print on the history of religious education per se. This history of Chautauqua is, therefore, especially welcome. Although Chautauqua has become a center for general cultural leisure education, it began as a center for Sunday school workers. The beginnings, under Vincent and Miller, are given in fascinating and informative detail.

259 Muirhead, Ian A. *Education in the New Testament*. New York: Association Press, 1965.

> "Religious education is an activity to be theologically understood both ecclesiologically and in the light of a special kind of divine revelation which has called the church into being. It involves the dynamic activity of the Spirit in the church, Christ who remained the teacher in his church, and is inseparable from the wholeness of the life of the Christian community. Its teaching cannot but reflect the quality of the church's worship, of its fellowship, and of its service in the world, for it is precisely the entry into that worship, fellowship, and service, in the most 'worthy' way which is the theme and goal of Christian teaching."

260 Murphy, James. *Church, State and Schools in Britain, 1800-1970*. London: Routledge and Kegan Paul, 1971.

> Seeks to unravel the complex relationships of church and state in education in Britain, 1800-1970. Early arrangements are discussed, followed by a systematic treatment of the Education Acts of 1870, 1902, and 1944, together with later developments in the period of "the end of 'passionate intensity.'"

261 Neill, Stephen Charles, and Hans-Reudi Weber. *The Layman in Christian History*. Philadelphia: Westminster Press, 1963.

> A scholarly review of the role of the laity in each period of church history, in the major geographical areas, and within the various traditions. Indispensable background for discussion of the theology and ministry of the laity. Howard Grimes contributes the chapter that reviews the role of the laity in Christian education in the United States, and Weber provides the chapter on the "rediscovery of the laity in the ecumenical movement." See also 295, 792, 854, 956, and 1167.

262 Ognibene, Richard. "Catholic and Protestant Education in the Late Nineteenth Century." *Religious Education* 77 (1982):5-20.

> Religious education is sometimes described as a discipline without a memory. With this in mind, Ognibene asks three questions that require knowledge of the late nineteenth century: What accounts for the parochial school system? Were Protestants satisfied with the Sunday school as an effective vehicle for religious education? Did Protestants genuinely accept the public system of education even as that system became increasingly secular? In dealing with the first question, a balanced picture of the controversy within the Catholic church over schooling emerges. Inquiry on the other questions produces a negative answer to both, setting the stage for more productive dialogue in the present day.

263 Parker, Inez Moore. *The Rise and Decline of the Program of Education for Black Presbyterians of the United Presbyterian Church, U.S.A., 1865-1970*. San Antonio, TX: Trinity University Press, 1977.

> Immediately after the Civil War, the Presbyterian church mounted a program for the education of the black people of the South. The work proliferated into many community-based schools, today consolidated into a few mission schools and

colleges of high grade. This detailed history tells the story, school by school, stressing the impact of the schools on their communities.

264   Power, Edward J. *Catholic Higher Education in America*. New York: Appleton-Century-Crofts, 1972.

Power previously wrote general histories of education and Catholic higher education, but in this volume he reexamines "the history of the nineteenth century Catholic higher education from a broader perspective," adding to it interesting and significant interpretations of twentieth-century developments in Catholic colleges and universities. The periods treated are 1786-1870, 1870-1940, and 1940-1970.

265   Praetz, Helen. *Building a School System: A Sociological Study of Catholic Education*. Melbourne: Melbourne University Press, 1980.

Traces the recent history of developments in Catholic education in Australia--the period in which an educational system has begun to take shape where before there were varieties of schools run by different orders and other bodies, without too much coordination. The focus is on changes in curriculum and administration, the thesis being that theological positions "become manifest in the tightening bonds of an administrative system."

266   Ravitch, Diane. *The Great School Wars, New York City, 1805-1973*. New York: Basic Books, 1974.

A major contribution to the history of education and, since religious factors have always played a key role in public schooling in New York City, to the history of religion in relation to education. Massive in detail, but clear in outline and interpretation.

267   Reiher, Dieter, ed. *Kirchlicher Unterricht in der DDR 1949-1990*. Göttingen and Zürich: Vanderhoeck und Ruprecht, 1991.

Traces the development of religious education under communism in East Germany. In spite of the pressures of the totalitarian regime, the churches maintained a great degree of independence and integrity in their educational programs and materials. What emerged may be characterized as authentically Christian, ecumenical, personally transformative, and socially responsible.

268 Sawicki, Marianne. "Educational Policy and Christian Origins." *Religious Education* 85 (1990):455-77.

The *Religious Education* research article for 1990 draws on insights from the field of Christian origins to discover why some patterns of "identity-propagation" became dominant in the first century Christian education while others were suppressed.

269 Sawicki, Marianne. *The Gospel in History: Portrait of a Teaching Church: The Origins of Christian Education*. New York: Paulist Press, 1988.

Sawicki uses two lenses for looking at the gospel in history. Arguing that "different historical eras tended to adopt one or another characteristic style of understanding according to the level of the culture of the times," Sawicki views the origins of Christian education through the lens of cognitive development. Her second lens consists of three ministries of the church: ministries of the Word, ministries of the sacraments, and ministries of service.

270 Schisler, John Q. *Christian Education in Local Methodist Churches*. Nashville: Abingdon Press, 1969.

A systematic tracing of the record from Wesleyan days through 1955. Schisler and those who completed the book after his death leave critical interpretation to the reader. Major values: providing a running account of a great denomination's parish education work, and locating areas for further historical and critical research.

271 Schmidt, Stephen A. *A History of the Religious Education Association*. Birmingham, AL: Religious Education Press, 1983.

The author, in this history with an argument, sees the Religious Education Association as representative of a movement to mobilize forces of both church and school on behalf of a "progressive democratic vision" and a "public vision." The vagaries of the organization (and the movement) through its almost eighty years are traced to the point where it serves as a pluralistic forum, with the public vision still to be realized.

272 Schmidt, Stephen A. "The Uses of History and Religious Education." *Religious Education* 80 (1985):345-72.

Pleading for a more sophisticated method in historical research and interpretation in religious education, Schmidt takes issue with those who reviewed his history of the Religious Education Association, and with Lynn's 1972 article. Rejecting the aims and methods of historicism, he sees the historian "nudging the present into the future...with a biased agenda. Both contribute to [the] search and [the] conclusion, but each is subjected to the rigid examination of primary sources." See also 250.

273 Seymour, Jack L. *From Sunday School to Church School: Continuities in Protestant Church Education in the United States, 1860-1929*. Washington, DC: University Press of America, 1982.

One of the most thorough histories of Christian education yet available. Maintains that the character and agenda of the church school were set by the Sunday school in the late nineteenth century, and that the liberal period did not effect the changes that were assumed. Now "the purpose of church education transcends the nursery of the church to become the education of the public, the form moves from the school to education, and the scope embodies a new Christian education ecology."

274 Seymour, Jack L. "The Future of the Past: History and Policy-making in Religious Education." *Religious Education* 81 (1986):113-33.

> "History fundamentally contributes to the discussion of who a people are: what visions focus their imaginations, and what strategies guide their interactions with each other....This task is summarized in the phrase policy-making. History is to contribute to the shaping of the policies that guide a people. The historian does this by clarifying the context within which the meanings and activities of a culture emerge....[History assists] in understanding the origin of present aims, issues and strategies in religious education, and consequently their continuing power. Moreover, it provides a means to clarify the role of religious institutions in the formation, maintenance, and transformation of the public."

275 Slaght, Lawrence T. *Multiplying the Witness*. Valley Forge, PA: Judson Press, 1974.

> A 150-year history of the educational work of the American Baptists, written in popular style and liberally illustrated. Covers Sunday schools, youth work, educational institutions, leadership education, and publications. A mine of detailed information.

276 Sloan, Douglas, ed. *The Great Awakening and American Education: A Documentary History*. New York: Teachers College Press, 1973.

> A key period in American church history is examined and revealed in its educational significance. Concentrating on leaders like Frelinghuysen, the Tennents, Edwards, and Whitefield, the educational issues that developed are identified and the related new educational situations (academies and colleges) are examined.   Some parallels with the contemporary educational situation are suggested.   All the readings but one come from or refer to the period of 1740-1761.

277 Stabler, Ernest. *Education Since Uhuru: The Schools of Kenya*. Middletown, CT: Wesleyan University Press, 1969.

> Reviews educational developments in Kenya, especially since independence. In the process, the author presents almost a case study of mission education and Christian education in the schools. This becomes especially vivid because it seems unintentional and is entirely within the larger context of the whole educational enterprise.

278 Towns, Elmer L., ed. *A History of Religious Educators*. Grand Rapids, MI: Baker Book House, 1975.

> Twenty-six articles, by individual authorities, on the persons who have been most important in the development of religious education from the beginning of the Christian era to the beginning of the twentieth century. A useful source and checklist for the serious student. Where else can you find anything in print on Francke, for instance?

279   Tyms, James D. *The Rise of Religious Education Among Negro Baptists.* Washington, DC: University Press of America, 1979.

A useful reference work in the history of religious education. Reflects the interests and concerns of the 1940s (when the study originated), brought up to date in the early 1960s. The emphasis is on the development of an indigenous church and its adaptation of the Sunday school to meet its educational needs.

280   Ulich, Robert. *A History of Religious Education.* New York: New York University Press, 1968.

A renowned scholar in the history of ideas in education here provides a substantial and rich text in the history of theory and practice in religious education. Not very profound on the critical or interpretative side, but authentic, clearly outlined, balanced, and full of fascinating detail. A unique blend of text and primary sources.

281   Wiater, Werner, ed. *Religionspädagogische Reformbewegung, 1900-1933.* Hildesheim: Georg Olms Verlag, 1984.

The basic documents—Catholic and Protestant—of the movement for the reform of religious education in Germany, from 1900 up to the Third Reich.

282   Worley, Robert C. *Preaching and Teaching in the Earliest Church.* Philadelphia: Westminster Press, 1967.

A reexamination of C.H. Dodd's kerygma-didache thesis, culminating in its rejection. An alternative theory of teaching-preaching in the early church is offered, and its implications for theory and practice touched on.

283   Yulish, Stephen M. *The Search for a Civic Religion: A History of the Character Education Movement in America, 1890-1935.* Washington, DC: University Press of America, 1980.

Details the history of the character education movement in America. As schools became secularized, their imperative for moral education remained. The phenomenon of character education came in to replace the sanctions of religious moral education, but in the process became a factor in the determination of a "civic religion," a set of values (patriotism, loyalty, obedience, and adjustment to the socioeconomic order) that came to have quasireligious force.

BEHAVIORAL STUDIES OF RELIGION

284   Adams, Carol Markstrom. "A Qualitative Analysis of the Impressions and Experiences of Religious Minority Students." *Religious Education* 84 (1989):417-27.

This qualitative study focused on middle-class Anglo-American adolescents who were members of a Presbyterian church in a community where 90 percent of the population was Mormon. Symbolic interaction provided the theoretical framework of the study, which was designed to understand how these adolescents were affected by living in a predominately Mormon community. While the adolescents in the study did not explicitly define themselves as a religious minority, they did manifest an "us-versus-them" mentality.

285 Argyle, Michael, and Benjamin Beit-Hallahmi. *The Social Psychology of Religion*. London: Routledge and Kegan Paul, 1975.

Summarizes the results of experimental research in religious behavior (thus shedding a great deal of light on the factors associated with religious experience) and uses these results to assess the value of "reductive" theories of religious behavior. The summaries of these theories are in themselves valuable.

286   Batson, C. Daniel, and W. Larry Ventis. *The Religious Experience: A Social-Psychological Perspective*. New York: Oxford University Press, 1982.

Two social psychologists collaborate in the study of religious experience. Especially useful for its definitions, frank analyses of methodology, and findings. Religious experience is a matter of coming to grips with existential questions. The social psychologists' method may be both phenomenological and empirical. The findings include significant steps in personal recreation, assessment of "facilitators" in religious experience (drugs, meditation, religious language), and contributions of religious experience to personal freedom, mental health, and love of others.

287 Benson, Peter L. and Carolyn H. Eklin. *Effective Christian Education: A National Study of Protestant Congregations*. Minneapolis: Search Institute, 1990.

This summary report on faith, loyalty, and congregational life was presented at a conference of denominational representatives in March of 1990. The study involved more than 11,000 people in 561 congregations. Both quantitative and qualitative methods were used. Researchers found that growth in faith and loyalty to a person's congregation and denomination was closely related to involvement in an effective Christian education program.

288 Benson, Peter, Dorothy Williams, and Arthur Johnson. *The Quicksilver Years: The Hopes and Fears of Early Adolescence*. San Francisco: Harper and Row, 1987.

Search Institute, at the behest of thirteen national youth-serving agencies conducted a research of 8,000 fifth- to ninth-graders and 11,000 of their parents, the results of which were reported to the sponsors in 1984. The research covers current issues of concern and also provides data on the importance of religion to young adolescents and their beliefs and pervasive themes. See also 930 and 946.

289 Berger, Peter L., and Thomas Luckmann. *The Social Construction of Reality*. Garden City, NY: Doubleday and Company, 1966.

A cogent summary of the dynamics of knowing, and the ramifications of knowing in grasping and building the lived world, according to the sociology of knowledge. Especially useful in understanding such aspects of religious experience as the development of symbolic universes, the conceptual and social processes of maintaining and using those symbolic constructs, and the ways in which they are changed (which the authors call "alternation," and religious educators will recognize as conversion). See also 344.

290 Berkowitz, Leonard. *The Development of Motives and Values in the Child*. New York: Basic Books, 1964.

A critical review of theory and research on child rearing, citing particularly the contrasting views of those who hold to "the necessity of both loving and training the child" over against those who "place greater emphasis on gratifying the child's needs." Concludes that "mothers and fathers who would cultivate achievement motivation and morality in their offspring must teach their children standards of excellence and proper conduct and with love and understanding make the youngsters want to live up to such standards....The theorists of self-actualization have an oversimplified picture of child development. The child's personality is much more of a tabula rasa than they would have us believe, and parents must become involved in shaping the personality."

291 Booth, Howard J. *Edwin Diller Starbuck: Pioneer in the Psychology of Religion*. Washington, DC: University Press of America, 1981.

Starbuck was the pioneer of the modern discipline of psychology of religion. He was also one of the chief figures in the character education movement of the 1920s. This book traces both his personal life and his career and analyzes his academic and practical contributions from 1897 to 1945.

292 Brekke, Milo. *How Different Are People Who Attended Lutheran Schools?* St. Louis, MO: Concordia Publishing House, 1974.

The research data upon which this book is based are taken from the Youth Research Center's *A Study of Generations*. The findings show significant differences in belief, church loyalty, and church activity. Not so clear are personal attitudes and practices. Not much difference was discovered in social prejudice and social action.

293 Browning, Don S. *Generative Man: Psychoanalytic Perspectives*. Philadelphia: Westminster Press, 1973.

A basic theoretical work in the psychology of religion. On the premise that psychoanalytical models of human life are replacing other models in the modern consciousness, four such models (Freud, Brown, Fromm, and Erikson) are examined. Browning's judgment is that Erikson's model of "generative man" is the most useful, and he develops its implications for future thought.

294 Byrnes, Joseph F. *The Psychology of Religion*. New York: Free Press, 1984.

A historical and functional account of the status of the discipline of psychology of religion. Organized around the paradigm of Augustine's conversion experience, it analyzes the contributions of psychologists (the tradition of William James, personality theorists, social interactionists, current research, and therapists) in establishing and utilizing a vocabulary adequate to the analysis of the phenomena of religious experience. Useful also in seeing how a discipline deals with data that proliferate without coalescing.

295   Campbell, Thomas C., and Yoshio Fukuyama. *The Fragmented Layman.* Philadelphia: Pilgrim Press, 1970.

A model research in sociology of religion, investigating the relationship of types and degrees of church participation to changes in social attitudes. The subjects were a cross section (8,000) of members of the United Church of Christ. At the end of the book the authors turn into practical theologians, making suggestions on implications of their findings for church practice. See also 261, 792, 854, 956, and 1167.

296   Carrier, Hervé. *The Sociology of Religious Belonging.* New York: Herder and Herder, 1965.

The structure and functioning of the religious group as a social system, related to the modal personality types and the personal needs of the system's members. Reviews the data available in theory and research and develops a new conceptual scheme for understanding religious socialization. Religious educators will especially value chapters on early education, religious instruction, weakening of religious commitment, and stability and maturity of the religious attitude.

297   Cavalletti, Sofia. *The Religious Potential of the Child: The Description of an Experience with Children from Ages Three to Six.* New York: Paulist Press, 1983.

Cavalletti, a religious educator in her own right, early joined forces with the followers of Montessori, elaborating a system of careful induction of the child into doctrine and liturgy, but building on the child's native religious experience. Jerome Berryman provides an invaluable biographical and theoretical preface. Word pictures of typical experiences are given, and there are theoretical discussions of the method of "signs" and the identification and use of "sensitive periods" in the child's religious development, supplemented by appropriate drawings by the children themselves. See also 139, 591, 676, 873, 1017.

298   Coles, Robert. *The Spiritual Life of Children.* Boston: Houghton Mifflin Company, 1990.

Like *The Moral Life of Children* (1986) and *The Political Life of Children* (1986), this book reports the fruit of a psychiatrist's research and reflection on interviews with more than 500 children. Coles interviewed children in North America, South America, Africa, the Middle East, and Europe. The result is a thoughtful portrait of children's spirituality.

299   Cruchon, Georges. *The Transformations of Childhood.* Dayton, OH: Pflaum, 1969.

An extremely useful guide to Christian "pedagogical psychology," which is to say developmental psychology for the Christian parent and teacher. Research based, the age span covered is birth through twelve. A major strength is thorough attention to religious development. Has a fine concluding chapter that gives a short history of child psychology in international perspective.

300   Deconchy, J.P. *Structure Génétique de l'idee de Dieu chez des Catholiques Francais*. Brussels: Lumen Vitae, 1966.

An empirical research, involving several thousand French schoolchildren (elementary and secondary), inquiring into the relation of personality and view on God. A good example of the excellent studies sponsored by Lumen Vitae, the Roman Catholic education center.

301   de Lorimier, Jacques, Roger Graveline, and April Aubert. *Identity and Faith in Young Adults*. New York: Paulist Press, 1973.

A Canadian research on the religious education of the 18-21 age group. Behavioral and theological data are used to set the basis for religious education. Principles and plans are proposed. The results of three experimental programs are reported. An unusually fine example of the use of research in program planning.

302   Dumoulins, Anne, and Jean-Marie Gaspard. *Les méditations religieuses dans l'universe de l'enfant*. Leuven, Belgium: Leuven University Press, 1973.

One of the splendid and massive research studies in psychology of religion from Lumen Vitae in Belgium. This one deals with prayer and Communion in the experience of six- to twelve-year-olds.

303   Erikson, Erik. *Childhood and Society*. New York: W.W. Norton, 1963.

The second edition, revised and enlarged, of one of the most influential books in education, presenting a psychoanalytic and anthropological approach to human development. Includes the famous "eight stages of man." Not substantially changed from the former edition; the author has included notes indicating the subsequent development of his thought and addressing the comments of his critics. See also 319 and 476.

304   Erikson, Erik. *Identity, Youth and Crisis*. New York: W.W. Norton, 1968.

Erikson's own review of the life-cycle and self-identity. Additional essays deal with youth, womanhood, and race.

305   Faber, Heije. *Psychology of Religion*. Philadelphia: Westminster Press, 1975.

The first part of the book consists of a review and critique of the contributions of Freud, Jung, Rümke, Fromm, and Erikson to the understanding of religion and religious experience. The author reveals himself (in chapter 9) as very much aware of the differences that developmental stages make in Christian education. This is reflected in the second part of the book, which is in effect a developmental psychology of religion in psychoanalytic light.

306 Fairchild, Roy W., and John Charles Wynn. *Families in the Church: A Protestant Survey*. New York: Association Press, 1961.

> A report of the intensive research conducted by the United Presbyterian Church in the U.S.A. into the theology of family life, the contemporary picture of Protestant parents and their religious ideas and practices, and the ministry of the church to families. Deals directly with problems of Christian education program and curriculum as they are related to parents and families. A milestone in religious research and a major contribution to the sociology of religion.

307 *Faith Development in the Adult Life Cycle*. Minneapolis: Faith Development in the Adult Life Cycle, 1987.

> The full report, with supporting data, of the Religious Education Association's research project on adult faith development (1981-1986). The main body of the report is in part 1, whose highlights are the sections that summarize the findings and that develop "some insights for ministry." The two research modules used in the study are reported in parts 2 and 3.

308 Fee, Joan L., Andrew M. Greeley, William C. McCready, and Teresa A. Sullivan. *Young Catholics*. New York: William H. Sadlier, 1981.

> A report of research that cuts deeply into common assumptions about the church and its youth. Points to the need for renewed interest in Catholic schools, augmented youth programs, increased professional effectiveness on the part of the clergy, evangelization of the family as such, and rehabilitation of and increased attention to traditional religious symbols and practices.

309 Ferm, Deane William. *Alternative Life-Styles Confront the Church*. New York: Seabury Press, 1983.

> Beginning with a documentation of the shift in America from the nuclear family as normative to other life-styles, a detailed treatment of programs, both national and local, is given to indicate approaches the churches are taking to ministry to the family, and to singles, the handicapped, the homosexual, and others. The book concludes with the author's own views of what should be done.

310 Fiske, Marjorie, and Chiriboga. *Change and Continuity in Adult Life*. San Francisco: Jossey-Bass Publishers, 1990.

> This longitudinal study indicates a blurring of the eras of adulthood and increased diversity in the way adults move through life. Fiske and Chiriboga tracked four groups of adults over a twelve-year period. High school seniors, newlywed young adults, empty nest early middle-age adults, and pre-retirement late middle-age adults were first interviewed in 1968. Four subsequent interviews were conducted in three-year intervals starting in 1970-71.

311 Fowler, James W. *Becoming Adult, Becoming Christian*. San Francisco: Harper and Row, 1984.

> Fowler sees a real crisis in vocation (by which he seems to mean personal meaning and purpose) and thinks that contemporary "stages of life" theories (Erikson's, Levinson's, Gilligan's, and his own) hold promise of providing something of a new "way of salvation" for the modern adult. The book thus represents his constructive answer to those who have seen his work as too generic and not sufficiently specifically Christian.

312 Fowler, James W. *Stages of Faith: The Psychology of Human Development and the Quest for Meaning*. San Francisco: Harper and Row, 1981.

> Here Fowler gives us the mature statement of his research-based "stages of faith development." With a warning that theory must not be limiting, this full presentation of his theory is set in a profoundly challenging psychological and theological context. At the same time it is a personal document in which he discloses his own faith development and invites the reader to do so as well. Useful also in making his research methods clear. See also 42, 307, 313, 357, 372, 374, 423, 621, 684, 877, and 1152.

313 Fowler, James W. "Stages of Faith: Reflections on a Decade of Dialogue." *Christian Education Journal* 13, no. 1 (Autumn 1992):13-23.

> Ten years after the publication of *Stages of Faith* (312), Fowler offers some reasons for the responses his book has evoked and responds to three critical questions evangelical Christians raise with regard to his work. These questions have to do with how grace and sin are understood by faith development theory, the relation of salvation to faith stage theory, and the centrality of biblical authority.

314 Fowler, James W., *et al. Trajectories in Faith*. Nashville: Abingdon Press, 1980.

> Biographical examinations of the faith stories of "world transformers"—Malcolm X, Anne Hutchinson, Blaise Pascal, Ludwig Wittgenstein, and Dietrich Bonhoeffer. Their faith histories are analyzed with the use of Fowler's "stages in faith development."

315 Friedman, Edwin H. *Generation to Generation: Family Process in Church and Synagogue*. New York: Guilford Press, 1985.

> A groundbreaking book in the use of family therapy in three areas: the counseling of families, the congregation as a family, and the leader's own family. The key is not expertise but self-definition and self-understanding in these "family situations," where the dynamics at work are essentially the same. The author sees unusual opportunity in the pastoral role because of the pastor's involvement in life-cycle events ("hinges of time" on which the doors can open or close for generations) and over long periods of time.

316 Furushima, Randall. "Faith Development in a Cross-Cultural Perspective." *Religious Education* 80 (1985):414-20.

Stage views are usually claimed to be sequential, invariant, hierarchical, and universal. To test such claims with regard to James Fowler's stages of faith, this research was undertaken with a group of Japanese Buddhists in Hawaii. The study found that there were areas of faith that could be accounted for within Fowler's faith development framework, but the findings also included the identification of ten hypotheses that might be subjected to further investigation.

317   Gillespie, V. Bailey. *The Experience of Faith*. Birmingham, AL: Religious Education Press, 1988.

Three opening chapters present the basic assumptions of this study. Succeeding chapters trace faith experience from early childhood ("Borrowed Faith") through older adulthood ("Resolute Faith"). Each of these chapters first describes the characteristics of faith experience and then discusses facilitating faith experience in that period of life.

318 Gillespie, V. Bailey. *Religious Conversion and Personal Identity*. Birmingham, Al: Religious Education Press, 1979.

There are few recent books that deal thoroughly with the psychology of religious conversion. This book, from within a conversionist framework, takes account of the relevant research and theory on the matter and can serve as a summary volume from which further research and theory may develop.

319   Gleason, John J., Jr. *Growing up to God*. Nashville: Abingdon Press, 1975.

From a clinical background, the author addresses the question of a theological-psychological approach to religious development. Using Erik Erikson's eight stages, he interprets each in theological as well as psychological light and indicates, among other things, implications of his findings for religious education. See also 303 and 476.

320 Godin, André. *Le Dieu des Parents et le Dieu des Enfants*. Paris: Casterman, 1966.

Godin is the leading investigator in the area of psychology of religion who is also attempting to develop the relationship of that field to religious education. Here he presents three research-based reports: (1) conceptions of God held by parents and children, (2) the priest and his image, and (3) psychological belief and Christian prayer.

321 Godin, André. *The Psychological Dynamics of Religious Experience*. Birmingham, Al: Religious Education Press, 1985.

Bridging the fields of psychological research and religious education, Godin here shares the methodological difficulties he has encountered (particularly in working in a field in which theology and behavioral studies have to mesh), and his findings on religious experience and growth.

322 Goldman, Ronald. *Religious Thinking from Childhood to Adolescence*. London: Routledge and Kegan Paul, 1964.

One of the most influential books of its generation in religious education, both in England and the United States, this study of cognitive developmental processes in religious growth is based upon the author's own extensive research. Cognitive content must be taken into account in using religious subject matter with children of various age levels; levels of operational thinking impose severe limits on the understanding of such subject matter; religious education for children should be appropriately child-centered rather than centered upon biblical concepts that can be appropriate only for adults. See also 334, 1067, and 1169.

323 Goleman, Daniel. *The Varieties of Meditative Experience*. New York: John Wiley and Sons, 1977.

Combining a personal story and scholarly research, the author uses the Buddhist Visuddimagga as his model for meditative experience, calling it "a map for inner space." Eleven other meditative methods (including Jewish Kabbalah, Christian Hesychasm, and Transcendental Meditation) are explained. The book concludes with a critical comparison of the twelve methods.

324 Grams, Armin. *Children and Their Parents* (The Lutheran Study Series, vol. 3). Minneapolis: T.S. Denison, 1963.

The director of parent education at the Merrill-Palmer Institute sketches a Christian (avowedly Lutheran) concept of the nature of personality and its development, "the relation between concepts of faith, hope, and love, and the notions of dependence, independence, and interdependence," through the life span. Presented at an elementary level, yet with reference to significant studies in psychology and family life.

325 Greeley, Andrew M. *Ecstasy: A Way of Knowing*. Englewood Cliffs, NJ: Prentice-Hall, 1974.

"A pragmatic, skeptical, hard-nosed analysis of both the mystical experience and the mystical revival." The author keeps close, in definition and delimitations, to the Christian mystical experience. But his study is based on contemporary empirical research. Since it is an investigation in how persons engage in and explain religious experience, it is important for religious educators.

326 Greeley, Andrew M. *The Religious Imagination*. New York: William H. Sadlier, 1981.

A report of national surveys of Catholics on various factors relating to the religious imagination, that being assumed to be basic to religious experience. Among the findings: While a particular teacher may have a profound effect on the religious imagination of the youth (religious imagination being a product of relationships), the effect of the classroom as such is nil. Advocates a return "to the basic story" and "to the fireside around which the story is told."

327 Greeley, Andrew M., and Peter H. Rossi. *The Education of Catholic Americans*. Chicago: Aldine, 1966.

A report on a survey centering on problems in and opinions of Catholic education. The results show surprisingly little influence of Catholic education on behavior and attitudes, either positive or negative, and lead to the conclusion that Catholic schools are not necessary for the survival of American Catholicism.

328 Grom, Bernhard. *Religionspädagogische Psychologie*. Düsseldorf and Göttingen: Patmos Verlag and Vandenhoeck und Ruprecht, 1981.

An exhaustive scholarly investigation of the psychological sources for, and hindrances to, mature religious experience. The author uses examples from both European and North American research and is clear on his theological norms and his prosocial approach to conscience formation. Specific implications are drawn for religious education, from the preschool level through youth.

329 Grom, Bernhard. *Religionspsychologie*. Munich and Göttingen: Kösel-Verlag and Vanderhoeck und Ruprecht, 1992.

Using the most recent psychological findings, the author provides an overview of contemporary religious experience, maintaining a balance between the influences of culture, religions, and confessions on the one hand, and the inner experiences of the person on the other. Those inner experiences, formative of religious experience, are developed as psychosocial and intrapsychic impulses, the complexities of normal and abnormal emotional development, as well as the varieties of conditions of the ego and consciousness.

330 Hall, Brian P. *The Genesis Effect: Personal and Organizational Transformation*. New York: Paulist Press, 1986.

Brian Hall works and publishes in the field of values education. Here he presents a system, experimentally tested, by which values may have their intended transforming effects on both persons and organizations. Incorporating insights from processes of spiritual formation, this manual, though technically complex, suggests important ways of testing for values structures and guiding in the dynamics of transformation.

331 Hardy, Alister. *The Spiritual Nature of Man*. Oxford: Oxford University Press, 1979.

This is the fifth publication of the Religious Experience Research Unit, Manchester College, Oxford, and is thus a substantive contribution to the psychology of religion. Discusses "the whole range of religious experience as revealed by an examination of the first three thousand personal accounts (descriptions of individual religious experience) sent in to the Unit."

332 Hill, Michael. *A Sociology of Religion*. New York: Basic Books, 1973.

> The emphasis is on sociological theory in the study of religion, with a method that avoids the extremes of "religious sociology" and socioeconomic reductionism. Introduces the major themes of the discipline (typologies of religious organization, the Weberian thesis, charisma and religious authority, etc.). The reader is rewarded with a critical knowledge of the main leaders, theories, and research in the field.

333 Hummel, Gert. "Religion and Psyche: Some Considerations on the Experience of Faith." *Dialog, A Journal of Theology* 21 (1982):25-31.

> The traditional forms of religious expression are in crisis, in part because of the growth of new forms of religious experience. The author relies mainly on Jung for the reformulation of religion in light of this phenomenon. Religious experience here is seen as unconditional and holistic encounter with the presence of the Spirit, requiring new symbols for expression. In the course of development religion is experienced in different ways and takes on different shapes. "What is at stake is the experience of perfect community of all reality, the experience of the Spirit."

334 Hyde, Kenneth E. *Religion in Childhood and Adolescence: A Comprehensive Review of the Research*. Birmingham, AL: Religious Education Press, 1990.

> Provides a new generation of religious educators and youth workers with the first comprehensive review of the research on religion in childhood and adolescence since the publication of *Research on Religious Development: A Comprehensive Handbook* in 1971 (1169). Religious thinking, religious experience, religious beliefs, and religious attitudes are among the areas covered in Hyde's review. An invaluable reference. See also 322 and 1169.

335 Johnson, Douglas W. *Growing up Christian in the Twenty-first Century*. Valley Forge, PA: Judson Press, 1984.

> An example of responsible "futuring" that bases itself in continuities on the one hand, and the identification of present issues that will inevitably influence the future on the other. Using the device of a hypothetical person, the author sketches Jill's life from the early teen pressures of 1990 by five-year intervals to "the long haul beginning in 2010."

336 Kay, William. *Moral Development*. London: George Allen and Unwin, 1970.

> Mainly a review of theory and research in character and moral development; intended as background guidance for British educators. Stresses: (1) the American work of Hartshorne and May and Havighurst and his associates, (2) the work of Piaget, and (3) British research like Goldman's. But comes to independent conclusions in a attitudinal model of moral development.

94 Religious Education

337 Kettler, Walter. *Von Gott und Jesus im Kindergarten reden*. Munich: Kösel-Verlag, 1979.

The findings of a three-year practical research on how to talk about God, Jesus, and other biblical and theological matters in the kindergarten.

338 Kohlberg, Lawrence. *Essays in Moral Development*. Vol. 1, *The Philosophy of Moral Development*. San Francisco: Harper and Row, 1981.

Philosophical essays undergirding Kohlberg's psychological work on moral development and his reports on experiments in educational practice, and dealing with the philosophical foundations of education, critical aspects of his delineation of moral stages, law and politics, and religion. A discussion of religion relates his thinking on moral development to that of Fowler on faith development, holding that moral development is necessary but not sufficient for religious development. See also 159, 312, 339, 350, 356, 368, 386, 427, 456, 457, 504, and 620.

339 Kohlberg, Lawrence. *Essays in Moral Development*. Vol. 2, *The Psychology of Moral Development*. San Francisco: Harper and Row, 1984.

Presents the background and development of Kohlberg's views, comparatively examined (part 1); an elaborate treatment of the formulation of the theory of moral development (part 2); and analyses of his research methods and their results (part 3). Fowler's influence is acknowledged in part 2. See also 338.

340 Koppe, William A. *How Persons Grow in Christian Community* (*Yearbooks in Christian Education*, vol. 15). Philadelphia: Fortress Press, 1973.

The report of the Lutheran Longitudinal Study, in which 10,000 Lutherans participated. Designed to study growth in church involvement over eighteen years, the results indicate a predominance of individual rather than demographic factors, an alternation between reliance on authority and self-development, and learning as maintenance of integrity rather than systematic accumulation of concepts, skills, and attitudes.

341 Lamport, Mark A. "Adolescent Spirituality: Age of Conversion and Factors of Development," *Christian Education Journal* 10, no. 3 (Spring 1990):17-30.

This article reports the findings of a research that investigated the age of conversion and developmental factors. The author affirms adolescence as a "prime age" for conversion and calls for a recommitment to fostering the spiritual development of adolescents. Adult mentors, peer leadership, servanthood, and the practice of spiritual disciplines are identified as four factors that can positively influence adolescents to have an "owned faith." See also 717 and 1169.

342 Lavoie, Marguerite. *Une Religion de Sens pour des Adolescents Nouveau*. Montreal: Editions Bellarmin, 1983.

A research involving middle adolescents, exploring the various facets of affective religious education. Using the premise that there are those who do not respond well to transmissive cognitive religious instruction, the study sees the possibility of an alternative approach, one in which "incarnational theology," drawing upon home, church, and society, uses an apprenticeship model.

343 Levinson, Daniel J., *et al. The Seasons of a Man's Life*. New York: Alfred A. Knopf, 1978.

This is the book that should have broken open the concern with stages in adult development, for it was on the basis of the research presented here that the popular literature (and controversy) that preceded its publication was based. The serious student of adult psychology will use it instead of its more popular counterparts.

344 Luckmann, Thomas. *The Invisible Religion*. New York: Macmillan, 1967.

An important sociological framework for the religious educator. Raises the question of the conditions under which "transcendent" superordinated and "integrating" structures of meaning are socially objectivated, and further, how these structures of meaning are then internalized subjectively. In addition, a new situation is described in which the human's place in society is related to powerful new structures of meaning, whose religious character is easily missed by those who identify religion with its usual institutions. See also 289.

345 Madge, Violet. *Children in Search of Meaning*. New York: Morehouse-Barlow, 1966.

A record of observational research in children's explorations and discoveries of religious and scientific meaning. In outline, method, and detailed recording of material, it suggests a simple basis for valuable action research that could be carried on by any sensitive and reasonably well-informed Christian educator. British; an interesting supplement to the work of Ronald Goldman.

346 Maslow, Abraham H. *Religions, Values, and Peak-Experiences*. Columbus, OH: Ohio State University Press, 1964.

Defining "peak-experiences" as "secularized religious or mystical or transcendent experiences," the author claims that "what the mystics have said to be essential to the individual's religion is now receiving empirical support." The conclusion for education is that "the teaching of spiritual values or ethical and moral values definitely does (in principle) have a place in education, perhaps ultimately a very basic and essential place....Precisely these ultimate values are and should be the far goals for all education." Makes a strong case for religious education, in the generic sense.

347 Maves, Paul B. *Faith for the Older Years*. Minneapolis: Augsburg Publishing House, 1986.

Maves is a specialist on religion and older persons. He wrote this book out of that background and out of personal experience as an older person. Thus the book is both professional and personal, packed with practical wisdom, presented in such a way that it may well be used by groups of older adults as a basis for study and discussion.

348 McAuley, E. Nancy, and Moira Mathiesen. *Faith Without Form: Beliefs of Catholic Youth.* Kansas City, MO: Sheed and Ward, 1986.

A study of the perceived transitions in belief, thinking, and practices in graduating Catholic high school seniors in the Archdiocese of Washington, D.C. Investigates questions of values and priorities, personal morality, specific religious faith, the church, the community, and vocation.

349 Mitchell, Marjorie Editha. *The Child's Attitude to Death.* New York: Schocken Books, 1967.

Death is changing in the modern world, and so are the attitudes toward it (people die older; they die in hospitals rather than at home; it is less talked about; medical postponement of death is a reality). This book examines what children and adolescents think, say, and are taught (in Great Britain) about death in the family, school, and church, to the end that educational approaches to the subject may be changed.

350 Munsey, Brenda, ed. *Moral Development, Moral Education, and Kohlberg.* Birmingham, AL: Religious Education Press, 1980.

Begins and ends with Kohlberg, with critical contributions from the fields of psychology (James Fowler and others) and philosophy. James Michael Lee (Christian) and Barry Chazan (Jewish) examine the implications and problems for religious education. James B. McDonald and others look at implications and problems for moral education. See also 159, 338, 356, 368, 386, 504, and 620.

351 Myers, William R. *Black and White Styles of Youth Ministry: Two Congregations in America.* New York: Pilgrim Press, 1991.

A qualitative study of mainline, church-based youth ministry programs in middle-class contexts funded by the Lilly Endowment. The study shows how a white suburban congregation implicitly teaches youth five dispositions that confirm the dominant culture and how a black urban congregation explicitly teaches youth five dispositions that question the dominant culture.

352 Nelson, C. Ellis, ed. *Conscience: Theological and Psychological Perspectives.* New York: Newman Press, 1973.

Nelson has made a specialty of examining the role of conscience in religious education. In this reader he has assembled thirteen articles on the theology of conscience and nine on its psychology. All shed light on the educational question of the formation of conscience.

353 Nepveu, Danielle. *Les Représentations Religieuses au Québec dans les Manuels Scolaires de Niveau Elementaire, 1950-1960*. Quebec: Institut Québecois de Recherche sur la Culture, 1982.

A research study of the ways (verbal and graphic) that religious matters and the life and work of the church have been represented in the French elementary textbooks used in the schools in Quebec. Piety, liturgy, and authority are prominent, along with some historical material.

354 Neville, Gwen Kennedy. *Kinship and Pilgrimage: Rituals of Reunion in American Protestant Culture*. New York: Oxford University Press, 1987.

Previous to the publication of this book, Neville joined John Westerhoff in writing *Generation to Generation* (740), in which she stressed the power of religious enculturation through kinship groups. Here she amplifies the theme, adding the figure of pilgrimage. The behavioral data are drawn from Protestant groups in the South and in Scotland. Pilgrimage here is pilgrimage back to your home place, to your roots. Kinship is the multigenerational extended family.

355 Nipkow, Karl Ernest. *Grundfragen der Religionspädagogik*. Band 3, *Gemeinsam leben und glauben lernen*. Gütersloh: Gütersloher Verlagshaus Gerd Mohn, 1982.

In previous books in this series, Nipkow dealt with social and theoretical bases for religious education and with the church's educational business. In this volume he concentrates on developmental, life-long, community, and specifically Christian aspects of the process, with the focus on the growth of faith. Nipkow is one of the few German theorists who gives serious attention in his work to theorists in the international community.

356 Oser, Fritz, and Paul Gmünder. *Religious Judgment: A Developmental Approach*. Trans. by Norbert F. Hahn. Birmingham, AL: Religious Education Press, 1991. Zürich-Köln: Benziger Verlag, 1984.

A translation of the 1984 work, *Der Mensch: Stufen seiner Religiösen Entwicklung*. With full recognition of the work of Piaget, Kohlberg, and Fowler, the authors concentrate on the religious consciousness, and more specifically religious judgment, as the key to the structural analysis of human personality. Stages are traced and research methods are explored and weighed, with a view to validating the stage concept and determining the horizons of the field of religious cognition. Five stages are suggested, culminating in "intersubjective religious orientation." See also 159, 338, 350, 368, 386, 504, and 620.

357 Parks, Sharon. *The Critical Years: The Young Adult Search for a Faith to Live By*. San Francisco: Harper and Row, 1986; HarperCollins, 1991.

Examines "the place of young adulthood and the role of higher education in the pilgrimage toward a critical and mature adult faith—a faith adequate to ground both an adult life and a more humane and life-giving culture." Drawing upon developmental psychology, the book emulates Fowler by using its data within the interdisciplinary study of faith development but stresses both structure and content, thus being explicit about "faith in what."

358   Peshkin, Alan. *God's Choice: The Total World of a Fundamentalist Christian School*. Chicago: University of Chicago Press, 1986.

A penetrating sociological study of the inner dynamics of a fundamentalist day school, done by a team from the University of Illinois with the cooperation of the school involved. Illuminating for its descriptive detail, its findings, and its methods of research.

359   Pohl, Rudolph. *Die Religiöse Gedankenwelt bei Volks und Hilfsschulkindern*. Munich: Ernst Reinhardt, 1968.

A report of a research into children's religious conceptualizations. The method used is an open-ended word association or definition technique. The population is sixty-six eighth and ninth year "Volksschule" students and ninety-five "Hilfsschule" (special school) students of the same school years. Six word clusters, comprehending much of the basic religious vocabulary, are used, and enough raw data are reported so that the reader may be intelligently critical of the interpretations. A plea is made at the end for a full-sensory approach to religious education.

360   Proudfoot, Wayne. *Religious Experience*. Berkeley, CA: University of California Press, 1985.

Proudfoot looks analytically and critically at the nature and authority of religious experience in the tradition of Schleiermacher and William James. He sees cognitive structures and content that have been subordinated to a dominant subjectivity, elements of religious thought that, when acknowledged and developed, may serve to elucidate, enrich, and correct the experience itself.

361   Pruyser, Paul W. *A Dynamic Psychology of Religion*. New York: Harper and Row, 1968.

Widely hailed as the most important book of its time in psychology of religion, this volume is approached by the author in distinctively psychological categories, thus applying the analytical tools of the discipline to the human experiences that are religious in character.

362   Reiser, Helmut. *Identität und Religiöse Einstellung*. Hamburg: Furche, 1972.

A very technical psychological approach to the question of personal identity and its relation to religious experience; the educational dimensions of the development of the religious attitude; and the specific implications of these for religious education.

363 Robinson, Edward. *The Original Vision: A Study of the Religious Experience of Childhood*. New York: Seabury Press, 1983.

> Having gathered thousands of autobiographical accounts of religious experiences in childhood, Robinson categorizes them helpfully and places them in philosophical and theoretical context. Thus they seem to span most of the traditional concerns of religion. He draws the conclusion that "the original vision" is a powerful form of religious knowledge, and that it need not be lost but may be nurtured and developed. John Westerhoff, introducing the book, points out its challenge to the now dominant developmentalism.

364 Rokeach, Milton. *The Nature of Human Values*. New York: Free Press, 1973.

> Rokeach's work in the field of human values has been recognized as having unusual significance for religious workers. This is a huge research report, complete with statistical tables and analyses, but at the same time it pulls together philosophical, social, scientific, political, and religious data on values and attitudes in such a way that religious educators can put handles on new insights on the nature of values and the ways in which they are changed.

365 Rosen, Bernard Carl. *Adolescence and Religion*. Cambridge, MA: Schenkman Publishing Company, 1965.

> A study of 859 Jewish adolescents in Philadelphia, New York City, and Omaha and Lincoln, Nebraska, done to ascertain empirically the meaning and function of the Jewish heritage and membership. A major contribution to the social psychology of religion.

366 Ross, Dorothy. *G. Stanley Hall: The Psychologist as Prophet*. Chicago: University of Chicago Press, 1972.

> A thorough and candid biography of the man most famous for introducing Freud to America, and for defining the modern understanding of adolescence. Here, however, is much more, including his contributions to the field of psychology of religion, education, religious education, and character education.

367 Russo, Anthony. *The God of the Deaf Adolescent*. New York: Paulist Press, 1975.

> There is very little attention paid to the religious education of exceptional persons, and very little substantial research in religious education. This book combines the two and thus makes a double contribution. It is an unabbreviated (about 300 pages) research report of an extensive study of the religious concepts and religious education of deaf youth.

368 Sholl, Doug. "The Contributions of Lawrence Kohlberg to Religious and Moral Education." *Religious Education* 66 (1971):364-72.

> Sees Kohlberg as drawing from Plato, Dewey, and Piaget. Carefully reviews his stages of moral development. Sees promise for moral and religious education in matching moral dilemmas to the developmental stage of the learner and creating structural dissonance, which then calls for the kind of coping that results in

growth. Brings into play the critique of theologians and theoreticians. See also 159, 338, 350, 356, 386, 504, and 620.

369 Spilka, Bernard, Ralph W. Wood, Jr., and Richard L. Gorsuch. *The Psychology of Religion: An Empirical Approach*. Englewood Cliffs, NJ: Prentice-Hall, 1985.

Combines an awareness of and appreciation for the historical tradition in psychology of religion (William James, *et al.*) with a contemporary treatment of research in the field. Basically topical, dealing with traditional (e.g., mysticism, conversion), developmental, and contemporary (e.g., the social psychology of religious organizations) areas of concern.

370 Stark, Rodney. "A Taxonomy of Religious Experience." *Journal for the Scientific Study of Religion* 5, no. 1 (Fall 1965):97-116.

Suggesting that the essential element characterizing religious experience is "some sense of contact with a supernatural agency," this study attempts to cope with the fact that "the term religious experience covers an exceedingly disparate array of events: from the vaguest glimmerings of something sacred to rapturous mystical unions with the divine, or even to revelations." The major categories are here sorted out as the confirming experience, the responsive experience, the ecstatic experience, and the revelational experience.

371 Stark, Rodney, and Charles Y. Glock. *American Piety: The Nature of Religious Commitment*. Berkeley, CA: University of California Press, 1968.

Findings of social scientists on the nature and varieties of American religious commitment. The religious educator will note the comparative effectiveness of "affective" education as against "cognitive" education implied in the study's findings.

372 Steele, Les L. "Research in Faith Development," *Christian Education Journal* 9, no. 2 (Winter 1989):21-30.

This is one of four papers (see also 418, 445, and 796) originally presented at the 1987 NAPCE Convention and selected for publication in the Winter 1989 issue of the *Christian Education Journal*. Steele traces the study of the religious dimension, starting with William James and continuing through the publication of *Research on Religious Development* (1971). The primary focus of the article, however, is on research associated with Fowler's work in faith development. Steele concludes by suggesting four potentially fruitful areas for further research.

373 Stewart, Charles William. *Adolescent Religion*. Nashville: Abingdon Press, 1967.

A study of the religious experience of several young adolescents drawn from the Menninger Foundation's Normal Development Project. Case studies of six boys and girls are interspersed with treatments of religious beliefs and practices, confirmation, vulnerability and religious experience, and faith and coping styles. Valuable for psychological detail, variety of frameworks for interpretation, and as an example of inductive method. But loosely organized, with religion vaguely defined, and no cohesive interpretative model.

374 Stokes, Kenneth, ed. *Faith Development in the Adult Life Cycle.* New York: W.H. Sadlier, 1982.

A solid contribution to the growing literature on faith development, resulting from the Religious Education Association's project on "Faith Development in the Adult Life Cycle." The basic contribution is four-fold: (1) A "hypotheses paper," laying out matters to be investigated, (2) five expert responses to the paper, (3) perspectives from various disciplines and professional orientations, and (4) projections for future study.

375 Stokes, Kenneth. *Faith Is a Verb: Dynamics of Adult Faith Development.* Mystic, CT: Twenty-Third Publications, 1989.

A readable account of research findings from the study of faith development and the adult life cycle sponsored by the Religious Education Association. A source of information about faith development in the adult life cycle as well as a resource for adult study groups.

376 Strommen, Merton P. *Five Cries of Youth.* New York: Harper and Row, 1974.

A brief but detailed report on a long and extensive interdenominational research on youth. The research reveals five major dynamics operating in the lives of church youth: low self-esteem, family conflict, social action orientation, closed-mindedness, and religious commitment. The particular elements found to be involved in each of these are delineated. The book is well written, challenging to the specialist and understandable by the layperson.

377   Strommen, Merton P. *Profiles of Church Youth.* St. Louis, MO: Concordia Publishing House, 1963.

Report of a vast four-year research by the American Lutheran Church and the Lutheran Church-Missouri Synod into the situation, ideas, and needs of Lutheran youth. Major findings: Adults do not have an accurate idea of youth; youth ministry needs to be unique to each congregation, because of variation of need from congregation to congregation; and the sense of God's forgiveness and justification by faith is poorly communicated, while information and propositional truth are stressed. A model of research design that should be of help to other communions in carrying through similar studies.

378 Strommen, Merton P., Milo L. Brekke, Ralph C. Underwater, Arthur L. Johnson. *A Study of Generations.* Minneapolis: Augsburg Publishing House, 1972.

Widely acclaimed as one of the best religious research projects ever undertaken, this study reports the cross-generational characteristics of American Lutheran youth and adults. Important for its methodology as well as for its findings.

379   Strommen, Merton P., and A. Irene Strommen. *Five Cries of Parents*. San Francisco: Harper and Row, 1985.

A companion to *Five Cries of Youth*, this book delves into parents' needs to understand themselves and youth, to know what makes for close family life, to understand and model moral behavior and purpose in their children, to know how faith may be made central in family life, and to know where to turn for help in crisis situations. Based on Strommen's extensive empirical research.

380   Taylor, Joanne. *Innocent Wisdom: Children as Spiritual Guides*. New York: Pilgrim Press, 1989.

The author offers "glimpses" (rather than scientific studies) into the authentic spirituality of children that makes them spiritual guides for adults. Excerpts from her interviews with children are accompanied by a focal quote from scripture, song, or religious figure; commentary; and twenty-three color reproductions of children's drawings. These are grouped into six kinds of spiritual guidance: angels, shepherds, justice seekers, doubters/believers, mystics, prophets, and those outside Christian faith.

381   Thompson, Andrew D. *That They May Know...* Washington, DC: National Catholic Educational Association, 1982.

The findings and implications of a vast study of religious outcomes (knowledge, attitude, practice) among Catholic youth of junior high and senior high age, focusing on God, Jesus Christ, church, grace, sacraments, conscience and moral principles, sexuality, social justice, prayer and spirituality, and Christian eschatology. The chief finding is the correlation between the religion of youth and "talking with my parents or family about religious/moral matters."

382   Vergote, Antoine. *The Religious Man*. Dayton, OH: Pflaum Press, 1969.

Massive review of research and theory in psychology of religion, having the great advantage of bringing together American and European sources. The approach is empirical, anthropological, and phenomenological. Concludes with brief but substantive chapters on genetic psychology of religion.

383   Vergote, Antoine, and Alvaro Tamayo. *The Parental Figures and the Representation of God: A Psychological and Cross-Cultural Study*. The Hague: Mouton Publishers, 1981.

Psychological analysis, with youth as the research subjects, of the symbolism of parental differentiation and integration. Among the results of the study are that the representation of God integrates the father-mother dimensions, the paternal factor being law and authority, the maternal factor being availability. Thus the integration takes place in thinking both of parents themselves and of God.

384   Warren, Michael. *Communications and Cultural Analysis: A Religious View.* Westport, CT: Bergin and Garvey, 1992.

Influenced by the work of Raymond Williams, Michael Warren seeks in this book to develop a religious theory of cultural influence. Warren critiques the influence of popular culture in the first chapter and offers a definition of culture in the second. These introductory chapters are followed by explorations of cultural reproduction, cultural analysis, image theory, and metaphoric images as signifiers. The concluding chapter discusses hegemony and contestation.

385   Webb-Mitchell, Brett. "Listen and Learn from Narratives that Tell a Story." *Religious Education* 85 (1990):617-30.

"Hearing the voice of people with mental retardation is crucial for religious educators as we begin to develop curriculum for people with mental retardation," writes Webb-Mitchell. Recognizing the significance of Coles's work with children's narratives (298, 411), Webb-Mitchell listened to the narratives of those with mental retardation as part of a nine-month ethnographic study conducted at London's l'Arche community. This article is his report.

386   Wilcox, Mary M. *Developmental Journey.* Nashville: Abingdon Press, 1979.

The author has mastered the developmentalists (Piaget, Kohlberg, and Fowler) and has explored theoretically, experimentally, and practically their relevance for education in school, church, and family. A first long, systematic look at the author's findings and their implications. See also 159, 338, 350, 356, 368, 504, and 620.

387   Woods, Ray T. and Gerald L. Klever. *World of Church Youth.* Philadelphia: Board of Christian Education, United Presbyterian Church in the U.S.A., 1971.

Strommen has studied Lutheran youth (377); Zuck and Getz, conservative Protestant youth (389). The Woods-Klever study is of active and inactive United Presbyterian youth and their leaders. An ambitious battery of research instruments was used, and the report gives the results in detail, providing the main value of the study. Interpretation was clearly difficult, and readers would do well to burrow through the data and try their hands at their own interpretations, comparing them with those of the researchers. Implications for youth work are briefly drawn, but more as hints from impressions than as considered findings from the research data.

388   Ziegler, Jesse H. *Psychology and the Teaching Church.* Nashville: Abingdon Press, 1962.

A brief but meaty treatment of four aspects of psychology as they contribute to religious education: personality theory, learning theory, group process, and human growth and development. Concludes with an analysis of "tensions systems in productive teaching-learning" as bases for a theory of religious education.

389 Zuck, Roy B., and Gene A. Getz. *Christian Youth—An In-depth Study*. Chicago: Moody Press, 1968.

A detailed analysis of a questionnaire study of 3,000 Christian (conservative evangelical) high school youth. The first of its kind, it is well done from a technical research standpoint. Reveals a great deal about the socialization of an "in-group," with occasional flashes of insight into the impact of changing cultural values (as in sex customs and secular amusements).

390 Zwergel, Herbert A. *Religiöse Erziehung und Entwicklung der Persönlichkeit*. Köln: Benziger Verlag, 1976.

Most developmental studies have very little to do with religious education, and when they do they depend almost entirely on some one theorist. This one is critical, comparative, and centered entirely on the guidance of religious education. Very substantive reference to the American and British literature as well as to the German. The thesis is that the task of religious education is the developmental nurture of religious identity.

BEHAVIORAL STUDIES OF EDUCATION

391 Aden, LeRoy, David G. Benner, and J. Harold Ellens, eds. *Christian Perspectives on Human Development*. Grand Rapids, MI: Baker Book House Company, 1992.

The sixth volume in the Psychology and Christianity series published jointly by the Christian Association for Psychological Studies (CAPS) and Baker Book House. Includes both original articles and articles previously published in the *Journal of Psychology and Christianity*.

392 Allport, Gordon W. *Pattern and Growth in Personality*. New York: Holt, Rinehart and Winston, 1961.

Allport's basic theory of personality. Emphasizes patterned individuality, the inner organization of motives, traits, and personal styles. Critical, constructive, and thorough.

393 Amos, Pamela T., and Steven Harrell, eds. *Other Ways of Growing Old: Anthropological Perspectives*. Stanford, CA: Stanford University Press, 1981.

Scholarly articles on the anthropology of aging in nine different cultures, and in groups of primates, with introductory articles on the anthropological and evolutionary approaches to aging. Useful not only for its specific data, but as a stimulus to cross-cultural understandings as well as perspective on a phenomenon that is sometimes misunderstood because it is too close at hand.

394 Austin, Gilbert R. *Early Childhood Education: An International Perspective*. New York: Academic Press, 1976.

> The results of a five-year, cross-cultural survey of early childhood education. Begins with a study of the American experience. The heart of the book is a series of detailed and very illuminating studies of early childhood education in Belgium, Canada, Germany, France, England and Wales, Italy, The Netherlands, and Sweden. Conclusions are drawn from the findings for the American situation—conclusions that are dependable because they are realistic and completely documented.

395 Ausubel, David P. *The Psychology of Meaningful Verbal Learning*. New York: Grune and Stratton, 1963.

> Proposes serious attention to cognitive structuring as the key to education's major task, making "discovery" through problem-solving secondary, and using motivational factors as instrumental to the major cognitive end. The view is compellingly developed, and can act as a corrective for educators who are prone to accept therapy-oriented rather than education-oriented views uncritically. A highly technical, tough, and sophisticated approach to an important and promising point of view.

396 Bar-Tal, Daniel. *Prosocial Behavior: Theory and Research*. Washington, DC: Hemisphere Publishing Company, 1976.

> Prosocial behavior encompasses various forms of altruism and outgoing attitudes and action--"good Samaritan" behavior. This book reviews and analyzes the meaning and development of this kind of moral thought and action and summarizes and evaluates the existing research in the area, including emergency and nonemergency situations, and behavior that is reciprocal and compensatory. Indispensable for the serious student of religious education in dealing with moral behavior and development.

397 Bar-Tal, David, and Leonard Saxe, eds. *Social Psychology of Education: Theory and Research*. New York: John Wiley and Sons, 1978.

> A thorough analytical and critical presentation of social psychology of education, exploring its major themes and showing its methodology, major conclusions, and developing concerns. Treats historical perspectives, the role of the social psychologist of education, methodological issues, individuals in the school, the classroom group, the school as an organization, and the school and the community.

398 Beeby, C.E. *The Quality of Education in Developing Countries*. Cambridge, MA: Harvard University Press, 1966.

> Deals with the way in which schooling grows and is up-graded in developing nations. Presents a helpful hypothesis of stages of educational growth (stages through which schooling develops) that should assist planners both as a direction-finder and as an evaluation device. Churches conducting enterprises in underdeveloped areas will find this book exceptionally useful.

399 Berger, Brigitte, and Peter L. Berger. *The War over the Family*. New York: Anchor Press/Doubleday, 1981.

> No institution has been buffeted by the winds of change, both in terms of changing mores and new ideologies, so badly as the family. The Bergers, in their usual stylish and challenging way, delineate the forces at work, weigh them, and set the problem in broad historical terms, using their well-known critique of modernity. Their aim is "to build bridges" and "recapture the middle ground."

400 Bloom, Benjamin S. *Stability and Change in Human Characteristics*. New York: John Wiley and Sons, 1964.

> A bold attempt to determine levels of development at which change does and does not take place in physical characteristics, intelligence, achievement, interests, attitudes, and personality, and to use the findings for predictive purposes. It is hypothesized that environmental factors operate most effectively to produce variations in characteristics at periods of most rapid change.

401 Boston, Bruce O. "Conscientization and Christian Education." *Colloquy* 5, no. 5 (May 1972):36-41.

> Written early, this article introduces Paulo Freire and education for liberation accurately and clearly. Unlike many other writings about Freire, offers practical implications for North American congregations. (David Ng) See also 152.

402 Braunius, Burt D. "Research in Ethnographic Methodologies." *Christian Education Journal* 10, no. 3 (Spring 1990):31-46.

> Recognizing the value of ethnographic research for Christian education, Braunius compares quantitative and qualitative research methodologies, defines and describes ethnographic research, and offers examples of ethnographic research in Christian education. He provides a beginning introduction to ethnographic research that touches on objectivity, validity, sampling, and generalizability. Attention is also given to the advantages and disadvantages of this approach to research.

403 Bronfenbrenner, Urie. *The Ecology of Human Development*. Cambridge, MA: Harvard University Press, 1979.

> A theoretical perspective for research in human development. The focus is on "development-in-context," emphasizing "the progressive accommodation between a growing human organism and its immediate environment, and the way in which this relation is mediated by forces emanating from more remote regions in the larger physical and social milieu." More simply, the idea is to observe children's behavior in natural settings, while they are interacting with familiar adults over prolonged periods of time.

404 Brown, Roger. *Social Psychology*. New York: Free Press, 1965.

> Discusses in exceptionally lively style many topics in social psychology that are
> of crucial significance for religious education: interpersonal relationships, role
> theory, socialization, language, morality, motivation, attitude change, group
> dynamics, and collective behavior. Emphasizes the variety of theoretical positions
> without attempting premature integration.

405 Cantor, Nathaniel. *Dynamics of Learning*. Buffalo, NY: Henry Stewart, 1956.

> A critical and constructive approach to the teaching-learning process, oriented to
> clinical psychological theory. "The points of view...are a radical departure from
> traditional methods of instruction. Their acceptance...will lead to the only kind
> of genuine education there is, self-criticism, self-discipline, self-motivation, and
> a willingness to be responsible for one's own decisions."

406 Carter, Elizabeth A., and Monica McGoldrick. *The Family Life Cycle: A Framework
for Family Therapy*. New York: Gardner Press, 1980.

> To add to the studies of "stages in the life cycle" this useful volume hypothesizes
> a "family life cycle" and investigates it both in terms of stages of family life and
> topics that bear on family life. The emphasis is on building a base for family
> therapy, but a wide variety of behavioral data are brought into the picture.

407 Cofer, Charles N., and Mortimer H. Appley. *Motivation: Theory and Research*.
New York: John Wiley and Sons, 1964.

> A very satisfactory, clearly written, broadly conceived weighing of the history and
> present status of theory and research in motivation. Takes into account the
> philosophic-theological tradition in motivation in a general way. The expository
> chapters are basically informative, the evaluative comments and attempts at unified
> theory (utilizing an equilibration model, and rejecting "drive") are stimulating, and
> the whole is tightly organized and well reasoned.

408 Coleman, James S. *The Adolescent Society*. New York: Free Press, 1961.

> Twelve high schools in northern Illinois are studied as social systems, and data are
> collected on the adolescent subculture, value climates in the schools, popular
> heroes and leaders, sports vs. studies and beauty vs. brains as paths to success,
> structures of association, psychological and social effects of the social system, and
> sources of adolescent value systems. "If secondary education is to be successful,
> it must successfully compete with cars and sports and social activities for the
> adolescents' attention, in an open market."

409 Coleman, James S., ed. *Youth: Transition to Adulthood*. Chicago: University of
Chicago Press, 1974.

> The report of the Panel on Youth of the President's Science Advisory Committee.
> The question is how youth enter satisfactorily and productively into adulthood in
> our society. Social, biological, and psychological background factors are outlined;
> contemporary issues are identified and sharpened; very specific recommendations

are made, aimed particularly at reassessment of schooling and entrance into the work force.

410 Coleman, John C. *Relationships in Adolescence*. Boston: Routledge and Kegan Paul, 1974.

A fresh study, based on empirical research, of the nature and functions of adolescence. Sees adolescence as one stage in which a series of rather stable relationships fluctuate between positive and negative experience: self, the opposite sex, parents, friends, and large groups. Interesting critical conclusions are suggested as to the interpretations of adolescence in role theory, "storm and stress," and stage theory, with the suggestion of a new "focal" model.

411 Coles, Robert. *The Moral Life of Children*. Boston: The Atlantic Monthly Press, 1986.

Coles is a master at uncovering data by talking one-on-one with those who deal with problems by living them through. He is after a "psychology of everyday life; a psychology of turmoil and response to turmoil." Here he reviews his studies in various sections and cultures of the United States and South America to pull out the moral problems (life and death issues in many cases) with which children have to deal, their resultant concepts of right and wrong, and the ways in which they develop moral strength in coping with them.

412 Cook, Bruce L. *Understanding Pictures in Papua New Guinea*. Elgin, IL: David C. Cook Foundation, 1981.

A detailed account of a research study on the use of pictures with preliterate people. The study takes account of the most important work done previously in the field and presents its own findings in ways that are of immediate use to teachers and curriculum builders. Avenues of future research are suggested.

413 Curran, Dolores. *Traits of a Healthy Family*. Minneapolis: Winston Press, 1983.

When it comes to sound, practical guidance for family life, this book is about the best of the lot. Fifteen "traits of a healthy family" (including teaching morals, enjoying traditions, sharing religion, and valuing service) are elaborated into specific guidelines, all presented as invitations rather than as guilt-producing directives.

414 Eisenstadt, S.N. *From Generation to Generation: Age Groups and Social Structure*. New York: Free Press, 1956.

For educators who are worried about the all-embracing phenomenon of age-grouping, this book is a real find. The rise of age-groups is interpreted in broad anthropological and sociological perspective, as a function of the inability of family and kinship systems to meet human needs in an age-heterogeneous way, thus throwing responsibility to other social structures including emergent age-homogeneous groups. Broad-ranging and highly technical, but clear, convincing, and extremely informative.

415 Elias, John L. *Psychology and Religious Education*. 2d ed. Malabar, FL: Robert E. Krieger Publishing Company, 1990.

> Since its first appearance in 1979, this book has proven to be a useful introduction to and summary of the field of psychology. Each chapter describes the work of a major figure and his or her relevance to religious education. Although the content has been updated, the writing style still does not reflect concerns for inclusive language.

416 Elizondo, Virgil. "A Bicultural Approach to Religious Education." *Religious Education* 76 (1981):258-70.

> The leading interpreter of Hispanic religious culture in the United States sees Hispanics as "one of the specific groups among several others which at this moment of history have much to offer towards a significant phase in the build-up of God's Kingdom among us." He analyzes Hispanic culture in the family, and attitudes to suffering and death, time, and an element that he calls "prophetic-festive." "Religious educators must situate themselves 1) within the tradition of their own people, and 2) in the midst of chaos, slavery, death, and division...not to uphold the cultural idols that we have grown comfortable with, but to shatter them with the teaching of the Father."

417 Elkind, David. *The Child's Reality: Three Developmental Themes*. New York: John Wiley and Sons, 1978.

> Elkind explores religious development, perceptual development in children, and egocentrism. The section on religious development centers on how children go about constructing conceptions of their religious denominations and prayer. Using a Piagetian empirical research method, Elkind discerns stages of development in both these areas of experience.

418 Elmer, Duane H. "Implications of Intercultural Research for the Christian Educator." *Christian Education Journal* 9, no. 2 (Winter 1989):31-40.

> Draws on a Canadian International Development Agency (CIDA) study of the effectiveness of overseas technical workers to report the primary and secondary findings and their implications for Christian educators to illustrate the relevance of intercultural research for Christian education. Interpersonal skills, which assume both an openness to learn from others and respect for others, was the most important variable identified in the CIDA study; self-identity and positive expectations were two secondary variables.

419 Empey, LaMar T. *American Delinquency: Its Meaning and Construction*. Homewood, IL: The Dorsey Press, 1978.

> "Enlightened" understandings of delinquency and its treatment are always under attack. The author deals with the situation by raising and analyzing a series of basic issues: the nature of childhood, rules that define delinquency, and the juvenile justice system. No ready solutions, but a review of the history, research, and theories involved.

420   Erdman, Daniel. "Liberation and Indo-Hispanic Youth." *Religious Education* 78 (1983):76-89.

> From familiarity with the culture and social situation of Indo-Hispanic youth in the southwestern United States and the promise and dynamics of liberation theology, the author suggests the use of a praxis action-reflection model of education, in which liberation is seen as "freedom from destructive ties to the past, from prejudice and fear, from self-hatred, from lack of identity [and] freedom to become who one really is, to find one's place in relation to God and the community of faith and the world, to extend oneself in love and service, and to live all of life with an aware openness to the inbreaking of the creative, life-affirming, loving spirit of Christ, the liberator and lord."

421   Erikson, Erik H. *Toys and Reasons*. New York: W.W. Norton, 1977.

> Play, according to Erikson, provides the infantile form of the human propensity to create model situations in which aspects of the past are relived, the present represented and renewed, and the future anticipated. Thus is laid the basis for adult thought and action. Erikson here links this concretely to the stages in the life cycle.

422   Farnham-Diggory, Sylvia. *Schooling*. Cambridge, MA, and London: Harvard University Press, 1990.

> While agreeing that schools should be reformed, the author draws on learnings from cognitive science to shape school reform along different lines from those called for by national studies and reports. Fractionated curriculum, grouping regulations, and test-driven planning are "wellsprings" of trouble in schools. Rather, an apprenticeship model which takes into account how the human mind works is called for. Complex, situated learning, participation of expert models, beginning where the student is, and the social nature of human learning are the major principles of the apprenticeship model.

423   Fowler, James W., Karl Ernst Nipkow, Friedrich Schweitzer, eds. *Stages of Faith and Religious Development: Implications for Church, Education, and Society*. New York: Crossroad, 1991.

> This volume makes two significant contributions to the ongoing discussion of faith development. First, it broadens the discussion to include British and European voices, such as Nicola Slee of the Rochampton Institute, Whitelands College, England, and Karl Ernst Nipkow of Tübingen University, Germany. Second, the work on religious development by Fritz K. Oser of Fribourg University, Switzerland, is brought into dialogue with Fowler's faith development theory. Critical voices and alternative perspectives are also included. See 312 and 356.

424   Gagne, Robert M. *The Conditions of Learning*. New York: Holt, Rinehart and Winston, 1965.

> A serious attempt to delineate the implications of learning theory and research for education. The author sees the need for a variety of theories to pair up with types of learning and selects eight for consideration (signal learning, stimulus-response

learning, chaining, verbal association, multiple-discrimination learning, concept learning, principle learning, and problem-solving). In light of this analysis he treats content, motivation, curriculum, decision-making, and instructional materials and methods.

425 Gardner, Howard. *Art, Mind, and Brain: A Cognitive Approach to Creativity*. New York: Basic Books, 1987.

Essays on creative processes. The social scientist, the philosopher, and the art historian are consulted, but the main sources have been investigations of the artistic processes in the normal child, the gifted child, the child who exhibits pathology, the normal adult, and the individual from a different cultural background. Presented as just a beginning at understanding creativity, "the ultimate goal is to illuminate artistry at its greatest heights." See also 202, 490, 495, 859, 878, and 967.

426 Gardner, Howard. *Frames of Mind*. New York: Basic Books, 1983.

Argues that the concept of human intelligence needs to be treated as holistic and expanded to include linguistic, musical, logical-mathematical, spatial, bodily-kinesthetic, and personal intelligences. Calls for "a position that takes seriously the nature of innate intellectual proclivities, the heterogeneous processes of development in the child, and the way in which these are shaped and transformed by the particular practices and values of culture." Implications for education are explored.

427 Gilligan, Carol. *In a Different Voice: Psychological Theory and Women's Development*. Cambridge, MA: Harvard University Press, 1982.

Both corrective and positive, this book seeks to call central attention to the difference that it would make in theories of human development if the nature, roles, and concerns of women were taken seriously. "The discrepant data on women's experience provide a basis upon which to generate new theory, potentially yielding a more encompassing view of the lives of both sexes." See also 338, 339.

428 Glock, Charles Y., Robert Wuthnow, Jane A. Piliavin, and Metta Spencer. *Adolescent Prejudice*. New York: Harper and Row, 1975.

A study of about 5,000 school young people and their teachers in the east, focusing on anti-Semitism. The problem is found to be very severe. A definite relationship is established between prejudice and lack of specific cognitive skills and sophistication. Training in logical inference, group differences, and individual differences is recommended.

429 Havighurst, Robert J., Paul Hoover Bowman, Gordon P. Liddle, Charles V. Matthews, and James V. Pierce. *Growing up in River City*. New York: John Wiley and Sons, 1962.

> A longitudinal study of eleven- to twenty-year-olds in a midwestern city, designed to show how social backgrounds and personal characteristics affect performance in growing up in the community. In many ways a companion to *Elmtown's Youth*. The emphasis is on the discovery of predictors: "Knowing these facts about boys and girls in the sixth grade, or in the ninth grade, what can we predict about their performance in the later years of high school, or after they graduate from high school?"

430 Jung, C.G. *Psychology and Education*. Princeton, NJ: Princeton University Press, 1969.

> Jung's various writings on childhood education are here excerpted from other sources and made easily available. His concerns are with the education of the adults who deal with children, and with the sources (sexual instinct and concept building) and nurturing processes by which the child's spiritual functions may emerge and be strengthened.

431 Karpel, Mark A., ed. *Family Resources: The Hidden Partner in Family Therapy*. New York: Guilford Press, 1986.

> Recognizing that "family therapy has long been able to identify patterns that weaken families and diminish the quality of daily life, patterns that impede individual growth and lead to the breakdown and cutoff of close relationships," this book seeks to "identify patterns that strengthen families, patterns that improve the quality of daily life, promote individuation and mutual care, buffer against the disorganizing effects of stress, and facilitate the resolution of conflict."

432 Keniston, Kenneth. *All Our Children: The American Family Under Pressure*. New York: Harcourt Brace Jovanovich, 1977.

> A study done under the aegis of the Carnegie Council on Children. Centering on the family, the study assesses the ways in which the family has changed yet remains basic to child nurture, the "odds against a decent life" experienced by American children, and the impact of technology on family life and structures. The major part of the book is prescriptive, mainly suggesting lines of public policy for strengthening the family and improving the "odds" for the good life for children.

433 Kett, Joseph F. *Rites of Passage: Adolescence in America, 1790 to the Present*. New York: Basic Books, 1977.

> The concept of adolescence was an expression of distinctive values relating to children and the family that originated in America as early as the 1830s. It was conditioned by social forces and reflected the demographic and industrial conditions of the late nineteenth and early twentieth centuries. Moral values that often masqueraded as psychological laws were at the root of the concept. These moral values grew out of a particular cultural heritage.

434 Kimball, Solon T. *Culture and the Educative Process*. New York: Teachers College Press, 1974.

An anthropological approach to analyzing and understanding education. Contains sections on anthropology and its role in education, the dynamics of culture and learning, and the way in which education may contribute to assisting underdeveloped areas in the world.

435 Lewis, Laura B. "Sunday School Teachers and Teaching: Memories and Metaphors," *Religious Education* 83 (1988):385-401.

Describes the memories and metaphors of twenty-four upper-elementary Sunday school teachers interviewed for a study Lewis conducted. Metaphors for teaching such as parenting, conversation, estrangement, discipleship, a job, and docentship were offered by the teachers during research interviews. The author examines the teachers' memories and metaphors in light of Philip Jackson's "mimetic" and "transformative" perspectives and finds them to fall more within the transformative tradition.

436 Lieberman, J. Nina. *Playfulness: Its Relationship to Imagination and Creativity*. New York: Academic Press, 1977.

Since religion is so highly affective, and since religious education necessarily reflects this, the more the religious educator can know about play and its relationship to imagination and creativity, the better. This is a highly technical book, reporting on research, but still putting the matter in a context that opens up the issues. It also provides sufficient interpretative material to be accessible to a reasonably well versed professional.

437 Lindholm, Charles E., and David K. Cohen. *Usable Knowledge: Social Science and Social Problem Solving*. New Haven, CT: Yale University Press, 1979.

Questions the dominant role of the social sciences in social problem solving (problem solving inquiry) in favor of other kinds of social interaction (ordinary knowledge, casual empiricism, and other nonscientific or nonprofessional methods of knowing and analyzing). To solve a social problem is not so much to understand the problem as to understand an outcome. "Practical judgment" is the key.

438 Littwin, Susan. *The Postponed Generation: Why American Youth Are Growing up Later*. New York: Morrow, 1987.

A study of the contemporary phenomenon of "perpetual youth," a generation that seems unable to grow up. One review comments: "These young people were all raised with a sense that they were special, that they were entitled to all the best that life has to offer—without commitment, hard work, sacrifice or the risk of choice. Now they drift, confused by their failure to find what they assumed was their birthright. They were raised with a combination of their parents' sense of alienation from traditional values, along with a rather unrealistic disenchantment with commitment, and a dogged preoccupation with self."

439 Lovell, R. Bernard. *Adult Learning*. New York: Halsted Press, 1980.

A thorough summary of psychological research and theory on the nature and processes of adult learning. The social context is also dealt with, as are the factors of planning and evaluation.

440 Manaster, Guy J. *Adolescent Development and the Life Tasks*. Boston: Allyn and Bacon, 1977.

Pulls a vast body of research together so as to provide the practitioner with exactly the organization of that material that is most useful. For the religious educator the basic pertinent material is there, readily available in the most useful form. Special value is to be found in the chapter on moral development, in the analysis of the life tasks of adolescence, and in the crucial emphasis on "the life-task—self" and "the existential task—religion."

441 Mann, John. *Changing Human Behavior*. New York: Charles Scribner's Sons, 1965.

A theoretically oriented scientific approach to the problem of consciously produced behavior change (the alteration of human behavior and the development of human potential). Believing that a model for behavior change can be discovered, experimental evidence from such fields as psychopharmacology, hypnosis, learning, psychotherapy, small groups, communications, mass media, intergroup relations, creativity, and eastern and western religions is reviewed. Proposes a "human development corporation" to coordinate research and development in this field.

442 Marrow, Alfred J. *The Practical Theorist: The Life and Work of Kurt Lewin*. New York: Basic Books, 1969.

The biography (largely the story of his work and that of his disciples) of Kurt Lewin. "Field theory in social science," "topological psychology," "group dynamics," "action research," "sensitivity training," and other well known ideas are the products of his thought and experiment.

443 Marschak, Marianne. *Parent-Child Interaction and Youth Rebellion*. New York: Gardner Press, 1980.

A wide-ranging research, international in scope, intended to clarify the nature and meaning of "youth movements." The focus is on the hippie movement in the U.S.A., the German Wandervogel, and the Israeli kibbutz, raising the question of why there is radical abandonment of identification with parents. The kibbutz is seen as an example of a youth movement that has been channeled into a reality-based, goal-oriented form of communal life.

444 Maslow, Abraham H. *Toward a Psychology of Being*. Princeton, NJ: D. Van Nostrand, 1968.

> The position of "Third Force Psychology"—an alternative to behaviorism and Freudianism. Maslow is concerned with the "transpersonal, transhuman, centered in the cosmos rather than in human needs and interest, going beyond humanness, identity, self-actualization, and the like."

445 McKean, Rodney B. "Research on Teaching for Christian Education," *Christian Education Journal* 9, no. 2 (Winter 1989):11-19.

> Originally a paper given at the 1987 NAPCE Convention, McKean here contrasts popular assumptions about teaching with the wisdom that can be drawn from the research on teaching. He identifies teacher effectiveness, teaching styles, and teacher decisions as the three research areas most relevant to Christian education. Following a summary of the three areas, McKean describes research methodologies and problems. He ends with a call for research on what teachers in Christian education actually do and on their selection, education, and supervision.

446 Mead, Margaret. *Continuities in Cultural Evolution*. New Haven, CT: Yale University Press, 1964.

> An inquiry into "the task of conscious intervention in the process of cultural evolution." Analyzes the basic processes of communication (imitation, identification, and empathy) involved in learning and teaching and stresses the emergence of originators and innovators in "the cluster of individuals with whom they interact and through whom they interact also with others." The potential significance of this cluster: "The combination of an atmosphere of freedom and choice and a setting in which spontaneous and voluntary commitments can be made provides the conditions within which intellectual friendships and clusters form from which we may expect ideas of evolutionary significance to emerge."

447 Middleton, John, ed. *From Child to Adult: Studies in the Anthropology of Education*. Garden City, NY: The Natural History Press, 1970.

> The process of "growing up," or "being brought up," in its educational implications, is examined by leading anthropologists. Margaret Mead provides a general interpretative article, comparing contemporary and primitive education. Others deal with the Hopi, the Papago, Guatemala, rural Mexico, the American inner city, etc.

448 Miller, Donald. "Religious Education and Cultural Pluralism." *Religious Education* 74 (1979):339-49.

> "Cultural pluralism threatens the religious enterprise, but only on the most superficial level. The relevance of religious institutions in an age of pluralism rests in their potential to forge identity....The purpose of the educative endeavor of the religious community is to nurture in individuals the formation of a unique and distinctive identity, one which faithfully represents the integrity and historical roots of the community of which one is a member."

449 Moriarty, Alice E., and Povl W. Toussieng. *Adolescent Coping*. New York: Grune and Stratton, 1976.

A study of midwestern adolescents that identifies four types of "coping": obedient traditionalist, ideological conservative, cautious modifier, and passionate renewer. Each is described as revealed by the data, including the correlated religious behavior. Additional valuable data are provided on religious beliefs and practices of those studied.

450 Morse, William C. *Socio-Emotionally Impaired Children and Youth*. Syracuse, NY: Syracuse University Press, 1985.

Combines research studies and personal experience to provide the psychological understandings and practical guidelines needed in the education of "disturbed" children: behaviorally disordered, emotionally disturbed, psychotic, autistic, socially maladjusted, etc.

451 Mowry, Bill J. "A Reflective Approach to Research: Applying the Research Paradigm of Post-Positivism to the Evangelical Church" *Christian Education Journal* 13, no. 2 (Winter 1993):51-67.

Seven basic presuppositions of the positivist research paradigm are compared to seven basic presuppositions of the naturalistic research paradigm. Finding that the aims and assumptions of positivistic research do not fit the research needs of the evangelical church, the author looks to naturalistic research for guidance and direction. Mowry's reflective approach to research combines qualitative research principles with Donald Schön's "reflection-in-action" approach.

452 Muuss, Rolf E. *Theories of Adolescence*. New York: Random House, 1962.

A review of the leading theories of adolescence. Educational implications are drawn, issues summarized, and generalizations stated. An invaluable guide to the literature and research in the field, and useful in itself to youth workers, who without such a guide may easily fall victim to limited points of view.

453 Nixon, Robert E. *The Art of Growing: A Guide to Psychological Maturity*. New York: Random House, 1962.

An arresting view, by a Vassar College psychiatrist, of the critical importance of middle adolescence, the "cognitive stage of self-awareness," in attaining maturity. Because of rapid social change, old cultural patterns will not do for the new generation. The key is "discovery-experimentation-mastery," applied to the whole of personal development. Special attention is given to problems of sex, anger, and anxiety. Simply written but soundly based in the social sciences, with some insight into religious experience. Equally useful for youth, parents, teachers, and leaders.

454 Norman, Jane, and Myron Harris. *The Private Life of the American Teenager*. New York: Rawson, Wade Publishers, 1981.

> The results of a survey of 160,000 young people. Adds to the stock of knowledge about youth in the areas of parents, sexual behavior and marriage, drinking and drugs, school, friends, personal questions, family situations, rules and responsibility, public ethics, religion, country, race and prejudice, and the future.

455 Peck, Robert F., and Robert J. Havighurst. *The Psychology of Character Development*. New York: John Wiley and Sons, 1960.

> Significant as indicating renewed interest in character on the part of general educators and behavioral scientists. Five character types are investigated: amoral, conforming, irrational-conscientious, and rational-altruistic. These are seen as related to succeeding stages in human development.

456 Piaget, Jean. *Science of Education and the Psychology of the Child*. New York: Orion Press, 1970.

> The great value in this book is that in it Piaget deals directly with the problems of education. It contains two documents; one he prepared in 1935 and the other in 1965. His thesis is that the psychology of the child has been neglected by educators in favor of the science of education, and he would like to see this reversed. Not addressed to an American audience.

457 Piaget, Jean, and Bärbel Inhelder. *The Psychology of the Child*. New York: Basic Books, 1969.

> Piaget and Inhelder here summarize, in briefest compass, the results of their studies in child psychology. Intended to present the essential concepts and findings and to serve as an introduction to their more detailed and technical works.

458 Reichert, Richard. *A Learning Process for Religious Education*. Dayton, OH: Pflaum Publishing Company, 1975.

> Suggests a four-stage learning process: starting point, significant experience, reflection, assimilation (an interesting blend of Herbartian and action-reflection models). Each stage is described, explained, and illustrated, with implications for lesson planning and for leadership roles. A valuable analysis of "starting points" by grades and a chart of "factors in human development" are included.

459 Reynolds, Maynard C., and Jack W. Birch. *Teaching Exceptional Children in All America's Schools*. Reston, VA: The Council for Exceptional Children, 1982.

> Deals with gifted and handicapped children and gives specific guidance in "mainstreaming," indicating that different skills are needed when exceptional children are in regular classes and taught by regular teachers, and where specialists play more of an advisory role. Such an approach has promise for the church but clearly calls for the kind of intensive teacher training expounded in detail in this book.

460 Roehlkepartain, Eugene C. *The Teaching Church: Moving Christian Education to Center Stage.* Nashville: Abingdon Press, 1993

The *Effective Christian Education* study was first reported in 1990. Roehlkepartain's book makes the fruit of this important research accessible to a wider audience in an understandable and usable form. "Must" reading for church educators and Christian education committees. Purchase of the book includes permission to reprint a number of helpful worksheets.

461 Rogers, Carl R. *Carl Rogers on Encounter Groups.* New York: Harper and Row, 1970.

Goes into every phase of encounter groups—describing, analyzing, explaining. Helpfully distinguishes the encounter group from other types of group experience. Provides historical and research background material.

462 Rychlak, Joseph F. *The Psychology of Rigorous Humanism.* New York: John Wiley and Sons, 1977.

A difficult but very important book that challenges psychologies that reduce behavior by the use of mechanical metaphors. The heart of the book for the religious educator is the presentation of logical learning theory, in which the assumption that human beings are meaning-processors is used to establish learning as meaning-extension.

463 Scott, John Finley. *Internalization of Norms: A Sociological Theory of Moral Commitment.* Englewood Cliffs, NJ: Prentice-Hall, 1971.

Advances a social psychology of moral commitment as moral learning, based on a selective fusion of the theories of B.F. Skinner and modern sociology. A thorough, rewarding, and critical study. Although "moral commitment" here has a totally secular meaning, and although the aspects considered are severely limited by the principle of scientific study, the religious educator is well served by a close study of the argument, involving as it does sharp analysis and comparison of divergent views.

464 Sell, Charles M. *Transition: The Stages of Adult Life.* Chicago: Moody Press, 1985.

An intricately detailed analysis, from a Christian perspective, of the stages and substages of adult growth and decline. Based on research studies and written in semi-popular vein.

465 Sherif, Carolyn, Muzafer Sherif, and Roger E. Nebergall. *Attitude and Attitude Change: The Social Judgment-Involvement Approach.* Philadelphia: W.B. Saunders, 1965.

Religious educators will find this book extremely helpful in clarifying the meaning and ingredients of attitudes and the process and conditions of attitude change. Attitudes resist change to the extent that they are ego-involved (as in religious attitudes). There are, however, predictable ranges, based on social judgment and ego-involvement, within which divergent communications (challenges to change) are assimilable, are rejected, and are treated noncommitally.

466 Sherif, Muzafer, and Carolyn W. Sherif, eds. *Problems of Youth: Transition to Adulthood in a Changing World*. Chicago: Aldine Publishing Company, 1965.

A technical work, reporting a number of projects in youth research, with major interest in the development and refinement of theory, operational definitions, and research methods. Distinctive thesis: "Whether youth behave or misbehave, set low or high goals for achievement, conform or rebel against adult values, they must ultimately be understood with reference to common psychological principles operating in different social environments. Within such a framework, the unique development of individual personalities may be explored more fruitfully and appreciated more fully."

467 Sherif, Muzafer, and Carolyn W. Sherif. *Reference Groups: Exploration into Conformity and Deviation of Adolescents*. New York: Harper and Row, 1964.

A study of adolescent boys (13-18) in their natural social groups, designed to shed light on the relationships of individual goals and group membership during the fairly prolonged period in which the adolescent is expected to reformulate ties with others in society. The theoretical structure, design, methodology, and findings are all illuminating. Suggests that the "grim" situation of delinquency may best be met by reorienting behavior of group members in their own settings.

468 Sherron, Ronald H., and D. Barry Lumsden, eds. *Introduction to Educational Gerontology*. Washington, DC: Hemisphere Publishing Corporation, 1978.

Among all the literature on aging and education in the older years, this is probably the most thorough and authoritative. The editors have chosen contributions that cover philosophical, psychological, political, social, and educational research, theory, and practice.

469 Smith, Ernest A. *American Youth Culture: Group Life in Teenage Society*. New York: Free Press of Glencoe, 1962.

A helpful and thorough analysis of the society of the "youth culture." Deals with causal factors, social relationships, internal structure and functions, the use of adult norms, and sex customs and relationships.

470 Snelling, Clarence H. "The Proper Study and the Chief End: The Relation of Religious Education and the Social Sciences." *Religious Education* 84 (1989):428-53.

The 1990 research article for *Religious Education* offers a personal view of the empirical method, anthropology, sociology of religion, sociology of knowledge (including concientization), participant-observer methodology, cross-cultural studies, community organization, psychology of religion, personality theory, structures of identity, behavioral psychology, confluent education, group work and family systems, conflict management and utilization, psychotherapy, and structural developmental theory as these relate to religious education.

471 Uthe, Edward W. "The Challenge of a Changing Culture." *Religious Education* 63 (1968):219-23.

> Christian education must be reinterpreted in terms relevant to the emerging culture—in particular, to the experiential environment, the intellectual environment, and social problems and social issues that are arising. The new culture "will present men and women with new issues and new ways to interpret the meaning of life....changes sharp enough to require modification of symbolic thought forms, language, and institutions."

472 Van Leeuwen, Mary Stewart. *The Person in Psychology: A Contemporary Christian Appraisal*. Grand Rapids, MI: William B. Eerdmans Publishing Company, 1985.

> A thorough and intriguing survey of the development of the field of psychology, historical and contemporary, as an interpreter of the nature of the human, cast against the background of a Christian view of human nature. Seeks for models that "do better justice to the whole range of human functions, and not only those that resemble the functions of machines or animals."

473 Walsh, Froma, ed. *Normal Family Processes*. New York: Guilford Press, 1982.

> A positive approach to understanding normality in family living and relationships. The editor provides a theoretical overview, which is followed by accounts of five research projects bearing on family normality. The heart of the book consists of contributions on the normal family's temporal context (e.g., the family life cycle), its structural varieties (and the ways it deals with the disruptions involved), and its sociocultural context (cross-cultural, ethnic, community networks, and historical developments and change).

474 Webster, Staten W., ed. *Knowing and Understanding the Socially Disadvantaged Ethnic Minority Groups*. Scranton, PA: Intext Educational Publishers, 1972.

> Through interviews and selected articles, information about and approaches to various American ethnic minorities are presented. Groups treated: Black Americans, Mexican Americans, Puerto Ricans, Indians, and Chinese and Japanese Americans.

475 Williams, Robin M. Jr. *Strangers Next Door*. Englewood Cliffs, NJ: Prentice-Hall, 1964.

> A detailed profile of ethnic relations in four American cities (Elmira, Steubenville, Bakersfield, and Savannah), based on an eight-year study conducted by researchers from Cornell University. Religious factors in prejudice and resistance to change are studied within the total constellation of behavioral forces operative in intergroup relations. Sheds clear light on the pervasiveness of "culture religion" in the United States and shows specific areas of weakness and need in religious education.

476 Wright, J. Eugene, Jr. *Erikson: Identity and Religion.* New York: Seabury Press, 1982.

> The chief value of this book is that it puts in one place Erikson's assumptions and findings about religion, religious experience, and religious growth, setting them clearly within the context of his more familiar views. Stresses the personal and social dimensions of his work and its ethical as well as religious dimensions. See also 303 and 319.

MULTIDISCIPLINARY FOUNDATIONS

477 Ashbrook, James B. *Humanitas, Human Becoming and Being Human.* Nashville: Abingdon Press, 1973.

> A pastoral theologian looks creatively, imaginatively, and very ecumenically at the constructive process of human becoming, developing its methods and means from a great variety of sources—psychology, the arts, etc. Suggestive to religious educators of the basic dynamics and resources for the transformation of personality.

478 Bergquist, William H., Elinor Miller Greenberg, and G. Alan Klaum. *In Our Fifties: Voices of Men and Women Reinventing Their Lives.* San Francisco: Jossey-Bass Publishers, 1993.

> A qualitative study of seventy-three men and women between fifty and sixty years of age using an extensive interview. The authors, themselves members of this decade in the adult life cycle, counter prevailing negative assessments of the fifties with findings of their four-year study (1987-1991). Chapters focus on self-image, priorities, and the emerging inner life; relationships with family and friends; work/career, leadership, and achievement/failure. Those interviewed for the study were mostly middle-class adults living in California.

479 Bettelheim, Bruno, and Alvin Rosenfeld. *The Art of the Obvious: Developing Insight for Psychotherapy and Everyday Life.* New York: Alfred A. Knopf, 1992.

> The authors offer a composite description of five representative seminar sessions for beginning psychotherapists which they led over a period of six years. The book is rich in insight, affording readers the opportunity to look over the shoulders of two experienced psychotherapists as they go about their teaching.

480 Browning, Don S. *The Moral Context of Pastoral Care.* Philadelphia: Westminster Press, 1976.

> The question, What is distinctively Christian about Christian education? has plagued the field incessantly. Pastoral care has also become conscious of the problem, as secular criteria and models have come to dominate functions like pastoral counseling. Here in historical, cultural, and theological analysis a leading pastoral theologian has done a critical and constructive job in reorienting the discipline to its Christian pastoral nature. What he has done serves as a model for the Christian educator troubled by the same problem.

481 Chittister, Joan D., and Martin E. Marty. *Faith and Ferment: An Interdisciplinary Study of Christian Beliefs and Practices*. Edited by Robert S. Bilheimer. Minneapolis and Collegeville, MN: Augsburg Publishing House and Liturgical Press, 1983.

An exceptionally meaty report of a research whose aims were "to discover the nature of the moral and spiritual concepts now alive among church members in Minnesota," and "to identify the social-psychological effects, ramifications, or complexities which flow from the beliefs of the Christian community." Technical presentation and analysis of the data are followed by a long interpretative essay by Martin Marty and shorter ones by lay people, clergy, and theologians.

482 Clouse, Bonnidell. *Moral Development: Perspectives in Psychology and Christian Belief*. Grand Rapids, MI: Baker Book House, 1985.

Analyzes and assesses five approaches to moral development: learning (moral behavior), cognitive (moral reasoning), humanistic (moral potential), psychoanalytical (moral conflict), and theological (morality as godliness). Sees the values in the first four caught up in the fifth. See also 583, 599, 620, 682, 692, 1093, 1102, 1126, and 1136.

483 Conn, Walter E. *Conscience, Development and Self-Transcendence*. Birmingham, AL: Religious Education Press, 1981.

A study of theological ethics with a focus on conscience. The theological position is correlated with insights from contemporary developmental psychology and is looked at philosophically through the lens of Lonergan. The result is a theory (and model) of "self-transcending subjectivity."

484 DeJong, Norman, ed. *Christian Approaches to Learning Theory*. Vol. 2. Lanham, MD: University Press of America, 1985.

Scholars review the learning theories of behaviorism, Kohlberg, and Piaget, evaluating them from the perspective of Christian learning. Providing the theological framework are Nicholas Wolterstorff (who deals with a biblically faithful learning model), Gregory J. Maffett (who writes from the perspective of Cornelius Van Til), Bert H. Hidges (on human identity), J. Marion Snapper (on the role of the Holy Spirit), and Norman DeJong (on divine revelation in learning).

485 Dykstra, Craig. "Transformation in Faith and Morals." *Theology Today* 39 (1982-83):56-64.

Examines the theme of religious transformation from the perspectives of theology, the social sciences, and the practical ministries of the church, concentrating on the major works of Lawrence Kohlberg, James Fowler, and James Loder. Kohlberg and Fowler agree that world and self are in constant interaction, shaping the person. Loder adds two other dimensions, "the void (the absence of being) and the Holy (felt when serenity comes up out of anxiety, joy out of depression, hope out of hopelessness, when goodness is returned for evil, forgiveness replaces retaliation, and courage triumphs over fear)."

486 Elias, John L. *The Foundations and Practice of Adult Religious Education*. Rev. ed. Malabar, FL: Krieger Publishing Company, 1993.

Originally published in 1982, this book has become a standard work in the field. The revised edition contains a bibliographic essay covering works between 1982 and 1992. The first part of the book covers foundations, including sociological, psychological, developmental, and historical perspectives. Program design, planning, organization, management, and evaluation are included in the second part, which focuses on practice. The author's approach in this comprehensive work is both ecumenical and interdisciplinary.

487 Elias, John L. *Studies in Theology and Education*. Malabar, FL: Robert E. Krieger Publishing Company, 1986.

Essays reflecting the author's particular interests: foundations of religious education; the religious education of adults; and theology, justice, and peace. Particularly challenging insights are found in the essays on moral education and the television culture. Uniquely informative is the essay on religion and adult education in Britain.

488 Fowler, James W. *Weaving the New Creation: Stages of Faith and the Public Church*. San Francisco: HarperSanFrancisco, 1991.

Weaves threads of faith development research and theory into the emerging fabric of interest in the public church. Four themes that constitute the "warp and woof" of the weaving are (1) constructive knowing, (2) vocation, (3) the sovereignty of God, and (4) hopefulness. Evaluates McFague's work on models of God in religious language (chap. 3) and reports on research on the public church undertaken with Tom Frank (chap. 6). Harris's (*Fashion Me a People*) five arenas of curriculum inform Fowler's approach to the formation of personal and public faith.

489 Franklin, R. William, and Joseph M. Shaw. *The Case for Christian Humanism*. Grand Rapids: Wm. B. Eerdmans Publishing Company, 1991.

In a period in which "humanism" has become suspect in some quarters of the Christian community, the authors set out to make a case for Christian humanism grounded in history, scripture, worship, and the trinitarian doctrine of God. This is the second book to emerge from Humanism in an Age of Limits: A Christian Perspective, a project sponsored by four colleges.

490 Gaebelein, Frank E. *The Christian, the Arts, and the Church*. Portland, OR: Multnomah Press, 1985.

D. Bruce Lockerbie, who edited this volume, identifies Gaebelein as a "renaissance man" and a "modern-day Christian humanist." The essays here gathered paint a picture of a life of deep faith and of rich and far-reaching Christian culture. Gaebelein ranges through a theory of the arts, education and the arts, and music and literature. Two essays deal with the uses of leisure. Here is a man one would want to have known and with whom one would want to have spent time. See also 202, 425, 495, 859, 878, and 967.

491 Gilbert, W. Kent. *Confirmation and Education*. Philadelphia: Fortress Press, 1969.

> Early in 1969 the Joint Commission (the American Lutheran Church, the Lutheran Church in America, and the Lutheran Church-Missouri Synod) on the Theology and Practice of Confirmation issued a searching restudy of the theory and practice of confirmation. The report is included in its entirety in the appendix of this volume. The volume itself is the first Yearbook in Christian Education published by the first two of the groups named above, and is intended as a series of studies (theological, psychological, developmental, sociological, educational, bibliographical, etc.) on the basis of which the report may be widely analyzed and evaluated.

492 Goodykoontz, Harry G. *The Persons We Teach*. Philadelphia: Westminster Press, 1965.

> Popularly written, this volume wrestles with the problem of the nature of the human in theological and psychological perspective, using Christian education as the context for discussion. Weaves together biblical, doctrinal, and Freudian ideas, but comes up with a personality theory like that of the ego-psychologists or field theorists. Contains useful summaries of learning theory and developmental psychology in Christian perspective. Serves to help Christian educators see the field of personality with greater understanding, and may intrigue them into following up the many clues to further study.

493 Greeley, Andrew M. *Unsecular Man*. New York: Schocken Books, 1972.

> A detailed exploration of the thesis that religion is a universal human phenomenon, maintaining that such a generalization, when sociologically studied, has not been invalidated by theories of secularization. Important data for the religious educator in understanding the nature and needs of both learner and teacher.

494 Hageman, Alice L. ed. *Sexist Religion and Women in the Church*. New York: Association Press, 1974.

> The Lentz Lectures at Harvard Divinity School, 1972-73, were devoted to the exploration of various aspects of the question of women and ministry. Some of the contributions are historical and sociological, some are theological. They all raise searching ethical and practical questions that apply (although the point is not made directly) to the religious educator as well as the pastor, the religious education graduate student as well as the candidate for ordination.

495 Harris, Maria. "Art and Religious Education: A Conversation." *Religious Education* 83 (1988):453-73.

> This 1988 research essay seeks to discover how religion and education are informed by art. After discussing religion, the aesthetic, and education in terms of meanings, appreciations, and resistances, Harris presents three models of art in religious education as a way of integrating religion, art, and education. See also 202, 425, 490, 859, 878, and 967.

496 Helminiak, Daniel L. *Spiritual Development: An Interdisciplinary Study*. Chicago: Loyola University Press, 1987.

> Spirituality is a matter of "authentic self-transcendence," and develops in adulthood through the stages of "conformist, conscientious conformist, conscientious, compassionate, and cosmic." With such a generic psychological description, the author goes on to show the meaning of spirituality in a theistic context. Human life is a process of divinization, responding to a "divinizing grace."

497 Holmes, Urban T., III. *Confirmation: The Celebration of Maturity in Christ*. New York: Seabury Press, n.d.

> Rich in personal pastoral experience and in theological and historical perspective, and reflecting the deliberations of the Episcopal Committee on Christian Initiation, this book basically suggests that confirmation be reconceived as a recognition of the crisis of faith that brings the person to Christian maturity (adulthood). Strangely, while the avowed basis of decision is theological and historical, most of the decisions are actually made on psychological and pragmatic grounds.

498 Howe, Leroy T. "Religious Understanding from a Piagetian Perspective." *Religious Education* 73 (1978):569-81.

> Sees religious understanding as a special case of human understanding and works through the insights of Goldman and Fowler (both of whom are indebted to Piaget). Concludes that "in Piagetian terminology, that cognitive structure which is most fundamentally involved in religious understanding is that structure which enables the consideration of alternative possibilities."

499 Hull, John M. *What Prevents Christian Adults from Learning?* Rev. ed. Philadelphia: Trinity Press International, 1991.

> The author seeks to answer the question posed in the title by drawing on the disciplines of sociology of religion and sociology of knowledge (chaps. 1 and 2), social psychology (chap. 3), depth psychology and developmental psychology (chap. 4), and theology (chap. 5). Unlike many secular studies of participation in adult learning, Hull pays more attention to the influence of ideology than to socioeconomic factors and motivational theories.

500 Jeeves, Malcolm A. *Psychology and Christianity: The View Both Ways*. Downers Grove, IL: InterVarsity Press, 1976.

> A useful analysis of psychological methods, findings, assumptions, and self-imposed limitations, raising the basic question of human nature. The Christian view of human nature and the sources and methods of Christian inquiry are compared with the psychological. Religious educators will be particularly interested in the sections on conversion (chap. 8) and moral learning and development (chap. 9).

501 Johnson, Robert K. *The Christian at Play*. Grand Rapids, MI: William B. Eerdmans
Publishing Company, 1983.

> Religious education has yet to come to grips with the role of the affective—the
> emotions, play, and the arts. This book helps in the understanding of play and its
> functions. Since our situation is one of increasing emphasis on leisure, the
> approach is to examine the meaning of play, the theological options in
> understanding and interpreting it, development of a biblical model of play, and
> relating play and work in the Christian life.

502 Kepes, Gyorgy, ed. *Education and Vision*. New York: George Braziller, 1965.

> "All the contributors to this volume agree on two points: 1) That there is a
> fundamental interdependence between perception and conception, between the
> visual and the rational. The experimental evidence in support of the idea that
> sensory functions belong to an interdependence system—that there is a primordial
> unity of sensory and motor processes—is extended to include a corresponding
> interdependence between the sensory and the intellectual: between art and science.
> 2) That because the visual factor has been for so long misunderstood and
> consequently neglected, there is an urgent need today for a re-evaluation of the
> education of vision."

503 Kotesky, Ronald L. *Psychology from a Christian Perspective*. Nashville: Abingdon
Press, 1980.

> The implications of a Christian worldview for the discipline (and subdisciplines)
> of psychology. The author systematically addresses the various branches of
> psychology (developmental, social, etc.) and its major themes (learning,
> motivation, personality, etc.) in an attempt to extract and synthesize a Christian
> psychology.

504 Kuhmerker, Lisa, with Uwe Gielen and Richard L. Hayes. *The Kohlberg Legacy for
the Helping Professions*. Birmingham, AL: Religious Education Press, 1991.

> Kohlberg's contributions to education, religious education, and counseling are the
> subject of this volume. The book opens with "My Personal Search for Universal
> Morality" by Kohlberg and ends with personal reflections by James Rest and Lisa
> Kuhmerker. See also 159, 338, 350, 356, 368, 386, and 620.

505 Kuhn, Alfred. *The Study of Society: A Unified Approach*. Homewood, IL: Richard
D. Irwin and The Dorsey Press, 1963.

> A "tightly integrated approach" to the understanding of society, based in political
> science, sociology, and economics. "It pulls all three disciplines apart, throws
> their components into a single pile, and then attempts to reconstruct them into a
> new, single discipline....The key analytical concepts in the new structure are
> transactions and organizations, each with an extremely broad definition, along with
> the   major   supporting   concepts   of   transformations,   decisions,   and
> communications."   Concepts from psychology, communications theory,
> information theory, psycholinguistics, systems of research, cybernetics, behavioral
> science, decision theory, and organization theory have also been used.

506 Lauer, Eugene, and Joel Mlecko, eds. *A Christian Understanding of the Human Person*. New York: Paulist Press, 1982.

A carefully selected and well-rounded set of readings on theological anthropology, in the broadest sense. Accomplishes for the religious educator what is a most perplexing responsibility—relating behavioral and theological approaches to personality.

507 Loder, James E. *Religious Pathology and Christian Faith*. Philadelphia: Westminster Press, 1966.

A study of the development of a theological-behavioral epistemology, needed in theological education (and religious education) because both disciplinary areas are involved in the one enterprise. Kierkegaard and Freud are the foci of the study, which proposes a "hypnagogic paradigm" as the clue to conflict resolution, and thus a model for the theological-behavioral epistemology that is sought (and thus also a model for the educational transaction). Specific implications for education are briefly drawn at the end of the book.

508 Loder, James E. *The Transforming Moment: Understanding Convictional Experiences*. San Francisco: Harper and Row, 1981.

Christian theology and the human sciences are brought to bear on the analysis and understanding of convictional experiences—those profound religious experiences of heightened awareness of the reality and presence of God. Such experiences are differentiated from mere subjectivity. They open up the dimensions of the lived world, the self, the void, and the holy. They are essentially christocentric. Such experiences direct, rather than follow, the course of religious development. A second edition was published in 1989 by Helmers and Howard, Colorado Springs, Colorado. It consists of the original text, plus an index, introductory chapter, epilogue, and glossary.

509 Marstin, Ronald. *Beyond Our Tribal Gods: The Maturing of Faith*. Maryknoll, NY: Orbis Books, 1979.

The business of the Christian and the church is the establishment of justice through action for the change of economic, social, and political structures that oppress. Such world-minded concern corresponds to the universal level of mature faith in James Fowler's work and its bases in Piaget and Kohlberg. This explains why other stages of faith exist and why they are inadequate. Action-based religious education for the maturing of faith is hinted at.

510 McCall, Emanuel L., comp. *Black Church Life-Styles*. Nashville: Broadman Press, 1986.

Explores the distinctive characteristics of the black Christian experience—historically, in terms of its practices (nurture, worship, hymns, and preaching), and in terms of its ways of evangelizing and relating to the community. Sees a "black church renaissance" on the way. The chapter on black nurture is scholarly and informative.

511 McFadyen, Alistair I. *The Call to Personhood: A Christian Theory of the Individual in Social Relationships*. Cambridge: Cambridge University Press, 1990.

> Finding both collectivist and individualist conceptions of the person unsatisfactory, the author seeks a third conception of personhood informed by Martin Buber's personalist philosophy, and its extension in the work of Karl Barth and Dietrich Bonhoeffer. Social interaction and communication theory also contribute to McFadyen's attempt to find a more satisfying alternative than those offered by the two competing theories for understanding personhood.

512 Mol, Hans J. *Identity and the Sacred: A Sketch for a New Social-Scientific Theory of Religion*. New York: The Free Press, 1976.

> Although mainly related to sociology of religion, this book "is an attempt to integrate anthropological, historical, psychological, and sociological approaches to religion in one conceptual scheme." That scheme consists of the theory that "religion is the sacralization of identity and that the mechanisms of sacralization consist of objectification, commitment, ritual, and myth." Foundational to the understanding of the religious process.

513 Moseley, Romney M. *Becoming a Self Before God: Critical Transformations*. Nashville: Abingdon Press, 1991.

> Reexamines current paradigms of moral and religious transformation. Brings moral, psychological, and theological perspectives together to critique developmentalism and religious triumphalism. Chapter 1 examines William James's phenomenology of religious faith and the moral life, and chapter 2 explores the relationship of pragmatism to Fowler's faith development theory. Dialectical psychology is used in chapter 3 to develop an alternative to Fowler's theory, and a discussion of Jung's analytical psychology follows in chapter 4. Repetition becomes a metaphor for the dialetical transformations of the self in chapter 5, while *kenosis* is the focus of chapter 6.

514 Nida, Eugene A. *Message and Mission: The Communication of the Christian Faith*. New York: Harper, 1960.

> A profound attempt to come to grips with the problems of Christian communication in behavioral and theological terms. Motivated by the task of Bible translation, the author has not been satisfied with answers until they have been checked in terms of all the reliable and relevant data available.

515 Palmer, Parker J. *The Company of Strangers: Christians and the Renewal of America's Public Life*. New York: Crossroad, 1981.

> An exposition of the theme of community, focused on the idea of the "public life," a via media between privatistic spirituality and imperialistic politicism. There are two chapters on "teaching the public life," and two others that deal specifically with congregational life.

516   Palmer, Parker J. "Learning is the Thing for You: Renewing the Vitality of Religious Education" *Weavings* 4, no. 5 (September-October 1989):6-19.

> Addresses how Western culture's desire for control has shaped knowing, teaching, and learning. This objectivism has resulted in the loss of inwardness and subjectivity and, in the church, it has led to the objectification of God, Jesus, scripture, faith, worship, and ministry. Sets up an alternate vision of a community of learning which allows for expression of "authentic subjectivity," recovery of "authentic objectivity," modeling of the connective nature of reality, and the experience of doing theology.

517   Pazmiño, Robert W. *Foundational Issues in Christian Education: An Introduction in Evangelical Perspective*. Grand Rapids, MI: Baker Book House Company, 1988.

> Seven foundations—biblical, theological, philosophical, historical, sociological, psychological, and curricular—are explored. The author seeks a holistic and integrated conception of Christian education in the search for principles to guide educational practice.

518   Richards, Lawrence O., and Hoeldke, Clyde. *A Theology of Church Leadership*. Grand Rapids, MI: Zondervan Publishing House, 1980.

> Manages in a fruitful way to provide a thoroughgoing and critical treatment of what is known about leadership from organizational management and social psychological points of view, but within a rich and consistent theological framework that makes that information useful to the church in authentic ways. Clarifies the nature of ministry, broadly understood, within the context of church renewal.

519   Roberts, J. Deotis. *Roots in the Black Future: Family and Church*. Philadelphia: Westminster Press, 1980.

> Particular cultural and ethnic backgrounds are a growing concern for religious education. This book by a theologian is useful in presenting in a broad and richly informed way the essence of the black experience in America, as developed through its major institutions, the church and the family.

520   Shorter, Aylward. *Toward a Theology of Inculturation*. Maryknoll: Orbis Books, 1988.

> An introduction to the basic terminology of inculturation and an examination of the relation of inculturation to theology, mission, and the teaching of the Roman Catholic church. Concludes with an exploration of future directions. Shorter writes: "The theology of this multicultural Church is Inculturation Theology, the recognition that faith must become culture, if it is to be fully received and lived."

521 Smart, Ninian. *The Science of Religion and the Sociology of Knowledge*. Princeton, NJ: Princeton University Press, 1973.

> An attempt to redefine the scientific study of religion by suggesting that (1) it become specifically "polymethodic," that is, that it make use of methods and data from many scientific disciplines, and that (2) the gap be closed between study about religion and its study from inside the experience of its adherents.

522 Steele, Les L. *On The Way: A Practical Theology of Christian Formation*. Grand Rapids, MI: Baker Book House Company, 1990.

> Attempts to integrate theology and psychology in this approach to Christian formation. Theology here means Christian formation as the gospels, the Pauline, and the general letters describe it. Psychology means primarily theories of developmental psychology. These two foundational disciplines are discussed in the first two parts; Steele's own integrative approach is presented in the third part and followed by a fourth, in which cycles of Christian formation are traced through childhood, adolescence, and adulthood.

523 Steward, David S., and Margaret S. Steward. "Cognitive Development and Ethnicity: Problems for Educational Ministry." *Religious Education* 70 (1975):308-16.

> Traces the growing openness to difference in the history of religious education and presents a research report intended to identify and understand the origin and meaning of two kinds of difference, cognitive development and ethnicity, that are significant for the church's educational ministry. Proposes work on both dimensions simultaneously in order to avoid religiously literate persons who have little sense of belonging, on the one hand, and a generation of "warm-hearted, empty-headed religious illiterates," on the other.

524 "Symposium: The Foundations of Religious Education." *Religious Education* 76 (1981):115-221.

> Articles include "Catechesis: An Enriching Category of Religious Education" (Michael Warren), "The Standpoint of Religious Education" (Mary Boys), "The Local Church as an Ecology of Human Development" (Kieran Scott), "The Church and the Task of Inhabiting the Symbol" (Michael Fuchs), "'Understanding' as a Purpose of Religious Education" (Charles Melchert), "Understanding the Place of 'Understanding'" (Craig Dykstra), "Religious Education in a Television Culture" (John Elias), and "Transformation in Christian Education" (James E. Loder).

525 Taylor, Charles. *Sources of the Self: The Making of Modern Identity*. Cambridge, MA: Harvard University Press, 1989.

> A major work which examines "an ensemble" of understandings of what it means to be a human agent in terms of inwardness, freedom, individuality, and embeddedness in nature. Taylor is concerned with how modern identity, in subtle and often unexamined ways, shapes philosophical thought, epistemology, and language. His examination takes a historical approach to three "major facets" of

modern identity: "Inwardness" (part 2), "The Affirmation of Ordinary Life" (part 3), and "The Voice of Nature" (part 4).

526 Thompson, William M. *Christ and Consciousness*. New York: Paulist Press, 1977.

In part prompted by the studies of development done by Piaget and Kohlberg, and using Jaspers's scheme for the historical development of consciousness, Thompson seeks to work out a theology of the development of consciousness (historic, generic, and individual) that takes the fact of Christ and the Christ-event seriously.

527 Ulanov, Ann, and Barry Ulanov. *Religion and the Unconscious*. Philadelphia: Westminster Press, 1975.

This interdisciplinary treatment of religion and depth psychology will be foundational for some religious educators, and, for others, at least full of insights. The psychological sources of religious experience are re-explored, together with the processes of religious communication and becoming, in primarily Jungian terms. Solid and rich, it challenges behavioristic bases of religious education, in favor of an open, adventurous, even risky approach.

528 van den Heuvel, Albert H. *The Humiliation of the Church*. Philadelphia: Westminster Press, 1966.

In spite of being a collection of occasional addresses and articles, this volume places such concerns as preaching, worship, and youth work under the searching light of theological debate and provides insights into the need for relevance, mission, and renewal. The chapter, "Young Adults in an Adolescent Society," will introduce the religious educator to the thought of such theorists and social scientists as Muchlow and Spranger.

Educational Theory

529 Adler, Mortimer J. *The Paideia Proposal: An Educational Manifesto.* New York: Macmillan Publishing Company, 1982.

Advocates a one-track curriculum for the nation's schools, with the same objectives for all without exception. Its goals are acquisition of organized knowledge, development of intellectual skills (learning skills), and enlarged understanding of ideas and values. Specific vocational training is not to be included, and there are to be no electives.

530 Banks, James A. *Multiethnic Education: Theory and Practice.* Boston: Allyn and Bacon, 1981.

"Designed to help preservice and inservice educators to clarify the philosophical and definitional issues related to pluralistic education, to derive a clarified philosophical position, to design and implement effective teaching strategies that reflect ethnic diversity, and to derive sound guidelines for multiethnic programs and practices." Describes actions educators can take to institutionalize educational programs and practices related to ethnic and cultural diversity.

531 Barrow, Robin. *Radical Education: A Critique of Freeschooling and Deschooling.* New York: John Wiley and Sons, 1978.

A critical examination of Rousseau, A.S. Neill, Paul Goodman, Reimer and Illich, and Postman and Weingarten, all radicals (in the sense of wanting to get at the root of today's educational problems) and romantics (in the sense of holding a belief in the basic goodness of the person). The challenge they give to education, but which they do not meet, is that of bringing up a generation of concerned and critical thinkers.

532 Belth, Marc. *Education as a Discipline.* Boston: Allyn and Bacon, 1965.

"A work of serious scholarship....The subject matter of education is the models by which knowledge is organized, transmitted, and extended....It is also the models of educating, of teaching, and their relations to the models of subject matter....Here we have described for the first time the structure of a discipline of education that is so discrete, complicated, and interesting that it will attract in the generation ahead some of the best scholars in our universities."

533 Benne, Kenneth D. *Education for Tragedy*. Lexington, KY: University of Kentucky Press, 1967.

Tragedy, identity, and community are among the themes explored in the attempt to get at an education for wisdom in times of crisis. A prime example of the "inevitability of religious dimensions in the search for the meaning of education."

534 Berman, Louise M., and Jessie A. Roderick, eds. *Feeling, Valuing, and the Art of Growing: Insights into the Affective*. Washington, DC: Association for Supervision and Curriculum Development, 1977.

Humanistic and affective education are themes that have been characteristic of certain strands of educational thought, and that have close affinity to some of the aims and methods of religious education. This book provides both theoretical and analytical background for understanding these emphases, has gathered commentary from representatives of the various disciplines involved (including Philip Phenix), and has shown how the practice of humanistic and affective education may be fostered in the schools.

535 Bronfenbrenner, Urie. *Two Worlds of Childhood, U.S. and U.S.S.R.* New York: Russell Sage Foundation, 1970.

The contrast, research based, is between the purposeful rearing of "the new Soviet man," and the laissez-faire processes that result in the American child's "unmaking." A short section at the end summarizes what could be done in American schools, families, and neighborhoods to change the pervasive child neglect built into American culture.

536 Bruner, Jerome S. *The Process of Education*. Cambridge, MA: Harvard University Press, 1960.

One of the most influential books in educational theory in America. The thesis is that basic concepts in any area may be grasped by persons of any age, and that the key to curriculum is the analysis of the basic structure of the subject matter field.

537 Bruner, Jerome S. *Toward a Theory of Instruction*. Cambridge, MA: Harvard University Press, 1966.

A series of essays following up the author's previous work in educational theory. His "theory of instruction" consists not so much in ideas for teaching techniques as in responsible curriculum building.

538 Courtney, Sean. *Why Adults Learn: Towards a Theory of Participation in Adult Education*. London and New York: Routledge, 1992.

> A volume in the Routledge Series on the Theory and Practice of Adult Education in North America, edited by Peter Jarvis. Presents a comprehensive and balanced review of the literature on participation in adult education (PAE). Attentiveness to the sociological dimension is an important contribution Courtney makes to the discussion of participation in adult education.

539 *Eighty-fourth Yearbook of the National Society for the Study of Education*. Chicago: University of Chicago Press, 1985.

> Part 1, "Education in School and Nonschool Settings," has an article by Burton Cohen and Joseph Lukinsky, "Religious Institutions as Educators" (140-158). Part 2, "Learning and Teaching the Ways of Knowing," has Dwayne Huebner's chapter, "Spirituality and Knowing" (159-173).

540 Elam, Stanley, ed. *Education and the Structure of Knowledge*. Chicago: Rand McNally, 1964.

> A follow-up of Bruner's *The Process of Education*. Three problems are dealt with: the structure of disciplines (the logical order of basic concepts in various fields of inquiry), the structure of knowledge (the interrelationships of the disciplines in ordering the whole of knowledge), and the educational and curricular implications of these concepts. Exploratory and technical in character, representing at least three different points of view on these questions.

541 Elias, John L. *Conscientization and Deschooling: Freire's and Illich's Proposals for Reshaping Society*. Philadelphia: Westminster Press, 1976.

> A splendid comparative analysis and assessment of Freire and Illich, pulling together for each one his theological, social, and educational views. Since the popular assumption is that both hold virtually the same views, the book provides a necessary corrective in differentiating sharply between them. The person who first reads this book will be ready to tackle the works of both with understanding. See also 152, 160, 549, 708, 710, and 728.

542 Ennis, Robert H. *Logic in Teaching*. Englewood Cliffs, NJ: Prentice-Hall, 1969.

> One of the learning tasks of Christian education is "to discover meaning and value in light of the gospel." Implied is a rigor of thought that involves logical operations. This book is the first to set forth the operations in the use of deductive logic in the classroom, especially in defining, explaining, and justifying. For those who would like more clarity and less muddle in discussions, question and answer sessions, and the like, this is a book with which to start.

543 Fasheh, Munir. "Community Education: To Reclaim and Transform What Has Been Made Invisible" *Harvard Educational Review* 60 (1990):19-35.

> Writing out of the Palestinian context, Munir Fasheh concerns himself with hegemonic education. He writes: "Hegemony is characterized not only by what it includes but also by what it excludes: by what it renders marginal, deems inferior, and makes invisible. As a result, the effects of hegemonic education make it possible to define the real environment by what formal education marginalizes or excludes." Fasheh sees community education responding to real needs, empowering people, building human resources and networks.

544 Fiedler, Ralph. *Die klassische deutsche Bildungidee*. Weinheim: Beltz Verlag, 1972.

> A thorough analysis and critique of the classical German concept of education, indicating its inadequacy for the present day. Urges curriculum reform toward a new humanism that takes the nature and needs of society into account.

545 Gage, N.L. *The Scientific Basis of the Art of Teaching*. New York: Teachers College Press, 1978.

> A strong case for the importance and adequacy of educational research in designing and selecting educational methods, in teacher education, and in the reexamination of educational paradigms. "Research on teaching promises no millenium; it merely holds out a reasonable prospect of improving the way teaching is."

546 Harris, Michael R. *Five Counterrevolutionists in Higher Education*. Corvallis, OR: Oregon State University Press, 1970.

> Critical reviews of the educational positions of Babbitt, Nock, Flexner, Hutchins, and Meiklejohn.

547 Hill, Brian V. *Education and the Endangered Individual*. New York: Teachers College Press, 1973.

> In its thesis (the importance of the individual) and insights for education (particularly in curriculum and method), this book is valuable in itself. In addition, it provides critical reviews of the thought of Kierkegaard, Nietzsche, Marx, Nunn, Mannheim, Dewey, Whitehead, Buber, Maritain, and Niebuhr.

548 Holt, John. *How Children Learn*. New York: Pitman, 1967.

> The author of *How Children Fail* turns to the positive side and, in a diary-like book, explores possibilities for conserving and enhancing the natural learning style of children.

549 Illich, Ivan. *Deschooling Society*. New York: Harper and Row, 1971.

> This is Illich's most finished statement of his views on education. His general
> approach is to raise the most basic questions about various human activities, and
> here he does so for schools and education, maintaining that the institutional form
> "school" has been substituted completely inadequately for education. He tells us
> what education actually is and makes suggestions for its accomplishment. See also
> 541, 572.

550 Jones, Richard M. *Fantasy and Feeling in Education*. New York: New York
University Press, 1968.

> "Bruner's advances toward a theory of instruction, made as they have been by
> half-steps, have revealed possibilities for the taking of full steps; that is, for the
> coordination of cognitive moves with emotional and imaginal ones." Brings
> psychodynamic principles and methods to bear on the educational process itself in
> a synthesis of Bruner, Piaget, Erikson, and others.

551 Joyce, Bruce, and Marsha Weil. *Models of Teaching*. Englewood Cliffs, NJ:
Prentice-Hall, 1986.

> An introduction to current educational theory, explicating models of teaching
> based on the work of Bruner, Ausubel, Piaget, Rogers, Glassner, Skinner, and
> others. They are grouped as "information processing, focus on the person,
> cooperative learning, and behavior theory." Concluding sections deal with
> educational outcomes and models of teaching, the student, and professional skill
> and knowledge.

552 Kennedy, William B. "A Radical Challenge to Inherited Educational Patterns."
Religious Education 74 (1979):491-95.

> Calls for the development of critical consciousness with regard to the powerful
> inherited structures that perpetuate injustice in education and society. Values must
> move from personal to social/political, behavior patterns from private to public,
> the scope of concern from local to global, and ethical motivation from charity to
> justice. Advocates direct engagement, careful reflection, and a strong community
> of support.

553 Kimball, Solon T., and James E. McClellan. *Education and the New America*. New
York: Random House, 1962.

> In this volume philosophy of education tries to come to terms with the
> urban-scientific-industrial culture in America. The concept of "commitment" is
> used as the key to a well-ordered society and to a heightened individuality at the
> same time. Commitment to what? The crux of the matter is education for mature
> disciplines of thought and action that release the uniqueness of the self and at the
> same time provide for social responsibility.

554   Kohl, Herbert. *On Teaching*. New York: Schocken Books, 1976.

   This book might be classified under "Administration" or under "Program, Curriculum, and Method," since it centers on the craft and politics of teaching. Yet its presentation of a mind and style of teaching runs so deep that it belongs in the category of educational theory. Any teacher—including any religious educator—will be challenged and inspirited by its sharp incisiveness, down-to-earth practicality, and high conception of what education is all about.

555   Krathwohl, David R., Benjamin S. Bloom, and Bertram B. Masia. *Taxonomy of Educational Objectives: The Classification of Educational Goals, Handbook II: Affective Domain*. New York: David McKay, 1964.

   The second volume of the taxonomy of educational objectives provides an analysis of objectives in the areas of awareness of and response to values, commitment, and the development of value systems. This analysis provides the basis for a review of methods for evaluating educational achievements in these areas. A basic contribution to the understanding of the religious aspects of educational experience.

556   Lather, Patti. *Getting Smart: Feminist Research and Pedagogy With/in the Postmodern*. New York: Routledge, 1991.

   A volume in Routledge's series, Critical Social Thought, edited by Michael Apple. Lather draws on feminism, Neo-Marxism, and poststructuralism in exploring oppositional theory and practice in her quest for nondominating and noncoercive knowledges. "Research as Praxis," "Feminist Perspectives on Empowering Research Methodologies," and "Student Resistance to Liberatory Curriculum" are among her themes in this volume.

557   Leonard, George B. *Education and Ecstasy*. New York: Delacorte Press, 1968.

   A rich challenge to the dull, the limiting, and the ineffective in education. The author is at one and the same time angry, visionary, and realistic. Accepted ways of educating will not do in these times of rapid change. "Open your mind to unfamiliar or even disreputable solutions if they are the ones that work, look upon all systems of abstractions as strictly tentative and throw out of the window every prior guideline about what human beings can accomplish....The goal of education [is] the achievement of moments of ecstasy."

558 Magendzo, Salomón. "Popular Education in Nongovernmental Organizations: Education for Social Mobilization?" Trans. by Cristina Cardalda. *Harvard Educational Review* 60 (1990):49-61.

> Magendzo distinguishes between education as a "functional activity," which fosters dependency in the learners, and education as a process, which emphasizes participation and social mobilization. State education, which uses the functional approach to education, involves social mobility, while social mobilization is the goal of the popular education practiced by nongovernmental organizations. Magendzo describes the efforts of one such organization associated with the Roman Catholic church in Chile, the Interdisciplinary Program for Research in Education (PIIE).

559 Marzano, Robert J. *A Different Kind of Classroom: Teaching with Dimensions of Learning*. Alexandria, VA: Association for Supervision and Curriculum Development, 1992.

> This model of classroom instruction draws on three decades of research on the learning process. It is based on the premise that the process of learning involves the interactions of five kinds of thinking: positive attitudes and perceptions, acquisition and integration, extension and refinement, meaningful usage, and productive habits of mind. Together, these five "dimensions" of learning constitute "learning-centered instruction" which is based on how the mind works when learning.

560 McClellan, James E. *Toward an Effective Critique of American Education*. Philadelphia: Lippincott, 1968.

> Seeks to establish a critical framework for examining educational policy decisions, using particularly the views of Conant, Brameld, Barzun, Skinner, and Paul Goodman for analysis.

561 Meyer, John R., ed. *Reflections on Value Education*. Waterloo, Ontario: Wilfrid Laurier University Press, 1976.

> A book of essays designed to stimulate thought in education in morality and values. The contributors are Dutch, American, and Canadian, and the contributions deal with certain theoretical problems (including a rundown on moral judgment by Kohlberg and his associates), the learning environment, and what is here called "the learning and helping facilitator." The most useful essay is the editor's summary, "Where Are We and Where Might We Go in Values Education?"

562 Mezirow, Jack. *Transformative Dimensions of Adult Learning*. San Francisco: Jossey-Bass Publishers, 1991.

> In this book, Mezirow presents a comprehensive statement of his critical theory of adult learning. Arguing that psychological theories do not explain the place of meaning in learning, he discusses meaning making and describes his concept of

"meaning perspectives" in the first two chapters. The next three chapters examine intentional learning, reflection, and assumptions. The remaining chapters deal with perspective transformation and the fostering of transformative learning.

563 Miles, Matthew B., ed. *Innovation in Education*. New York: Bureau of Publications, Teachers College, Columbia University, 1964.

Centers on the process of educational change—"how educational innovations are introduced and adopted—or rejected." Nine case studies are analyzed, research and theory reviewed, and the possibilities and probabilities in the American educational system discussed. Summary principles and warnings, set within an educational systems framework, are provided by the editor in the final chapter.

564 Moustakas, Clark. *The Authentic Teacher: Sensitivity and Awareness in the Classroom*. Cambridge, MA: Howard A. Doyle Publishing Company, 1966.

Considers in sequence the possibilities in teacher sensitivity to children and youth in their needs and possibilities, from kindergarten through high school. The teacher is to confirm the child as a being of noncomparable and nonmeasurable worth; to be authentically present, open to honest encounter with children, and a resource for learning and enrichment; and to make other resources available—colors, shapes, forms, audiovisual materials, and reference books—which can be encountered, explored, and tested in exercising capacities, in expanding awarenesses, and in developing skills.

565 Mphahlele, Es'kia. "Alternative Institutions of Education for Africans in South Africa: An Exploration of Rationale, Goals, and Directions." *Harvard Educational Review* 60 (1990):36-48.

"Alternative education" is the focus of this article by South African educator Es'kia Mphahlele. Alternative education is distinguished from informal education and continuing education. Mphahlele writes: "In my mind, alternative education is any form of education that is alternative to that which is provided, planned, and controlled by a political authority, whether on a local or a national level." The focus of alternative education is on integrated studies rather than education in which subjects are taught in a separate and unrelated manner.

566 Newton, Robert R. "Current Educational Trends and Strategies in Religious Education." *Religious Education* 67 (1972):253-58.

Argues that decisions in religious education are most often made out of context. In other words, directions are chosen from the educational options without taking philosophical and educational orientations into account. To counteract this trend, the author provides a detailed contextual analysis of three educational options: individual fulfillment, scholarly discipline, and behaviorist.

567 Novak, Joseph D. *A Theory of Education*. Ithaca, NY: Cornell University Press, 1977.

> Religious educators who emphasize values and the affective are reminded that learning religion also involves, in the overwhelming number of cases, learning concepts, and learning them accurately. Novak, building on Ausubel, develops a full treatment of educational theory and practice, from philosophical and psychological bases to curriculum design and instructional planning, oriented to what he considers to be a mature cognitive learning theory. The second part of the book consists of empirical validation of the theoretical section.

568 Palmer, Parker J. *To Know as We Are Known: A Spirituality of Education*. San Francisco: Harper and Row, 1983.

> A blistering attack on the inadequacies of his own education is balanced by the author's advocacy of an education that is spiritual formation, with method and content in harmony. The key is "to create a space in which obedience to truth is practiced." A final chapter deals with the spiritual formation of teachers.

569 Piening, Ekkehard, and Nick Lyons. *Educating as an Art*. New York: Rudolph Steiner School Press, 1979.

> A beautifully written and produced book setting forth and explaining the method of the Waldorf Schools, pioneered by Rudolph Steiner. The more esoteric of Steiner's views do not figure in his educational designs. Rather, we have here a prototype of the humane, the life-centered, and the integrated in education, with the arts (literature, folklore, dance, and others) giving the method focus, character, and unity.

570 Postman, Neil, and Charles Weingartner. *Teaching as a Subversive Activity*. New York: Delacorte Press, 1969.

> Sometimes sounds like a tract, but is in reality one of the most serious of books in educational theory and practice. (The theory is on the serious side; the practice tends to be tract-like.) Beamed at the experienced but frustrated teacher who is ready for reform, it puts religious experience in focus with the rest of experience in a functional and relevant education. The basic suggestion is that education be conducted as inquiry.

571 Raths, Louis E., Merrill Harmin, and Sidney B. Simon. *Values and Valuing*. Columbus, OH: Charles E. Merrill Publishing Company, 1978.

> The educational process of valuing is presented as a formal matter, the substance (values themselves) to develop as the process is used in the classroom and elsewhere. Examples and varieties of possibilities are amply presented, and there is a rundown of research in values clarification.

572 Reimer, Everett. *An Essay on Alternatives in Education*. Cuernavaca, Mexico: Centro Intercultural de Documentación, 1970.

> Reimer and Ivan Illich have worked closely together for many years, so that the analysis and position in this volume shed light on Illich's views as well as speaking for themselves. "Schooling" is society's answer to the educational problem. Yet schooling is not feasible in economic terms for much of the world, and may indeed be questioned on theoretical and pragmatic grounds as well. The alternatives are explored here in fresh and provocative ways. See also 549.

573 Rogers, Carl R. *Freedom to Learn*. Columbus, OH: Charles E. Merrill Publishing Company, 1969.

> After thirty-five years, this is Rogers's first book on education per se. An educational "practice for freedom" is illustrated, theorized, and supported philosophically. Concludes with "a plan for self-directed change in an educational system" and reports on the use of this plan in Immaculate Heart College in the Los Angeles area.

574 Shor, Ira. *Empowering Education: Critical Teaching for Social Change*. Chicago and London: The University of Chicago Press, 1992.

> Empowerment, problem-posing, critical thought, critical dialogue, critical teaching and classroom research, desocialization and critical consciousness, democratic authority, obstacles and resources, and transformative discourse are the themes of this book. Shor offers theoretical and practical perspectives for teachers who want to develop critical teaching skills that empower learners.

575 Skinner, B.F. *The Technology of Teaching*. New York: Appleton-Century-Crofts, 1968.

> The leading exponent of "reinforcement" and pioneer experimenter with teaching machines, primarily an experimental psychologist, addresses himself here systematically to educational theory.

576 Sloan, Douglas, ed. *Toward the Recovery of Wholeness: Knowledge, Education, and Human Values*. New York: Teachers College Press, 1984.

> Papers from a 1980 symposium in which representatives of the fields of natural science, philosophy, philology, sociology and anthropology, religion, and education addressed themselves to the "ways of knowing and thinking about the world that do, indeed, make meaning, purpose, and values central, and that require a radical new look at education in all its dimensions." International in scope, and addressed to the issues of positivism vs. humanism in education.

577 Spodek, Bernard, and Herbert J. Walberg. *Studies in Open Education*. New York: Agathon Press, 1975.

> In a sense, this is open education come of age. On the basis of research and experience, a group of experts gathers together what is known of open education, its achievements, shortcomings, and possibilities. The purpose of the book is to provide a solid foundation for understanding the movement and developing it further.

578 Sprung, Barbara, ed. *Perspectives on Non-Sexist Early Childhood Education*. New York: Teachers College Press, 1978.

> Explores the problems and conflicts involving sexism in education, reviews research on the matter, discusses non-sexist parenting, and provides resources and guidelines on the development and evaluation of unbiased educational materials.

579 "Symposium: Educational Theory and Religious Education." *Religious Education* 63 (1968):457-89.

> Articles include "A Churchman's Guide to Marshall McLuhan" (John M. Culkin), "The Significance of Jerome Bruner's Educational Philosophy for Religious Education" (Janet E. Shapiro), "A New Pedagogy for Theological Education" (Robert E. Karsten), "A Simulation Approach to Learning" (Lois Edinger), "The Import of the 'Bloom Taxonomies' for Religious Education" (D. Campbell Wyckoff), and "Towards a Definition of Teaching" (Joseph A. Browde).

580 "Symposium: Educational Theory and Religious Education." *Religious Education* 64 (1969):261-302.

> A continuation of the preceding symposium. Articles include "The Significance of Marc Belth for Religious Education" (Charles F. Melchert), "Educational Language and Logic: Israel Scheffler" (Frank W. Lewis), "The Educational Philosophy of Abraham J. Heschel" (Morton C. Fierman), "Religious Education as Sacred and Profane: An Interpretation of Martin Buber" (Lionel Etscovitz), "Some Aspects of the Educational Thought of Isaac B. Berkson" (Morton J. Merowitz), "Bushnell Revisited" (Garland Knott), and "Bushnell's Nurture Process: An Exposition" (David S. Steward).

581 Taylor, Harold. *The World as Teacher*. Garden City, NY: Doubleday, 1969.

> The result of a three-year study of teacher education in America. Teacher education must prepare persons for effective and responsible fulfillment in world terms. It must then bring students into direct contact with international affairs and with other cultures. Specific and detailed in its recommendations. Relevant to the training (and self-education) of religious educators.

582   Vaccaro, Liliana. "Transferica y Apropiación en Intervenciones Educativas Comunitarias: Un Marco de Referencia para su Análisis" *Harvard Educational Review* 60 (1990):79-95.

Vaccaro, like Magendzo (558), writes out of the context of popular education in Chile. Her concern in this article is with how various popular education projects achieve autonomy. She examines the "transference-appropriation" process in the Learning Workshops Program.

583   Wilson, John, and Barbara Cowell. *Dialogues on Moral Education*. Birmingham, AL: Religious Education Press, 1983.

John Wilson has written for many years on the subject of moral education and is joined in this book by Barbara Cowell. The discussion proceeds in the form of a Socratic dialogue, but livelier than the prototype. Cephalus is the authoritarian father, and Antiphon the relativistic son. Socrates is the voice of a reasonable moral stance. See also 599, 682, 692, 1093, 1102, 1126, 1136, and 1168.

584   Wright, Nathan, Jr., ed. *What Black Educators Are Saying*. New York: Hawthorn Books, 1970.

An informative symposium dealing with the black educator, the white establishment, the university scene, educational redefinition, and community involvement and action.

Religious Education Theory

585 Amalorpavadass, D.S. "Catechesis as a Pastoral Task of the Church: The Nature, the Aim, and the Process of Catechesis." *Lumen Vitae* 17 (1972):259-80.

Establishes evangelism as precatechesis. Catechesis then "consists in the dynamics or the dynamic procedure in which the catechized are guided from within, with due respect for their freedom, to interpret their life, to discover God, and to establish a genuine interpersonal relationship with God and others, through the Word proclaimed, in a vital context of relevance and transformation, leading to communion with God in prayer and in service to others and society at large."

586 Anthony, Michael J., ed. *Foundations of Ministry: An Introduction to Christian Education for a New Generation*. Wheaton, IL: BridgePoint Books, 1992.

The contributors to this comprehensive text are faculty members and graduate students in Christian education at Biola University and its Talbot School of Theology. Among the foundational elements are theology, history, philosophy, psychology (developmental and educational), cross-cultural perspectives, and moral and faith development. Lifespan concerns, in addition to the usual sections on children, youth, and adults, include special treatments of ministry to families and single adults. Special attention within the section on organization and administration is given to the leadership role of women and to legal and ethical issues. A section is devoted to specialized ministries (camping, parachurch programs, counseling, mission education, special education, and schooling).

587 Arnold, Eberhard. *Children's Education in Community: The Basis of Bruderhof Education*. Rifton, NY: Plough Publishing House, 1976.

A slim but significant collection of the educational writings of the founder of the Bruderhof. "With good teaching, the Spirit will be seen behind the history of religion and also behind arts and crafts, social studies, and everything in nature and history....Children discover Christ everywhere. He comes close to them as the One who fulfills mankind's religions through all ages, in all cultures, and on all continents."

588 Babin, Pierre, ed. *The Audio-Visual Man: Media and Religious Education*. Dayton, OH: Pflaum Publishing, 1970.

> This first full-scale treatment of the idea that "the medium is the message" in religious education is also a first-rate book in religious education theory. Deals with "the new person" who sees, hears, and communicates differently; and makes discriminating suggestions on the use of the media in religious education.

589 Batson, C. Daniel. "How Far Does One Teach the Truth Which Admits of Being Learned?: Toward a Model of Education for Creative Growth." *Religious Education* 66 (1971):180-91.

> Truth must be learned. It is not within every human being waiting to be brought to light but is revealed to learners from outside themselves through Jesus, the Christ. An indirect dialectical method of presentation is an attempt to bring the person into an experiential encounter with the Truth. The creative process may be stimulated through the unpacking of potentially creative symbols, but whether the learner acts creatively in the situation is a personal matter.

590 Baudler, George. *Korrelations-didaktik: Leben durch Glauben erschliessen*. Paderborn: Ferdinand Schöningh, 1984.

> Based in a rich theory of symbols and their role in human life, a theory of religious education is developed and illustrated, stressing open dialogue between life experience and Christian faith. The correlation of faith and life is made concrete in the use of such symbols as water and wind, and in the relationship of the sacraments to daily life.

591 Berryman, Jerome W. *Godly Play: A Way of Religious Education*. San Francisco: HarperSanFrancisco, 1991.

> For nearly twenty years, religious educators have had to rely upon articles in journals and periodicals for access to Berryman's work. *Godly Play* is a comprehensive presentation of his careful and thoughtful approach to religious education with young children. "Godly play," he writes, "is the playing of a game that can awaken us to new ways of seeing ourselves as human beings. It is the way to discover our deep identity as Godly creatures, created in the image of God." See also 139, 873.

592 Bodenstein, Walter. *Der Bankrott der gegenwärtigen Religionspädagogik*. Berlin: Verlag Die Spur, 1973.

> The author, a leading religious educator from Kiel, enters into critical dialogue with nine other religious education theorists on the basis and shape of religious education. His constructive suggestions include serious decision as to what is existentially significant, the upbuilding of the inner world, and the discovery of the fact of ultimate mystery.

593 Boehlke, Robert R. "Revelation, Insight, and Creativity, and Some Implications for Christian Education." *The East Asia Journal of Theology* 3, no. 1 (April 1985):36-55.

Proposes a parallelism of operation among the three experiences and suggests that conditions fostering insight and creativity are also valid for helping teachers and learners shape the learning context so that revelation may be more apt to be recognized when it occurs. RRB

594 Bowman, Locke E. Jr. *Teaching for Christian Hearts, Souls and Minds: A Constructive, Holistic Approach to Christian Education*. San Francisco: Harper and Row, 1990.

The author views Christian education as a conversation involving language, concepts, and moves. He introduces the notion of "magni-concepts," drawn from the work of Rabbi Max Kadushin, adding gospel and church to Kadushin's fundamental value concepts of the love of God, the justice of God, Torah, and Israel. Concepts are viewed as furnishings for the mind, which is understood biblically rather than psychologically.

595 Bowman, Locke E., Jr. *Teaching Today*. Philadelphia: Westminster Press, 1980.

A Christian education research specialist, theorist, and trainer who has done more than anyone else to detail the meaning and dynamics of the act of Christian teaching, here sets out his theory in the full context of the church's responsibility. He clarifies learning, teaching, and educational ministry, and brings them into focus.

596 Boys, Mary C. *Educating in Faith: Maps and Visions*. San Francisco: Harper and Row, 1989.

Drawing on the imagery of maps, Boys presents in part 1 four classical expressions of religious education: evangelism, religious education, Christian education, and Catholic education. In part 2, she scans the horizon for trends and finds four movements: "an expanded understanding of knowledge; the contribution of different voices, particularly feminists', to rethinking certain foundational questions; the maturation of the social sciences; and the emergence of a new vision of the public responsibility of the church."

597 Brousseau, Richard, ed. *Réflexions Chrétiennes sur L'Education*. Ottawa: Fides, 1964.

A fascinating glimpse of the beginning of ferment in Roman Catholic educational thought in Quebec. The focus is on questions of religion in higher education, but several of the authors (including Cardinal Leger) have the whole sphere of Christian education in mind.

598 Brown, Marion E., and Marjorie G. Prentice. *Christian Education in the Year 2000.* Valley Forge, PA: Judson Press, 1984.

A careful examination of the issues facing Christian education today precedes the use of a methodology for "futuring" that combines analysis of "success stories" and a sifting of the findings of the "students of the future." The result is an open-ended suggestion of guidelines for the future which combine the achievement of clarified purposes with the technical skills for accomplishing them.

599 Brusselmans, Christiane, ed. *Toward Moral and Religious Maturity.* Morristown, NJ: Silver Burdett Company, 1980.

A rich contribution to the literature of the field. An outgrowth of an international conference held in France, there are outstanding papers by William R. Rogers, James W. Fowler, Antoine Vergote, James E. Loder, Lawrence Kohlberg, Stanley Hauerwas, Thomas Lickona, and others. Provides a substantial reference work of permanent value.

600 Burgess, Harold William. *An Invitation to Religious Education.* Notre Dame, IN: Religious Education Press, 1975.

A splendid, well-documented, and much needed book in basic religious education theory. Traces the development of religious education through the "traditional theological approach," the "social-culture approach," and the "contemporary theological approach" to the "social-science approach." In each case, full, accurate, and well-integrated analyses of the key figures are given.

601 Byrne, H.W. *A Christian Approach to Education: A Bibliocentric View.* Milford, MI: Mott Media, 1977.

Clearly fundamentalist in orientation, the attempt here is to take a penetrating look at education and to work out a philosophy of education that will not do violence either to education itself or to conservative religious views. There are sections on learning theory, developmental theory, and the Christian day school.

602 Chamberlin, J. Gordon. *Freedom and Faith.* Philadelphia: Westminster Press, 1965.

Concerned that critical debate take place to bring a discipline of Christian education into being, the author discusses the views of Smart, Miller, and Sherrill before giving his own position. In a pluralistic context, "the end of Christian education is educated persons who have engaged in a self-conscious reexamination of their views of the meaning of existence, who have been confronted by a competent interpretation of the Christian faith, and who accept their responsibility for the many decisions of their lives in the light of their education." New and adequate institutional patterns will place major responsibility on local congregations rather than national boards and will give priority to adult education.

603   Clark, Robert E., Lin Johnson, and Allyn K. Sloat, eds.   *Christian Education: Foundations for the Future*.   Chicago: Moody Press, 1991.

> Designed as a general text in Christian education.   The contributors are distinguished evangelical scholars.   The usual topics (the nature of Christian education, teaching-learning process, the persons involved, educational strategies, and the church's allies in education) are covered in a more thorough and detailed way than is usual in such books.   Biblical and theological matters are made integral to the practical side of the discipline.   New concerns (cultural differences, computer use, and a global view of Christian education) are introduced.

604   Coleman, Lucien E., Jr. *Why the Church Must Teach*. Nashville: Broadman Press, 1984.

> A biblical-historical and functional treatment of the church's teaching ministry. A full and realistic analysis of Jesus as teacher is followed by an exploration of teaching in the early church.   Christian teaching is seen to be unique in content, focus, and context—basically theologically oriented—while Christian learning is seen as transforming dialogue with the Word.   Aspects of the teacher's role are delineated, forming the basis for an understanding of Christian teaching as a vocation, a calling.   The mandate to teach takes into account both the preservation of tradition and the demands of the technological world.

605   Cully, Iris V. *Christian Child Development*. San Francisco: Harper and Row, 1979.

> Contemporary psychological theories (Erikson, Skinner, Piaget, Bruner, Kohlberg) and theories of religious development (Goldman, Oraison, Godin, Fowler) are examined for their insights on child development in religion.   An overview of religious development is given, together with an analysis of the roles of church and family.   The book concludes with considerations of teaching methods and the use of the Bible.

606   Cully, Iris V. *Christian Worship and Church Education*. Philadelphia: Westminster Press, 1967.

> A more than usually thorough examination of the relation of worship and religious education.   Helpful in maintaining a balance among study, social action, and worship in religious education theory and practice.

607   Cully, Iris V. *Education for Spiritual Growth*. San Francisco: Harper and Row, 1984.

> Described as "encyclopedic," the book comes at spirituality and spiritual growth from a number of angles—human need, influences prompting spiritual growth, biblical understandings, the varieties of historical experience, spirituality and world religions, the conflict between inner spirituality and social responsibility, and theological, biblical, and psychological rootage.   The latter part of the book speaks to educational questions—developmental, corporate, methodological, and the interaction of the whole experience with its various elements.

150

608 Cully, Iris V. *Imparting the Word*. Philadelphia: Westminster Press, 1963.

A solid and insightful summary of biblical scholarship, drawing applications for religious education and especially for curriculum. An attempt to lessen the lag between the biblical field and the church's education.

609 Cully, Kendig B., ed. *The Episcopal Church and Education*. New York: Morehouse-Barlow, 1966.

Cully has brought together some of the best minds in the Episcopal church to examine critically the church's work in education. The complex educational operations of a church, and the varieties of opinion about them, emerge with unusual clarity. No attempt is made to arrive at a consensus or point of view. Instead, the contributors are given free rein to express their views and organize their material as they see fit. Therefore, a stimulating and provocative book.

610 Daniel, Eleanor, John W. Wade, and Charles Gresham. *Introduction to Christian Education*. Cincinnati, OH: Standard Publishing Company, 1987.

Another solid and substantial guide to Christian education thought and practice from a conservative Protestant point of view. The book is organized in a most useful fashion (foundations, materials and methods, administration, and paraparochial concerns). Topics sometimes neglected, like the Christian school and Christian camping, are treated in helpful detail.

611 Davis, Billie. *Teaching to Meet Crisis Needs*. Springfield, MO: Gospel Publishing House, 1984.

Makes excellent use of both the resources of faith and the behavioral sciences to enable the ministries of the church (particularly the teaching ministry through the Sunday school) to deal sensitively and effectively with a variety of life crises: single parenting and blended families (resulting from remarriage); adolescence; midlife; illness; dying, death, and grief; work, unemployment, and money; and identity. Specific guidance is given to the teacher.

612 DeBenedittis, Suzanne M. *Teaching Faith and Morals: Toward Personal and Parish Renewal*. Minneapolis: Winston Press, 1981.

A plea for "holistic catechesis." Making good use of current research in moral and faith development and guided by the church's definitive documents, the author is explicit about education for faith, morals, virtues, and wholeness. Assumes mutual involvement of the whole individual and the community of faith.

613 DeGraaff, Arnold H. *The Educational Ministry of the Church*. Grand Rapids, MI: William B. Eerdmans Publishing Company, 1966.

A Dutch doctoral dissertation that reviews Christian education theory on both sides of the Atlantic. Reasserts the role of catechetics as the proper fulfillment of the church's educational responsibility, but cautiously opens the way for the use of educational insights of an extrabiblical character.

614 Del Prete, Thomas. *Thomas Merton and the Education of the Whole Person*. Birmingham, AL: Religious Education Press, 1990.

Thomas Merton's life and work become the reference point for thinking about the education of the whole person. Del Prete explores Merton's notion that education means "the formation of the whole person." The whole person focus and the concept of self-discovery, central to Merton's educational thought, are presented.

615 Di Chio, Vito. *Didaktik des Glaubens*. Zürich: Benziger Verlag, 1975.

A theory of adult religious education stemming from the need to relate the Christian faith to the social reality of the adult world. The author uses Tillich's method of correlation to establish the relationship. Two exemplary adult education programs are described and analyzed: "Chantier" in Quebec, and "Experiment Isolotto" in Florence.

616 Durka, Gloria, and Joanmarie Smith, eds. *Aesthetic Dimensions of Religious Education*. New York: Paulist Press, 1979.

The editors believe that "unless the process [of religious education] is aesthetic it is not education and it is certainly not religious." Sections on the aesthetic quality of spirituality, the arts themselves, worship and educating the aesthetic sensibility, and aesthetic theory. Maria Harris provides specifics. The rest of the contributors (artists, theologians, and religious educators--including Westerhoff, Thompson, Miller, Peatling, Moran, Slusser, and Loder, among others) provide raw materials for anyone working in the arts in religious education.

617 Durka, Gloria, and Joanmarie Smith. *Modeling God: Religious Education for Tomorrow*. New York: Paulist Press, 1976.

The term "philosophy of religious education" is thrown around loosely, but not in this book. Realism as a base for religious education is rejected in favor of a process philosophy of religion in which our way of perceiving is through the eyes of faith. The term, "modeling reality," is used to indicate how faith is the lens by which reality is seen by the religious person. The ultimate object of learning, the process of learning, and the process of teaching are then reinterpreted to involve the religious educator in this "processive model."

618   Dykstra, Craig. "Christian Education as a Means of Grace." *Princeton Seminary Bulletin* 13, no. 2 (1992):164-75.

An essay honoring Freda Gardner on her retirement from the faculty of Princeton Theological Seminary. The core of the essay is a retelling of Philip Haillie's *Lest Innocent Blood Be Shed: The Story of the Village of Le Chambon and How Goodness Happened There* as a case study of Christian education as a means of grace.

619   Dykstra, Craig. "The Formative Power of the Congregation." *Religious Education* 82 (1987):530-46.

Argues that the congregation in itself is not a strong mediator of the faith but is shot through with destructive cultural assumptions. Yet "in the midst of its sinfulness, rather than just apart from it, the congregation has power to mediate the gospel in [a way that] can restructure and transform human personal and social life." That power is worship, in which it can "acknowledge its participation in patterns of mutual self-destruction (confession), articulate its incapacity to secure itself (repentance), and recognize, proclaim, and celebrate the establishing and sustaining power which belongs to God alone (proclamation and prayer)."

620   Dykstra, Craig. *Vision and Character: A Christian Educator's Alternative to Kohlberg.* New York: Paulist Press, 1981.

After a thorough analysis of Kohlberg's "juridical ethics," which he finds not compatible with theological ethics and thus not of direct service to Christian education, Dykstra develops "visional ethics" as an alternative. Its dynamics are imagination and revelation, and its disciplines are repentance, prayer, and service. How the church may appropriate moral education is summed up in the model on page 121. See also 159, 338, 350, 356, 368, 386, and 504.

621   Dykstra, Craig, and Sharon Parks, eds. *Faith Development and Fowler.* Birmingham, AL: Religious Education Press, 1986.

Starting with an exposition of the theory by Fowler himself, the book moves to a series of evaluations by Dykstra, Fernhout, Broughton, and Harris. Three articles on enhancing the theory follow (Parks, McLean, and Nelson and Aleshire). Uses of faith development theory in ministry are explored by Lyon and Browning, Schneider, and Dykstra. Concludes with an exciting commentary by Fowler on his critics. See also 312, 357, 372, 374, 877, and 1152.

622   "Education and the Nature of Man." *Dimensions in Christian Education* 17, no. 8 (May 1968):9-15, 33-41.

A document from the Joint Study Commission on Education of the World Council of Churches. Concerned that in many countries educational theory has little relationship to religious ideas, twelve ecumenical educators met in 1965 and drew up this study paper. The paper attempts to address educational theory in terms of religious values, but in secular language, so far as possible. Concludes with six appendices, the last of which addresses the situation in explicitly biblical and theological terms.

623 Ernsberger, David J. *Education for Renewal*. Philadelphia: Westminster Press, 1965.

A complete rethinking of the educational work of the local church, from the point of view of training for the ministry of the laity. The clue is new forms of adult education, specifically "concern groups."

624 Esser, Wolfgang G. *Religionsunterricht*. Düsseldorf: Patmos Verlag, 1973.

Proposes a reorientation of religious education toward existential phenomenology. Explores the options of religious education as proclamation of the gospel, as transmissive and interpretative, and as problem oriented. The position espoused, however, is that religious education must probe the meaning of existence. Bultmann and Buber are used as bases for the position. Practical plans are suggested, and the responsibilities of school and church differentiated.

625 Evans, Alice Frazer, Robert A. Evans, and William Bean Kennedy. *Pedagogies of the Non-Poor*. Maryknoll, NY: Orbis Books, 1987.

The concern is for education that not only raises consciousness for the middle class but also develops actions to change oppressive structures. Eight existing programs for "education of the non-poor" are presented and discussed. Included are an interview with Paulo Freire, a theoretical article, and a set of educational guidelines.

626 Evenson, C. Richard, ed. *Foundations for Educational Ministry*. Philadelphia: Fortress Press, 1971.

Reflects the work of the Lutheran curriculum review, central to which is the restatement of a "central objective for educational ministry in the parish." Having formulated this central objective (the document appears as the appendix to the volume) those responsible have subjected it to thorough and rigorous analysis and criticism—theological, educational, and technical. Contributors and critics are staff members and outside specialists.

627 Fallaw, Wesner. *Church Education for Tomorrow*. Philadelphia: Westminster Press, 1960.

Recognizing that teaching is one of the church's most serious concerns, but maintaining that the church has not taken it seriously enough, Fallaw makes the radical proposal (for the church of tomorrow) that teaching be done by professional "pastor-teachers," trained clergy.

628 Foster, Charles R., ed. *Ethnicity in the Education of the Church*. Nashville: Scarritt
Graduate School, 1987.

Emphasizes the interplay of assumptions and expectations about the nature and
character of religious education indigenous to the various ethnic constituencies in
the church, in order to gain understandings, approaches, program, method, and
curriculum that grow out of their own ways of living, seeing, thinking, and
learning. Treats the experiences of Pacific Asian Americans, Blacks, Anglos, and
Mexican Americans and suggests an agenda for multicultural Christian religious
education.

629 Foster, Charles R. *Teaching in the Community of Faith*. Nashville: Abingdon Press,
1982.

The specific concern of this book is "the way we respond to the increasing loss
of status and place of the Christian community in our larger society." Its
suggestion is a new stance that stresses the transmissive function of the church
(since outside influences may no longer be counted on) at the same time that the
Christian community stays alert and responsive to changes in the world around it.
An emphasis on childlikeness is seen as the clue.

630 Frik, Helmut. *Evangelium und Gruppenpädagogik*. Stuttgart: Calwer Verlag, 1976.

Frik, a religious educator who is an astute theologian and psychologist, is not one
to be taken in by every new idea that floats by. His treatment of group method
in critical theological perspective is a model of the Christian educational theorist
developing a theology of relationships that is completely and normatively
Christian, and drawing sharp conclusions for religious education practice.

631 Gangel, Kenneth O., and Warren S. Benson. *Christian Education: Its History and
Philosophy*. Chicago: Moody Press, 1983.

A remarkably comprehensive history of ideas in Christian education, from Hebrew
and Greek roots to the present, orienting the reader to the major philosophers,
theorists, and constructive and critical practitioners in educational and church
history. The critical stance is a strict evangelicalism, applied with a view to
"authentic interaction."

632 Gilbert, W. Kent. *As Christians Teach*. Philadelphia: Lutheran Church Press, 1962.

A fine one-volume presentation of the curriculum theory and design developed by
the Lutheran Church in America as a basis for a new approach to Christian
education in their churches. This model stimulated other churches and will send
the reader back to the original documents that the book summarizes.

633 Giltner, Fern M., ed. *Women's Issues in Religious Education*. Birmingham, AL: Religious Education Press, 1985.

>   Eight women who are involved in religious education—from various confessions, most being lay professionals—were asked to write on issues of choice and importance to them in religious education. The result is a rich blend: some autobiographical, some professional, some on feminist issues, some on peace and violence, some dealing with institutional process.

634 Glen, J. Stanley. *The Recovery of the Teaching Ministry*. Philadelphia: Westminster Press, 1960.

>   A profoundly theological call for the release of the teaching ministry from its position of subordination in the church.

635 Graendorf, Werner C., ed. *Introduction to Biblical Christian Education*. Chicago: Moody Press, 1981.

>   An omnibus treatment of Christian education from conservative Protestant points of view. Thirty articles treat the biblical bases, issues of process, learner and teacher, the family, organization (including supervision, leadership training, and curriculum), the school (including the Christian school and college), and other perspectives (parachurch vocations, special education, urban Christian education, and Christian education and missions).

636 Grierson, Denham. *Transforming a People of God*. Melbourne: The Joint Board of Christian Education of Australia and New Zealand, 1984.

>   A penetrating study of the dynamics of education in the church, aimed at discovering the forms, shapes, and systems which sustain a faith community. The author's assumption about Christian education is that "it is the culture of the people as a faith community that must be transformed." Both theological and functional in its approach, the book provides a way of exploring congregational reconstruction and renewal as the key to vital parish education.

637 Groome, Thomas H. *Christian Religious Education: Sharing Our Story and Vision*. San Francisco: Harper and Row, 1980.

>   One of the great books in religious education. Groome presents his "shared praxis" model fully developed and in the richest possible context. A critical review of basic theory is informed by comprehensive historical, biblical, theological, philosophical, and educational materials.

638   Groome, Thomas H. *Sharing Faith: A Comprehensive Approach to Religious Education and Pastoral Ministry—The Way of Shared Praxis*. San Francisco: HarperSanFrancisco, 1991.

> This extensive work appears eleven years after the publication of *Christian Religious Education: Sharing Our Story and Vision* (637). The nature and purpose of Christian religious education, epistemology, and the dimensions and dynamics of being are discussed in part 1. Part 2 updates and expands Groome's earlier description of the five movements of shared praxis. Appendices offer specific illustrations and examples. The focus of Groome's interest is expanded to include liturgy and preaching, justice and peace, and pastoral counseling in part 3. In the fourth and concluding part, Groome shares his fourteen-article pedagogical creed.

639   Habermas, Ronald, and Issler Klaus. *Teaching for Reconciliation: Foundations and Practice of Christian Educational Ministry*. Grand Rapids, MI: Baker Book House, 1992.

> Written as a textbook for Christian education courses at the college and seminary level. Uses reconciliation as the central concept for organizing the foundations and practice of educational ministry. Foundations and practice represent the two major sections of the book. Reversing the common pattern, in part 2 the focus on teaching begins with adults and then moves to youth and children.

640   Halbfas, Hubertus. *Fundamentalkatechetik*. Stuttgart: Calwer Verlag, 1968.

> A treatment of the role of language and practical experience in religious education. The orientation is to German Catholic education, but the sources and interpretations are broadly ecumenical in character. A plan for religious education follows the more theoretical material.

641   Harper, F. Nile. "Social Power and the Limitations of Church Education." *Religious Education* 64 (1969):390-98.

> The church is called to educate for social justice but is limited in being able to do so. A carefully analytical definition of Christian education makes it clear that it is in the context of its servant role that the church must educate for its mission, including its mission of establishing social justice. But political power is lacking. Programs concentrate on children, and where adults are involved the materials do not include the means for involving persons in action around the issues. The needed focus is on disciplined action-reflection groups.

642   Harris, Maria. *Teaching and Religious Imagination*. San Francisco: Harper and Row, 1987.

> A book teachers will want to live with. In a profoundly theological way, Harris helps us stop, listen, and reflect, and in the process gain a vision of what our teaching can be and who we can be as teachers. Her chapters on Mary Tully as a teacher, and on her own teaching, give us models to which to aspire.

643 Heckman, Shirley J. *On the Wings of a Butterfly: A Guide to Total Christian Education*. Elgin, IL: Brethren Press, 1981.

A theory of Christian education, interlaced with much personal experience and many practical illustrations and exercises, developing what it means to be an educating community of faith and action. A good balance is maintained between education into the community and educating for freedom, creativity, and responsibility. Comes close to a whole Christian nurture.

644 Hill, Brennan R. *Key Dimensions of Religious Education*. Winona, MN: St. Mary's Press, 1988.

A fresh approach to the definition, understanding, and practice of religious education. Instead of setting religious education off as a discipline of its own, the author sees it encompassed by the larger aspects of religious and educational experience. He thus explores the "dimensions" of religion, faith, theology, educational theory, culture, freedom, spirituality, social justice, and the Scriptures for their implications for religious education. Generally, religious education is seen as an aspect of the liberation of the individual and society as life is lived within these dimensions. Some attention is paid to the role of directors of religious education, the role of teachers, the audiences for religious education, and the content of training for directors and teachers of religious education.

645 Hofinger, Johannes. *Evangelization and Catechesis*. New York: Paulist Press, 1976.

The "new catechetics" pioneered in relating Roman Catholic education to the needs, capacities, and experiences of the learner. Here one of its main proponents deals with the question of whether at the same time the nature of the gospel was not sufficiently understood and emphasized. Put in the context of evangelization, this has profound impact on Christian education.

646 Holley, Raymond. *Religious Education and Religious Understanding*. Boston: Routledge and Kegan Paul, 1978.

Based in a philosophical analysis of personhood, the author argues that "religiously educational situations are those which sensitize children to the mysteries of life and enable them to view the cosmos, and their place in it, in spiritual terms if they so wish." A basic differentiation is also made between the study of religion (which is about religion), and religious education (which is a matter of personal search, discovery, and decision). The milieu is the British school.

647 Huebner, Dwayne. "Christian Growth in Faith." *Religious Education* 81 (1986):511-21.

"We change—in form, structure, complexity, and relationships--with time and experience." Thus, we grow. But faith itself does not grow. "Rather it becomes more and more a part of the complex evolving structures that involve us in the rest of the universe." Faith does not replace other schema and structures of our being but infuses, transforms, and sanctifies them. This is an act of God's grace, a mystery to be acknowledged with thankfulness and to be acted upon faithfully.

648 Hug, James E., ed. *Tracing the Spirit: Communities, Social Action, and Theological Reflection*. New York: Paulist Press, 1983.

One of the most promising models of religious education is that of action/reflection. This book is a detailed analysis of the dynamics involved, based on actual instances of the model's use. "The focus is theological reflection on experience as it is (or can be) carried on in small communities of people engaged in the struggle for social justice." Linking social action and spirituality, the goal of such theological reflection "is pastoral and practical: it aims at transformation of social structures and institutions and at fuller personal integration and conversion."

649 Hull, John, ed. *New Directions in Religious Education*. Lewis, Sussex: The Palmer Press, 1987.

British religious education has entered a new period, which is characterized by its development as a virtually new educational subject. In it, religion is studied in depth as a human phenomenon that has doctrinal, literary, aesthetic, moral, and behavioral aspects. Its research base and varieties of rationale, curriculum, and method are here delineated. A situation of cultural pluralism is assumed.

650 Hunter, David R. *Christian Education as Engagement*. New York: Seabury Press, 1963.

A brief but major statement of Christian education theory by the then director of the Department of Christian Education of the Episcopal church. Hunter speaks as an individual but nevertheless provides deep insight into the principles and design of the Seabury Series. Engagement is the moment of God-human encounter, and thus the goal of Christian education at every level.

651 Johnson, Susanne. *Christian Spiritual Formation in the Church and Classroom*. Nashville: Abingdon Press, 1989.

Johnson brings biblical and theological perspectives to bear on the contemporary interest in spirituality. Concerned about the potential for narcissism in contemporary spirituality, Johnson links spirituality to the realm or reign of God. She focuses on the teaching ministry of the church: "The process of initiating persons into the Realm of God links the teaching office of the church with its office of spiritual direction."

652 Kelsey, Morton. *Can Christians Be Educated?* Mishawaka, IN: Religious Education Press, 1977.

The author brings rich experience as parish priest, Jungian psychologist, mystic, scholar, theologian, and graduate university professor to bear on the questions of religious education. Highly motivated by a successful experience in intensive religious education in his own parish, he moves on to deal with education in praying, love, and communication. Religious education is also seen as concerned with wholeness, with emotion and affect, and with one's world view.

653   Kennedy, William B. "Education for Liberation and Community." *Religious Education* 70 (1975):5-44.

In preparation for the 1975 Assembly of the World Council of Churches in Nairobi, the council's education unit reviewed its constitution and mandate and suggested new priorities. Looking back, it determined to "see education whole." Looking forward, it discerned great promise in the process of "conscientization." Dealing with representative statements from around the world, given here in detail, the priorities of education for liberation and community emerged, with radical implications for schools and churches.

654   Kennedy, William B. "Toward Reappraising Some Inherited Assumptions About Religious Education in the United States." *Religious Education* 76 (1981):467-81.

Cites and discusses nine assumptions about religious education that are considered to be faulty: (1) The ethos of U.S. society supports the general values and purposes of Jewish and Christian education. (2) The Christian faith is to become triumphant worldwide. (3) Written materials and literacy are central. (4) Religious education will continue to be supported by the sale of study materials. (5) Cognitive knowledge leads to action. (6) School is the sole or prime setting for religious education. (7) Schooling is normal and neutral. (8) Human development, personal or global, is progress in a straight-line sequence. (9) Learning is basically individualistic.

655   Koulomzin, Sophie. *Our Church Our Children*. Crestwood, NY: St. Vladimir's Seminary Press, 1975.

Fills a gap by providing an introduction to religious education in the Orthodox tradition. A strong plea for religious education partnership between the home and the church. Community and world are alien, so that the task is the formidable one of the shaping of Christian faith and practice where outside influence and support may not be counted on. A five-fold approach to the task is used to deal with the key issues of freedom and authority, individual and church, and the central tradition. Curriculum guidelines are developed in some detail along lines suggested by Ronald Goldman's work.

656   Kraybill, Donald B. *Mennonite Education*. Scottdale, PA: Herald Press, 1978.

Summarizes a series of research studies on Mennonite education and draws conclusions for the assessment of Mennonite schools. Part 1 is, in effect, a short treatise on how a researcher handles fallacious assumptions. Part 2 summarizes the data and findings of the studies. Part 3 discusses basic changes in the Mennonite situation and the consequent role of schooling.

160

Religious Education

657 Krych, Margaret A. *Teaching the Gospel Today*. Minneapolis: Augsburg Publishing House, 1987.

> Influenced by Tillich's theology and Loder's theories of the transformational process, Krych has written a basic theory of religious education combined with a practical introduction to teaching and learning method. She introduces and illustrates the central use of the transformational narrative as fundamental method.

658 LeBar, Lois E. *Focus on People in Church Education*. Westwood, NJ: Fleming H. Revell, 1968.

> The key to all Christian education planning is personal relationships. The book moves from theology to theory to practice in terms of this principle. Conservatively oriented, yet basically consistent with a concern for change and relevance. Detailed enough to be used as a guidebook.

659 Lee, James Michael. *The Content of Religious Instruction*. Birmingham, AL: Religious Education Press, 1985.

> The third of Lee's monumental trilogy, further developing his "social-science approach" to religious instruction. Content is interpreted broadly as all subject matter and experience that may be pertinent to religion. It is analyzed in terms of nine dimensions of experience, culminating in "life style content," defined as the overall pattern of a person's activities. Voluminous, closely argued, combative, and challenging—a permanent resource for religious education theory.

660 Lee, James Michael. *The Flow of Religious Instruction*. Dayton, OH: Pflaum/Standard, 1973.

> Lee has been carefully building a new "social-science" theory of religious education, and this is the second of three volumes in which it is fully developed. This volume propounds the thesis that "attention to and control of the teaching act together constitute the most direct and most practical way of improving the quality of religious instruction." Included is a set of generalized, effective pedagogical guidelines that (1) are derived both from the facts of learning and the facts of teaching, and (2) are anchored in sound theory of instruction.

661 Lee, James Michael. *The Shape of Religious Instruction*. Dayton, OH: Geo. A. Pflaum, Publisher, 1971.

> The first volume of Lee's trilogy. Pressing for a "social-science" approach to religious instruction, the attempt is "to work out the principles of formulation, methodology of study, scope of content, direction of activity, and evaluative-corrective norms [for religious instruction]—all within a broad framework of a systematized, taxonomic set of principles and procedures."

662 Liégé, André. "The Ministry of the Word: From Kerygma to Catechesis." *Lumen Vitae* 17 (1962):21-36.

The whole ministry of the word in the church is to be faithful, not only to the contents of revelation, but also to the forms of pedagogy used by God in manifesting himself in the history of salvation. Implications for catechesis: It flows from the gospel; it must unify the different aspects of the Christian mystery and preserve the organic balance of revelation; it creates a Christian community; it is dogmatic, moral, and liturgical; in its expression it must retain traditional Christian language, while creating a modern Christian vocabulary.

663 Lines, Timothy Arthur. *Systemic Religious Education.* Birmingham, AL: Religious Education Press, 1987.

Taking religion generically, a systemic perspective on religious education is proposed, in "an integrative, transdisciplinary, and dynamic venture that perceives religious education from a teleological viewpoint." The perspective "uses the organism as its primary metaphor, where interrelated and interdependent elements interact to create a dynamic and transforming whole." Sets a theoretical base from which program implications may emerge.

664 Little, Sara. *To Set One's Heart: Belief and Teaching in the Church.* Atlanta: John Knox Press, 1983.

Provides a balance to the emphasis on deschooling and the affective at the expense of the cognitive, by insisting on the basic function of thought—belief—in Christian teaching, set within the dynamics of Christian community. Five models of teaching are suggested for functional and selective use: information-processing, group interaction, indirect communication, personal development, and action/reflection.

665 May, Philip. *Which Way to Educate?* Chicago: Moody Press, 1975.

A seasoned British educator discusses ways in which the Christian faith may penetrate the whole educational enterprise as the Christian teacher participates in the determination of aims, approaches to the learner, the content of the curriculum, and other practical aspects of the matter. Roots everything in a Christian philosophy of education and carries it through to the teaching of morality and presence of the Christian teacher.

666 Mayr, Marlene, ed. *Does the Church Really Want Religious Education?* Birmingham, AL: Religious Education Press, 1988.

Well known and respected religious educators representing Roman Catholic, Eastern Orthodox, Lutheran, Episcopal, Presbyterian/Reformed, United Methodist, Southern Baptist, evangelical, and black protestant perspectives respond to the question asked by the book's title. Their answers could be summed up as, Yes, churches *do* want religious education, but are either unwilling to pay the price or want a religious education that is different from that deemed desirable by a particular respondent.

667   Mayr, Marlene, ed. *Modern Masters of Religious Education*. Birmingham, AL: Religious Education Press, 1983.

Having been asked to recount the persons, events, and ideas that most shaped their thinking, twelve leaders in religious education—a wide span of Roman Catholics and Protestants—provide what amount to intellectual autobiographies. The result is a series of very personal statements that give decisive clues to why religious education is what it is today, and where it is going.

668   McBride, Alfred. *Heschel: Religious Educator*. Denville, NJ: Dimension Books, 1973.

An all too brief study of the great Jewish educator, Abraham Heschel. His life is outlined, and his rootage in and use of the Talmud is developed. The heart of the book is an exposition of his "transcendental themes," which are then explored for their religious education values. An appendix gives one of Heschel's best known addresses on religious education.

669   McKenzie, Leon. *The Religious Education of Adults*. Birmingham, AL: Religious Education Press, 1982.

A good example of the ways in which the science of education and its supporting research may inform both theory and practice in the religious education of adults. Takes a negative attitude toward present church practice and separates the roles of theological and educational insights in determining content and process.

670   Miller, Donald E. *Story and Context: An Introduction to Christian Education*. Nashville: Abingdon Press, 1987.

Using the model of the faith community as teacher, the author deals with the structure of Christian education and the way its issues—revelation and instructional content; growth, maturation, and conversion; common faith and public responsibility; and the support and renewal of the religious community—are being discussed. The context is the community of faith, locally and broadly defined. The story is our stories and the Christian story.

671   Miller, Donald E. *The Wing-Footed Wanderer: Conscience and Transcendence*. Nashville: Abingdon Press, 1977.

An exciting book that will help the religious educator, through Freud, Erikson, Piaget, Kohlberg, and others, to a Christian view of conscience, moral development, and moral education. A phenomenological analysis is followed by a confessional treatment in which awareness is transformed into God's presence, actuality into God's creativity, intentionality into God's Spirit, and conscience into God's righteousness.

672 Miller, Randolph Crump. *Christian Nurture and the Church*. New York: Charles Scribner's Sons, 1961.

A sequel to *The Clue to Christian Education* (1950) and *Biblical Theology and Christian Education* (1956), this volume deals with the theology of the church and its implications for parish life, especially the educational functions of instruction and nurture. The emphasis is on the dynamics of nurture in the communities of church and family through the person's entire life-span.

673 Miller, Randolph Crump. *Education for Christian Living*. Englewood Cliffs, NJ: Prentice-Hall, 1963.

The second edition of Miller's full-scale treatment of all the major concerns of Christian education: principles, Christian education agencies, methods, and administration. Especially valuable bibliographies and suggestions for further reading.

674 Miller, Randolph Crump. *The Language Gap and God*. Philadelphia: Pilgrim Press, 1970.

A serious attempt to develop the implications of analytic philosophy and language analysis for religious education. Primary attention is paid to Ramsey, Bushnell, Drinkwater, and Evans, with secondary attention to van Buren, Whitehead, Belth, and Peters. Specific implications for religious education are drawn in each chapter. See also 63, 136, 153, 163, 173, and 674.

675 Miller, Randolph Crump. *The Theory of Religious Education Practice*. Birmingham, AL: Religious Education Press, 1980.

Miller explores the meaning and implications of process theology for religious education in the fabric of his life's thought. He thus develops his testament as a religious educator who is concerned with practice that is fully informed by theory, as well as thoroughly theological in character. See also 82, 141, and 158.

676 Montessori, Maria. E.M. Standing, ed. *The Child in the Church*. St. Paul, MN: Catechetical Guild, 1965.

A revised and greatly augmented version of Montessori's basic treatment of religious education. Seeing childhood as having an integrity of its own, and with the conviction that the child has a close feeling for God, the approach to religious education is highly catechetical, liturgical, and sacramental. Like all Montessori methods, the approach is extremely practical, centering on "hands on" experience. See also 297, 591.

677   Moore, Allen H., ed. *Religious Education as Social Transformation*. Birmingham, AL: Religious Education Press, 1989.

>   An effort to introduce a new generation of religious educators to the social dimension of religious education.   Family, gender, politics, work, and environment are among the critical contexts in which the authors explore social transformation and religious education. Authors include: Charles R. Foster, Mary Elizabeth Moore, and James M. Wall.

678   Moore, Mary Elizabeth. *Education for Continuity and Change: A New Model for Christian Religious Education*. Nashville: Abingdon Press, 1981.

>   The model proposed is called a "traditioning model," and it "maximizes persons' connectedness with the past so that transformations taking place in their life will be rooted and will be all the richer," at the same time that it "maximizes persons' changing so that their connectedness with the past will help them live in the changing world and with God's call forward."

679   Moran, Gabriel. *Design for Religion: Toward Ecumenical Education*. New York: Herder and Herder, 1970.

>   Incisive thinking on theology and education, leading to the conclusion that traditional religious education has actually lacked the essential religious quality, and that henceforth it must be set firmly in an ecumenical framework—that is, with a concern for all that is human.

680 Moran, Gabriel. *Education Toward Adulthood: Religion and Lifelong Learning*. New York: Paulist Press, 1979.

>   Moran is very particular about his use of language, finding clues to practice in the exact use of terms and value in naming the as yet unnamed processes of ordinary experience.   From a discriminating definition of adulthood he moves to a "laboratory" model of adult education. Corresponding insights on the family/community and on learning are developed. He concludes by weighing the pros and cons of professional leadership.

681 Moran, Gabriel. *Interplay: A Theory of Religion and Education*. Winona, MN: St. Mary's Press, 1981.

>   Moran is concerned for a religious education that is ecumenical in the most extended sense and that is committed to the emergence of new dimensions in education. "Religious education may be defined as the attempt to keep education open to the undreamt possibilities of the human race."   Dimensions like professionalization, adult education, moral education, and religious education for justice are examined.

682 Moran, Gabriel. *No Ladder to the Sky: Education and Morality*. San Francisco: Harper and Row, 1987.

> A challenge to the images—mainly hierarchical and developmental—that have governed our understandings of the moral life. Broadening the concept of morality to include religion, and of education to make it more than schooling, Moran's thesis is that morality is, far from being static, a product of a process that is essentially educational.

683 Moran, Gabriel. *Religious Education as a Second Language*. Birmingham, AL: Religious Education Press, 1989.

> Written as an "invitation" to those who teach in churches and in schools, this book challenges assumptions and questions conventional wisdom about religion and education. Moran argues that religious education has the characteristics of a language people learn after they have learned their native language. He views learning this second language as crucial to world peace.

684 Moran, Gabriel. *Religious Education Development*. Minneapolis: Winston Press, 1981.

> Using his characteristic method of intricate linguistic analysis, Moran gives us two things--a critique of current developmentalists and a constructive theory of religious development. His alternative to Piaget and Kohlberg is "the ethic of virtue/care/character/community." His alternative to Fowler is a three-stage religious development: the simply religious, acquiring a religion, and the religiously Christian, which for religious educational purposes he correlates with the six educational stages.

685 Moran, Gabriel. *Vision and Tactics: Toward an Adult Church*. New York: Herder and Herder, 1968.

> Moran is convinced that the aim of religious education is that persons shall grow up into Christ. This is the theological vision from which might come the concrete steps (tactics) to initiate change that might take a generation to accomplish. The implication is priority to adult education.

686 Myers, William R. "Youth Between Culture and Church" *Theology Today* 47 (1990-91):400-409.

> Traces the history of the emergence of adolescence in North American culture and shows how cultural values became virtually synonymous with Christian values. Argues that the church, like the culture, has abandoned its youth: "Most youth ministry handbooks read like cultural handbooks for middle-class survival instead of books concerned with youth ministry." Calls the church to a reassessment of the faith story and the cultural context in the effort to recover the bedrock of youth ministry. See also 717, 867, 896, 930, 981, 1014, 1032, and 1049.

687 Nebreda, Alfonso M. *Kerygma in Crisis?* Chicago: Loyola University Press, 1965.

In reestablishing dialogue with the modern world, the major difficulties and objectives of the church's mission are brought into focus by the problem of pre-evangelization (a stage of preparation for the kerygma that, taking humans as they are and where they are, makes a human dialogue possible and awakens in them the sense of God). The three stages that normally characterize the journey of an adult to faith are pre-evangelization, kerygma (evangelization, the dynamic heralding of the substance of the Christian message, having as its goals personal conversion or initial acceptance of Christ as the Lord), and catechesis proper, which systematically develops the message, initiating humans into Christian life and building within them Christian personalities.

688 Nelson, C. Ellis, ed. *Congregations: Their Power to Form and Transform*. Atlanta: John Knox Press, 1988.

Why people congregate, fostering the growth of vision and energy in a congregation, the role of meditation in the life of a congregation, *paideia* and leadership, informal conversation, and the call to teach are among the topics covered. Maria Harris, Charles Foster, Janet Fishburn, Donald Miller, David Steward, and Mary Elizabeth Moore are among the authors.

689 Nelson, C. Ellis. *How Faith Matures*. Louisville, KY: Westminster/John Knox Press, 1989.

This "essay in practical theology" offers in part 1 a critical assessment of contemporary North American culture and its influence on religious experience. In part 2, it presents a biblical model of experience. In part 3, implications for Christian education in the congregation are drawn.

690 Nelson, C. Ellis. *Where Faith Begins*. Richmond, VA: John Knox Press, 1967.

Faith is a thing that happens in persons; it has priority over the various means by which it is communicated. But its communication (as its biblical inception was also) is within a community of Christian experience. In practical terms this is the congregation, which as a community of faith uses processes of socialization and instruction to recreate the faith experience in the persons of the new generation. A final chapter supplies practical guidelines.

691 Neville, Gwen Kennedy, and John H. Westerhoff, III. *Learning Through Liturgy*. New York: Seabury Press, 1978.

A fitting sequel to *Generation to Generation*. In part 1, Neville continues her reports of anthropological research into ritual and its role in developing and sustaining the religious life. In part 2, Westerhoff explores the dynamics of liturgy in relation to catechesis, the development of the life of the spirit, Christian initiation, and Christian identity.

692 Nipkow, Karl Ernst. "Education's Responsibility for Morality and Faith in a Rapidly Changing World." *Religious Education* 80 (1985):195-214.

Since responsibility for young people is the primary concern of education, it is of vital importance that youth are experiencing basic changes in values. These changes provide a frame of reference for education. In this light, moral education has to be education for peace, realized through action for justice, peace and justice being the two most lasting Christian social values. Biblical realism prevents us from adopting an unrealistic historical optimism in the process, but also makes possible a deep trust in the way of the future.

693 O'Hare, Padraic, ed. *Education for Peace and Justice.* San Francisco: Harper and Row, 1983.

Most considerations of peace and justice are political and lack educational perspective. This exceptionally well thought out and tightly integrated book reverses the emphasis, grappling with the issues foundationally, educationally, and in relation to other functions of ministry. Justice is not only an issue of the church in the world, but also of the church in relation to itself. Distinguished contributions here come from men and women, and from representatives of various ethnic groups.

694 O'Hare, Padraic. *The Way of Faithfulness: Contemplation and Formation in the Church.* Valley Forge, PA: Trinity Press International, 1993.

An integrative understanding of faithfulness, education, religious community, and contemplation frames O'Hare's proposal to link formation in the church with contemplation. He draws on Christian traditions, as well as Jewish, Taoist, and Buddhist sources; the works of Gabriel Moran and Gustavo Gutierrez; and the ideas and insights of religious educators such as Maria Harris, Parker Palmer, and Craig Dykstra. Having explored contemplation, faithfulness, and religious education in the first three chapters, O'Hare turns to sketching a vision for practice in the context of work, home, and church in the remaining three chapters.

695 Osmer, Richard Robert. *A Teachable Spirit: Recovering the Teaching Office in the Church.* Louisville, KY: Westminster/John Knox Press, 1990.

Seeing the reestablishment of a "vital teaching ministry" as a critical task for mainline Protestant churches, Osmer first analyzes the present state of mainline Protestant denominations .and their North American cultural context. He then examines the teaching office found in Calvin and Luther and in the *magisterium* of the Roman Catholic tradition. Finally, he describes what the three functions of the teaching office—transmission, reinterpretation, and educational institutionalization—mean for seminaries, congregations, and denominational boards and agencies.

696   Pazmiño, Robert W. *Principles and Practices of Christian Education: An Evangelical Perspective*. Grand Rapids, MI: Baker Book House, 1992.

In this sequel to *Foundational Issues in Christian Education* (517), Pazmiño seeks to provide an evangelical philosophy of Christian education. Central elements include two forms and two complementary principles. The two forms are the "educational trinity" of content, persons, and context and the five tasks of proclamation, community, service, advocacy, and worship. Conversion and connection are the complementary principles.

697 Pietri, Charles, ed. *Transmettre la Foi, La Catéchèse dans l'Eglise*. Paris: Editions Beauchesne, 1980.

An edition of the Parisian journal devoted to catechetics. Four studies deal with the history of catechetics; four explore various influences and options; three look at catechetics in the school, the Soviet Union, and Poland; the issue concludes with four case studies. Few innovative stirrings have been heard from France. This volume seems to break open the possibilities of change.

698 Pilch, Judah, and Meir Ben-Horin, eds. *Judaism and the Jewish School*. New York: Bloch, 1966.

A comprehensive reference volume on the variety of viewpoints in Jewish education, intended to clarify the basis for the reformulation of aims for Jewish schools and other educational enterprises. "The essays collected here reflect the whole range of Jewish educational thought and seek to clarify the implications for Jewish education of the varieties in outlook on Jewish existence. They represent the wide diversity of views from Jewish orthodoxy to reform and to secularism, from activity programs to subject-matter methodology."

699 Piveteau, Didier-Jacques, and J.T. Dillon. *Resurgence of Religious Instruction*. Notre Dame, IN: Religious Education Press, 1977.

Part 1 traces the path of religious education's development, 1955-75, in critical detail. Part 2 assesses the situation as "change-in-process" and makes this concrete in the understanding of humanity, God, alternatives to schooling, and ways of teaching. Part 3 sees the promise of the future as emphasis on "persons-in-community," with special focus on family, the world around, crises of change, and the faith community.

700 Preiswerk, Matias. *Educating in the Living Word: A Theoretical Framework for Christian Education*. Maryknoll, NY: Orbis Books, 1987.

A small but significant book. Christian education theory is first analyzed comparatively (on a grid, one axis of which is economic, philosophical, political, theological, and pedagogical; the other axis being spiritualistic, liberative, and liberal Christian education), then historically. A final section deals with "the marks of a liberative Christian education," laying out the chief implications of a liberative approach for education.

701 Price, Elizabeth Box, and Charles F. Foster, eds. *By What Authority: A Conversation on Teaching Among United Methodists*. Nashville: Abingdon Press, 1991.

Eight chapters constitute this volume. Price introduces the conversation in the first chapter. A historical context is provided by Richard Robert Osmer (Luther and Calvin) and Thomas A. Langford (a Wesleyan perspective) in chapters two and three. Robin Maas and Mary Elizabeth Mullino Moore discuss scripture and theology as guidelines for the conversation on teaching (chaps. 4 and 5). Cross cultural contexts (Joseph V. Crockett), a feminist paradigm (Nelle G. Slater), and educational insights (Allen J. Moore) are the subjects of the last three chapters which are grouped under the heading, "Voices That Need to Be Heard."

702 Roloff, Marvin L. ed. *Education for Christian Living*. Minneapolis: Augsburg Publishing House, 1987.

One of the values of this introductory book is that the issues with which it deals (and thus the way it is structured) match the questions that most religious educators in congregations are facing. With a good mixture of foundational material (historical, theological, and behavioral), theory (considerations of basic objectives and principles), and practice (method, curriculum, and administration), it is a dependable and resourceful guide.

703 Rolston, Holmes. *The Bible in Christian Teaching*. Richmond, VA: John Knox Press, 1962.

A simple and clear presentation of an approach to the study of the Bible which recognizes its basic character as witness to the revelation event. Critical problems are discussed and principles of interpretation suggested. The emphasis is on biblical education through personal and corporate involvement, and a curriculum that views all experience in the perspective of the Word of God. Concludes with an analysis of settings and methods for Bible study.

704 Rood, Wayne R. *Understanding Christian Education*. Nashville: Abingdon Press, 1970.

A splendid addition to the major literature in Christian education theory. Organizes a wealth of historical, philosophical, and theological material around four key figures: Horace Bushnell, John Dewey, George Albert Coe, and Maria Montessori. A concluding chapter spells out the author's own position analytically, critically, and comparatively.

705 Rummery, R.M. *Catechesis and Religious Education in a Pluralistic Society*. Huntington, IN: Our Sunday Visitor, 1976.

Specifically British and Roman Catholic, but ecumenical in import. Sees religious education (1930-70) as having developed through traditional, pedagogical, kerygmatic, life-centered and situational, and group-centered stages, to the point where "education of [the] faith" is appropriately called for. At the same time, pluralism forces a choice among "teaching that, educating in, teaching how, and teaching about," which also points to the need for "education of [the] faith," which is "growth in faith leading to further knowledge and love of God, and ratification of personal faith as a life-task."

706   Russell, Letty M. "Changing My Mind About Religious Education." *Religious Education*: 79 (1984):5-10.

In an autobiographical reflection, Letty Russell ponders the continuities and changes in her thought and practice of Christian education. She sees education as "a process of actualizing and modifying the development of the total person through dialogical relationships." Her roots are in the Reformed tradition; her starting point is biblical and christological. Elements that have entered into the dialogue to effect change are an emerging feminist consciousness and critique, and the openness of liberation themes and action.

707   Russell, Letty M. *Christian Education in Mission*. Philadelphia: Westminster Press, 1967.

The educational minister of the East Harlem Protestant Parish puts the emphasis in Christian education back where it belongs—in the nurturing power of every aspect of the worship and work of the witnessing community. Strongly theoretical (biblically and theologically) and richly practical (stemming from fourteen years of experimental educational ministry).

708   Schipani, Daniel S. *Conscientization and Creativity: Paulo Freire and Christian Education*. Lanham, MD: University Press of America, 1984.

Schipani here establishes himself as a major voice in Christian education, and one of the few able to deal with the discipline internationally. His close examination of the thought and work of Paulo Freire reveals its affinity for and need of the creative process, and links it, after critical theological analysis, with the central doctrine of the kingdom of God. This provides the basis for developing a full theory of Christian education whose implications are rooted in, but also transcend, cultural differences. See also 152, 160, 541, 710, and 728.

709   Schipani, Daniel S. *El reino de Dios y el ministerio educativo de la iglesia*. San José, Costa Rica and Miami: Editorial Caribe, 1983.

Closely paralleling his *Conscientization and Creativity*, Schipani makes his theory and practical ideas on Christian education available in Spanish. The fundamental elements are human development, conscientization, and creativity, critically appropriated through his theology of the kingdom of God.

710   Schipani, Daniel S. *Religious Education Encounters Liberation Theology*. Birmingham, AL: Religious Education Press, 1988.

Schipani begins with a thorough discussion of Paulo Friere's work. He then explores in each of the four succeeding chapters one of the major areas in which religious education and liberation theology challenge one another: "Prophetic and

Utopian Vision," "Praxis Way of Knowing," "Faith Seeking Understanding," and "The Oppressed and the Base Community." See also 160, 541, 708, and 728.

711 Schonherr, D. Albrecht. "The Evangelical Church as a Learning Community in a Changing World." *Religious Education* 78 (1983):398-412.

The author reflects on the changes in thought, institutions, and action that have resulted from the challenge to Christian faithfulness the church has faced in East Germany under the Communist regime. In the process he sees the church as a community being forced to find new ways of faithfulness, and he interprets this experience as a process of corporate Christian learning.

712 Seymour, Jack L., Margaret Ann Crain, and Joseph V. Crockett. *Educating Christians: The Intersection of Meaning, Learning, and Vocation.* Nashville: Abingdon Press, 1993.

Examples drawn from Christian communities and exercises inviting personal reflection by the reader make this book very concrete and very practical. Three key words in the subtitle frame the three major parts of the book: "Meaning and Faith," "Educating Toward Vocation," and "Christian Education." The authors hold that "religious education begins with the basic human need to make meaning."

713 Seymour, Jack L., and Donald E. Miller, eds. *Contemporary Approaches to Christian Education.* Nashville: Abingdon Press, 1982.

A serious and detailed assessment of the state of Christian education theory. The options explored are religious instruction, nurture in the faith community, spiritual development (working through Piaget, Kohlberg, and Fowler), a liberation approach that takes account of the North American situation, and a hermeneutic approach that roots in narrative and involves the dialectic of self with tradition and community.

714 Seymour, Jack L., Robert T. O'Gorman, and Charles R. Foster. *The Church and the Education of the Public: Refocusing the Task of Religious Education.* Nashville: Abingdon Press, 1984.

Reminds the church and religious educators of their neglected role in relation to public education. While a historical review makes clear that the stance of previous years cannot be regained, the task remains. Education does not fulfill its own ends without achieving a religious level of experience and responsibility that involves deep commitment to shared values on the part of the public.

715 Shapiro, Alexander M., and Burton I. Cohen, eds. *Studies in Jewish Education and Judaica in Honor of Louis Newman.* New York: KTAV Publishing House, 1984.

A *festschrift* providing significant glimpses of Jewish education in America. Newman was influential in camping (Ramah), schooling (the Akiba Academy), practice-oriented research (the Melton Research Center), and in regional supervision (the Boston Bureau of Jewish Education), in all of which his major concerns were reflected: a total Jewish education involving the whole child and the whole community, a focus on the growth of the individual, and an insistence on the priority of moral responsibility. Short writings of his are included.

716 *Sharing the Light of Faith: National Catechetical Directory for Catholics in the United States*. Washington, DC: United States Catholic Conference, 1979.

The official text of the *National Catechetical Directory*. Against the background of cultural and theological factors, catechesis and the catechetical ministry are set forth; the essential Christian message analyzed; and catechetics for a worshiping community, for social ministry, and toward maturity in faith developed in some detail. Concludes with a treatment of personnel, organization, and resources.

717 Shelton, Charles M. *Adolescent Spirituality: Pastoral Ministry for High School and College Youth*. Chicago: Loyola University Press, 1983.

Foundational and practical but not programmatic, this book works from the thesis that "the adolescent's response to Jesus' call is inextricably tied to the beckoning of grace as it is experienced at his or her developmental level and in the context of his or her own life experience." Three foundations are used: Ignatius of Loyola, the developmentalists (from Piaget to Fowler), and the demand of pastoral ministry to youth. The dominant themes are spirituality, morality, and maturity. See also 341, 686, 867, 896, 930, 981, 1014, 1032, 1049, and 1169.

718 Shinn, Roger L. *The Educational Mission of Our Church*. Philadelphia: United Church Press, 1962.

Presents the basic principles and plans of the new curriculum of the United Church of Christ, as seen by a professor of applied Christianity who was closely associated with the development of that curriculum. Reflecting basic theological concern, forthright explanation is made of the detailed decisions made at various steps in the curriculum's development.

719 Sisemore, John T., ed. *The Ministry of Religious Education*. Nashville: Broadman Press, 1978.

Carefully planned as a representative, though not official, account of Southern Baptist religious education (church education), this book includes treatments of foundations (biblical, theological, learning theory, teaching), programs (Bible teaching, church training, missions, and music), and vocational roles (the various educational ministries). It reflects the deepening and professionalization of religious education thought and practice in the denomination. Contributors are professors, denominational executives, and local practitioners.

720 Snyder, Ross L. *A Church as a Learning Community*. Boston: Division of Christian Education, United Church of Christ, 1962.

Explores: (1) the internal dynamics of a congregation as a caring fellowship that embodies and develops truth, (2) the nature of ministry that takes seriously its corporate responsibility to history and to the future, (3) a style of life for the church with focus on expectant and functional learning, and (4) the deepening of that learning so that it transforms the individual and infuses the life of the faith community.

721 Snyder, Ross L. *On Becoming Human*. Nashville: Abingdon Press, 1967.

An exploratory book, designed to help people interpret themselves in their world in terms of basic meaning and direction. At the same time the book reveals the author's existential-phenomenological approach to Christian education, one of the most important types of theoretical stance available to the religious educator.

722 Sparkman, G. Temp. *The Salvation and Nurture of the Child of God*. Valley Forge, PA: Judson Press, 1981.

Emulating Rousseau's Emile and Pestalozzi's Leonard and Gertrude, Sparkman tells the story of the salvation and nurture of Emma as she moves from infancy to adulthood (a cumulative process of sonship-daughtership, belonging, affirmation, and creative trusteeship). An introductory chapter summarizes the theory of salvation and nurture and its theological, educational, and behavioral foundations. Extensive appendices detail the critical material upon which the theory rests.

723 Stewart, Donald Gordon. *Christian Education and Evangelism*. Philadelphia: Westminster Press, 1963.

Defines evangelism as the decisive communication of the gospel against the background of the ethical demands of the complete social environment. Makes the point that education, in its nurturing and teaching functions directed toward the person's maturation and attainment of reverence and discipleship, is integral to the attainment of evangelism's goal with both children and adults. Gives the minister a key role in maintaining the evangelistic integrity of the teaching ministry. Proclamation "must proceed in an educational context." Sustains keen dialogue with the most active theological minds of the time.

724 Stinnette, Charles R., Jr. *Learning in Theological Perspective*. New York: Association Press, 1965.

"If Christ is to be formed in us, the task requires an openness to change—an openness which is sustained only through membership in an enabling community. The inevitable shock of recognition attendant upon learning requires both a means of participation (ego-involvement) and a social matrix in which threat is reduced and one is able to try out new ways of behaving. The task of critical self-analysis and prophetic renewal is sustained only by membership in an abiding community of values...a prophetic community which in its life and action raises up a bold witness to the power of God to transform every human predicament."

725 Sturm, Wilhelm. *Religionsunterricht Gestern, Heute, Morgen.* Stuttgart: Calwer Verlag, 1971.

At the time of its publication probably the best available comprehensive review and assessment of religious education thought in Germany. Contains systematic treatments of the leading theorists and places them within the total context of the discussion.

726 Sutcliffe, John M. *Learning Community.* Nutfield, Surrey: Denholm House Press, 1974.

A popular version of the report of the Consultation on Evaluating the Sunday School Contribution to Church Education in Europe Today (1973). Indeterminate so far as the future of the Sunday school is concerned (there seems to be a good deal of vitality there still), the report suggests alternatives for Sunday and weekdays, but in the main maintains that church education is "a subtle combination of education and a sense of security created by the loving, understanding relationships experienced within the community which point to the love of God, to set people free." See also 760 and 838.

727 "Symposium: Religious Education: A Jewish Perspective." *Religious Education* 78 (1983):153-216.

Articles include: "Reform Judaism and the Day Schools: The Great Historical Dilemma" (Daniel Syme), "Jewish Schools and American Society" (Michael Zeldin), "Curriculum, Philosophy of Education and the Jewish Religious School" (Samuel Joseph), "The Jewish Identity of Confirmation: Problem and Proposal" (Steven Sager), and "Jewish Education and Dying" (Elliot Salo Schoenberg).

728 "Symposium: Religious Education in Latin America." *Religious Education* 66 (1971):403-41.

Articles include: "New Theological Perspectives" (José Miguez Bonino, response by Paul Verghese), "Education as an Idol" (Ivan Illich), "The Thought of the Church and the Future of Catholic Education in Latin America" (Patricio Cariola), "Some Notes on Parish Education in Latin America" (Federico J. Pagura), "Education for Liberation: Conscientization in Comerio" (Clifford J. Wright), "New Educational Perspectives" (Birgit Rodhe), with the "Message to the Churches from the World Council of Christian Education Assembly, at Haumpani, Peru, July 14-21, 1971." See also 160, 541, 708, and 710.

729 Taylor, Marvin J., ed. *Religious Education: A Comprehensive Survey.* Nashville: Abingdon Press, 1960.

> A compendium, by forty authors, of information and outlook on religious education's major concerns: principles; program, materials, and methods; administration; and agencies and organizations. Contains an extremely valuable bibliography. [Marvin Taylor's subsequent volumes, all published by the Abingdon Press, updated the treatment of the field periodically: *An Introduction to Christian Education* (1966), *Foundations for Christian Education in an Era of Change* (1976), and *Changing Patterns of Religious Education* (1984).]

730 Warford, Malcolm L. *The Necessary Illusion: Church Culture and Educational Change.* Philadelphia: Pilgrim Press, 1976.

> New hope for education in the conscienticised congregation. The liberated congregation is the basis for the liberation of the individual, and the transcendence required for such liberation is expressed in a myth of integrity and transformation rooted in an incarnational theology. Christian education's task is the rediscovery and communication of the radical gospel, and the critique of everyday life in terms of that gospel.

731 Warren, Michael. *Faith, Culture, and the Worshiping Community.* New York: Paulist Press, 1989.

> A collection of ten essays held together by a concern for the integrity of a gospel-based way of life in the midst of a consumeristic culture. Titles include "Religious Formation in the Context of Social Formation," "Liturgy and Catechesis as Counter-Cultural," and "Catechesis and the Problems of 'Popular' Culture."

732 Warren, Michael, ed. *Source Book for Modern Catechetics.* Winona, MN: St. Mary's Press, 1983.

> A meaty compilation of texts and articles intended to provide historical, theoretical, and practical orientation for the catechetical function. The focus is on Roman Catholic thought and practice, but Protestant and Jewish perspectives are included. Serves the religious educator with information essential for a clear sense of roots, identity, and purpose.

733 Westerhoff, John H., III. *Bringing up Children in the Christian Faith.* Minneapolis: Winston Press, 1980.

> A quick survey-theological, psychological, historical, and functional--of stages of faith learning in the context of parents' responsibilities and opportunities. Chapters trace the faith journey through childhood, youth, and adulthood.

734 Westerhoff, John H., III. *Building God's People in a Materialistic Society*. New York: Seabury Press, 1983.

> In this thoroughly developed treatment, Westerhoff offers "an introduction to practical theology by focusing on the catechetical dimension as it is related to the liturgical, moral, spiritual, and pastoral aspects of ministry." Its focus is on "an understanding of stewardship as a useful theological perspective from which to reflect on our communal life in church and society in the light of the Christian story."

735 Westerhoff, John H., III. *Living the Faith Community*. San Francisco: Harper and Row, 1985.

> Westerhoff explores and expands his concept of Christian education as catechesis, a vital nurturing function of the church as a faith community. "Catechesis is comprised of two interrelated processes: formation and education....Catechesis as formation inducts persons into the church and its story. Catechesis as education aids persons in making the community's faith more living, conscious, and active in their lives."

736 Westerhoff, John H., III. *Tomorrow's Church*. Waco, TX: Word Books, 1976.

> "Christian education has to unite concerns for tradition, persons, and society, with concerns about how people think, feel, and act. God's Word must be known, understood, lived, and acted upon....Our educational goal is best expressed as enabling groups of persons to do God's Word....A worshiping, learning, caring, witnessing community of faith, memory, hope, and power is affirmed as basic to the learning process." Four chapters on Christian education's foundations, and one on theory, containing a plan for leader training.

737 Westerhoff, John H., III. *Values for Tomorrow's Children*. Philadelphia: Pilgrim Press, 1970.

> An exciting and challenging book for religious educators, evaluating past and present plans and performance and presenting vigorous alternatives for the future. Westerhoff knows and appreciates what has gone into the religious education tradition and program in the past and seeks a correspondingly new vitality for the future of the enterprise.

738 Westerhoff, John H., III, ed. *Who Are We? The Quest for a Religious Education*. Birmingham, AL: Religious Education Press, 1978.

> A reader consisting of twenty-one articles, twenty of them drawn from the publications of the Religious Education Association, particularly from its journal, *Religious Education*, from 1903 to 1974, arranged in chronological order. The editor provides an introduction, prefatory interpretations of each article, and a conclusion (in which he calls for four concurrent emphases: religious education, Christian or Jewish education, church or synagogue education, and

catechesis—with greatest weight given to the last). A meaty and illuminating contribution to the history of ideas in the field.

739 Westerhoff, John H., III. *Will Our Children Have Faith?* New York: Seabury Press, 1976.

Proposes "a community of faith-enculturation paradigm" as a substitute for the schooling-instructional paradigm of the past in religious education. Sinking his roots deeply in religious education history and theory, Westerhoff sees this alternative as demonstrably effective in providing education in biblical faith, in the church as a community with a meaningful history and relevant present, and in a personal faith that is doctrinally and theologically informed and mature.

740 Westerhoff, John H., III, and Gwen Kennedy Neville. *Generation to Generation*. Philadelphia: Pilgrim Press, 1974.

An anthropologist and a religious educator team up to deal with religious socialization and its implications for religious education. The book is cast in a dialogical form, and consists of a variety of materials put together to provide data upon which the reader may base further investigations and judgments. The two main sections of the book deal with the dynamics of religion, cultures, and education and with the processes of their interaction through the life-cycle.

741 Wickett, R. E. Y. *Models of Adult Religious Education Practice*. Birmingham, AL: Religious Education Press, 1991.

Canadian religious educator R.E.Y. Wickett offers practitioners in the field of adult religious education a helpful survey of relevant models for use in their work. He surveys both the traditional andragogical model of Malcolm Knowles and alternatives such as self-directed, small group, and intergenerational models. See also 762, 770, 795, 798, and 811.

742 Wilhoit, Jim. *Christian Education and the Search for Meaning*. Grand Rapids, MI: Baker Book House, 1986.

Designed to establish a rationale for Christian educators that will serve to clarify their purpose. The biblical doctrine of the priesthood of all believers establishes the requirement of personal and social responsibility—undergirded by knowledge of God, the Bible as the guide to spiritual maturity, the work of the Holy Spirit, and a realistic view of human nature as known to the social sciences and as needing transformation.

743 Wilson, John. *Education in Religion and the Emotions*. London: Heinemann, 1971.

A substantive theoretical contribution to understanding moral education, stemming from the work of the Farmington Trust. Emphasizes the affective in religious and moral education.

744   Wolterstorff, Nicholas P. *Educating for Responsible Action*. Grand Rapids, MI:
William B. Eerdmans Publishing Company, 1980.

A provocative and helpful discussion of what the author calls "tendency learning,"
that is, learning that results in tendencies to act. Some religious educators would
refer to it as an "ethical action" approach.   Against the background of rival
educational theories, the case is made for discipling and modeling as appropriate
dynamics, coupled with internalization. A major treatment of a significant aspect
of a Christian philosophy of education.

Administration of Religious Education

745 Allen, Dwight, and Kevin Rya. *Microteaching*. Reading, MA: Addison-Wesley Publishing Company, 1969.

> Microteaching is a technique for teacher training in which the trainee teaches a small class for a short time with a specific objective. Often the session is videotaped. This is followed by analysis and evaluation and repetition of the experience with a new group.

746 Anderson, Andy, and Linda Lawson. *Effective Methods of Church Growth*. Nashville: Broadman Press, 1985.

> It is generally recognized that the phenomenal growth of Southern Baptist churches is due in very large part to the ways in which their Sunday schools have been used as means of evangelism. This book shows in detail how recruitment, training, follow up, and incorporation into the working life of the church are accomplished. Combines the theory behind the process with many practical suggestions for carrying it out.

747 Argyris, Chris. *Increasing Leadership Effectiveness*. New York: John Wiley and Sons, 1976.

> To effect societal change, change the individual's theory of action. This book is the detailed recounting of a long-term experiment in the continuing education of leaders, in which they learn to learn and act effectively by identifying and reexamining their theories-of-action-in-use, inventing and producing while discovering, and developing effective ways of intervention. The significance, beyond the training, is in a theory of adult learning, learning for effective leadership, and the development of an open learning environment.

748   Arn, Charles, Donald McGavran, and Win Arn. *Growth: A New Vision for the Sunday School*. Pasadena, CA: Church Growth Press, 1980.

> Applies the principles of the church growth movement to the Sunday school. Combines the rationale and principles involved with an exploratory program by which the reader may weigh the principles and procedures and decide on an appropriate course of action.

749   Barrett, Lois. *Building the House Church*. Scottdale, PA: Herald Press, 1986.

> Out of her experience as minister to a cluster of house churches in Kansas, the author discusses the house church's character, structure, functions, and qualities. The religious educator will find interesting alternatives in the chapters on teaching and learning and on children.

750   Belknap, Ralph L. *Effective Use of Church Space*. Valley Forge, PA: Judson Press, 1978.

> A very practical guide that actually delivers what the title promises and much more. The basic position is one that integrates responsible stewardship with a philosophy of beauty. The planning process is detailed, and six planning options are presented. Two chapters deal with conserving energy and with the use of solar energy. Two other chapters give wise guidance on financing.

751   Bennis, Warren G., Kenneth D. Benne, and Robert Chin. *The Planning of Change*. New York: Holt, Rinehart and Winston, 1961.

> A comprehensive book of readings dealing with the dynamics and practicalities of the social planning process. Rooted in behavioral research and sensitive to the needs of such institutions as the church.

752   Bormann, Ernest G., and Nancy C. Bormann. *Effective Committees and Groups in the Church*. Minneapolis: Augsburg Publishing Company, 1973.

> A basic manual for churches on group dynamics, leadership, and communication in small groups.

753   Bossart, Donald E. *Creative Conflict in Religious Education and Church Administration*. Birmingham, AL: Religious Education Press, 1980.

> The author makes a wide survey of behavioral and theological understandings and models of conflict, coming to the conclusion that conflict in the church (and in the person) holds promise of insightful breakthrough and creative resolution. Ways are suggested for structuring such conflict into religious education processes, and particular strategic models for doing so are outlined.

754 Bower, Robert K. *Administering Christian Education*. Grand Rapids, MI: William B. Eerdmans Publishing Company, 1964.

> The first book in Christian education administration to integrate research and theory from the behavioral sciences, business, and education. Centers upon the functions of planning, organizing, delegating, staffing, coordinating, and controlling.

755 Bowman, Locke E., Jr. "Teacher Education: New Possibilities for the Churches." *Andover Newton Quarterly* 12, no. 3 (January 1972):140-51.

> An action research project that was part of the Arizona Experiment. It used sophisticated methods of analysis of teacher-pupil interaction in the classroom to help teachers develop more effective instructional strategies. Its best known aspect was INSTROTEACH (Instrument for the Observation of Teaching Activities in the Church).

756 Bowman, Locke E., Jr., Thomas H. Metos, and Frederick D. Levan. *Education for Volunteer Teachers*. Scottsdale, AZ: National Teacher Education Project, 1971.

> The Arizona Experiment was begun in 1956 as a project for improving the teaching competence of volunteers in the church. It was succeeded in 1968 by PACE (Project for the Advancement of Church Education), consisting of widespread INSTROTEACH workshops for training teachers according to carefully developed criteria of good teaching, and a learning laboratory designed to foster research and innovation in church teaching. This report consists of both popular and technical reviews of research on the project, together with recommendations for the furthering of its aims and methods. It was later renamed NTEP (National Teacher Education Project).

757 Browning, Robert L., ed. *The Pastor as Religious Educator*. Birmingham, AL: Religious Education Press, 1989.

> Charles Foster writes about the pastor's role as an "agent of vision;" Robert Browning explores the educative power of the sacraments in relation to the pastor's role; Joanmarie Smith sees spirituality as the opportunity for the growth of both pastor and congregation; and Robin Maas stresses the importance of the pastor's love for scripture in the role of biblical interpreter and teacher. These are among the contributors to this diverse collection of articles.

758 Burns, Ridge, with Pam Campbell. *Create in Me a Youth Ministry*. Wheaton, IL: Victor Books, 1986.

> An experienced, innovative, and reflective youth minister reviews the course of his ministry in an informal, autobiographical way, allowing the essential directives, guidelines, and qualities to emerge. Eagerness to experiment and down-to-earth practicality are combined with a clear sense of calling.

759 Chafe, Joanne M., ed. *Adult Faith, Adult Church*. Ottawa: Canadian Conference of Catholic Bishops, 1985.

> An official report of the National Advisory Committee on Adult Education, issued as a guide to Roman Catholic churches in Canada, with four foci: the faith community as educator, maturing adult believers, how adults learn, and structures that support adult religious education. Research and theory on adult faith development are skillfully summarized and made available to the church, with encouragement to explore programs and structures and to provide feedback to the national church.

760 Cully, Iris V. *New Life for Your Sunday School*. New York: Hawthorn Books, 1976.

> With the basic assumption that the life of the congregation is the actual educator, the author separates out and deals with "fundamental factors which do not depend on time, place, or method." Mostly a book on organization, management, and supervision in the Sunday school; the factors of purpose and age-level concerns are not neglected. See also 726, 838, and 857.

761 DeBoer, John C. *Let's Plan*. Philadelphia: Pilgrim Press, 1970.

> An analytical and practical handbook that puts the best of planning theory at the disposal of churches and other voluntary organizations. Shows the place for planning, the process of planning, and the role of research in planning. Detailed enough to be used by nonprofessional leaders.

762 DeBoy, James J., Jr. *Getting Started in Adult Education: A Practical Guide*. New York: Paulist Press, 1979.

> No church body has taken adult religious education more seriously than has the Archdiocese of Baltimore. In this book the director of the Division of Religious Education of the archdiocese summarizes in a clear and direct way the bases for adult religious education and the steps to take in setting up and maintaining a parish program of adult education. See also 741, 770, 795, 798, and 811.

763 De Pree, Max. *Leadership Jazz*. New York: Currency Doubleday, 1992.

> A collection of essays on leadership as seen through the lens of a jazz band: "Jazz-band leaders must choose the music, find the right musicians, and perform—in public. But the effect of the performance depends on so many things—the environment, the volunteers playing in the band, the need for everybody to perform as individuals and as a group, the absolute dependence of the leader on the members of the band, the need of the leader for the followers to play well."

764 Donnelly, Dody. *Team: Theory and Practice of Team Ministry.* New York: Paulist Press, 1977.

> The concept of team ministry is here broadly defined to include much more than teams of professionals. The fields of human relations, communication, and community building are elaborately schematized, so that the details of the process may be followed carefully and with understanding of what lies behind them. A product of experience worked through, the book specifically encompasses "theory, recipes, and dreams."

765 Drucker, Peter F. *Managing the Non-Profit Organization: Practices and Principles.* New York: Harper Business, 1990.

> Written for leaders of non-profit organizations, this book includes interviews with Max De Pree, Phillip Kotler, Dudley Hafner, Albert Shanker, Father Leo Bartel, David Hubbard, and Roxanne Spitzer-Lehmann. The interviews are used to illustrate basic principles outlined in each of the book's five sections. Each section ends with a summary of action implications. Drucker offers practical wisdom drawn from years of experience with a variety of non-profit organizations, ranging from the Girl Scouts to local congregations.

766 Edwards, Mary Alice Douty. *Leadership Development and the Workers' Conference.* Nashville: Abingdon Press, 1967.

> A thoroughgoing practical guide for the best use of various kinds of workers' conferences in religious education. Part 1 covers basic principles and practices. Part 2 consists of records of particular workers' conferences designed to accomplish various planning and training ends.

767 Emler, Donald G. *Revisioning the DRE.* Birmingham, AL: Religious Education Press, 1989.

> Emler is concerned that directors of religious education see themselves as professionals. Being a professional involves using theoretical principles and empirical research to evaluate the practice of ministry and to choose appropriate courses of action. The book is divided into two parts—"Revisioning the Basic Framework" and "Revisioning the Profession"—reflecting the dialogue between theory and practice which is so much a part of what it means to be a professional engaged in the practice of religious education.

768 Evans, David M. *The Pastor in a Teaching Church.* Valley Forge, PA: Judson Press, 1983.

> The church is challenged to be a teaching church, and the pastor's role is in relation to the church that sees itself this way and orders its life accordingly. Thus a team approach is established. A theology of church and ministry is made practical by cases and by the challenge to the reader to work it through in action.

769 Evans, David M. *Shaping the Church's Ministry with Youth*. Valley Forge, PA: Judson Press, 1965.

> A good example of the concept of youth ministry. Popularly presented but with the principles, possibilities, and problems involved in this approach clearly brought out. The keys are "ministry," "flexibility," and a combination of centralization and decentralization. In keeping with the approach, the book is not a manual, but more like an unfinished story to which readers must supply the next chapters out of their own situations.

770 Foltz, Nancy T., ed. *Handbook of Adult Religious Education*. Birmingham, AL: Religious Education Press, 1986.

> Provides a detailed overview of adult religious education, outlining its purpose, scope, and basic principles; reviewing the essentials of work with adults at various life stages as well as with adult educators; singling out major areas of concern (working with single parents, adults in separation and divorce, and adults in death-related circumstances); and assessing the future of the enterprise. Strengthened and enriched by the fact that the contributors are seasoned professionals in the field. See also 741, 762, 795, 798, and 811.

771 Ford, Richard S. "The Minister/Educator as Change Agent." *Religious Education* 71 (1976):171-86.

> In the context of increasing emphasis on the theology and ministry of the laity, churches want a professional educator who has, among other skills, the ability to enable a congregation to move ahead in its problem-solving and program planning. These are the skills of a facilitator or change agent. The processes of planning and implementing change are here spelled out in detail.

772 Foster, Charles R. *The Ministry of the Volunteer Teacher*. Nashville: Abingdon Press, 1986.

> Introduces the volunteer teacher to the full scope, implications, tools, and strategies of the task. Not accepting the notion of limitations because the person is a volunteer, it develops the theological, human, and practical aspects of the task in terms that are responsible and challenging, yet understandable and possible.

773 Fox, Zeni, Marisa Guerin, Brian Reynolds, and John Roberto. *Leadership for Youth Ministry*. Winona, MN: Saint Mary's Press, 1984.

> Well informed and practical guidance for leaders and coordinators of youth ministry in the parish. Here the concept of ministry is holistic, encompassing spiritual, educational, social, relational, and catechetical elements in a broad pastoral way. The ingredients are Word, worship, creating community, justice and service, guidance and healing, enablement, and advocacy.

774 Gangel, Kenneth O. *Competent to Lead*. Chicago: Moody Press, 1974.

> An exceptionally useful book on administration and leadership, seeking to "speak specifically to the issue of human relations in the church and its affiliate organizations....The pattern is to draw principles from both secular research and biblical text, in an effort to blend the two into a Christian philosophy of collective service and ministry." The author is unusually well read in the field, makes wise negative as well as positive judgments, and works judiciously from theory to practice.

775 Genne, Elizabeth, and William Genne. *Church Family Camps and Conferences*. Valley Forge, PA: Judson Press, 1979.

> A brief and very practical resume of information and guidance on family-type camps and conferences.

776 Glasse, James D. *Putting It Together in the Parish*. Nashville: Abingdon Press, 1972.

> A guide to the parish pastor in dealing with personal and professional plans and activities. Suggests specifics for examining and improving professional practice, including ways of dealing with conflict, methods of analyzing and prescribing for particular situations in ministry, and responsible career development. Directly adaptable to the situation of the professional religious educator.

777 Glickman, Carl D. ed. *Supervision in Transition: 1992 Yearbook of the Association for Supervision and Curriculum Development*. Alexandria, VA: Association for Supervision and Curriculum Development, 1992.

> Contributions to this yearbook are organized under the headings of context, practice, preparation, and reflection. Although the focus of many of the articles is limited to public schools, the context and theoretical perspectives have relevance for religious educators, especially Thomas J. Sergiovanni's concluding reflection, "Moral Authority and the Regeneration of Supervision."

778 Goldhammer, Robert, Robert H. Anderson, and Robert J. Krajewski. *Clinical Supervision*. New York: Holt, Rinehart and Winston, 1980.

> A revised edition of the best book in educational supervision ("clinical" here does not mean personal counseling; it means being of professional help to the classroom teacher). The process is made clear. Immediately applicable to religious education.

779 Greenleaf, Robert K. *Servant Leadership: A Journey into the Nature of Legitimate Power and Greatness*. New York: Paulist Press, 1977.

> A rambling and inspiring book, written out of thoughtful business experience around the thesis that persons "will freely respond only to individuals who are chosen as leaders because they are proven and trusted as servants." Chapters on

"The Servant as Leader" and "The Institution as Servant" are followed by applications of the thesis to particular fields, among them education and the church.

780   Hanisch, Helmut, *et al.*, eds. *Qualifiziert als Lehrer und Erzieher im Religionsunterricht: Zur Lehrerfortbildung im Medienverbund.* Stuttgart and Munich: Calwer Verlag and Kösel-Verlag, 1978.

A discussion of a unique experiment in leadership education for professional religion teachers in Germany. The experiment involves the use of a variety of media of communication, including broadcasting, and builds on previous experience in continuing education using independent study. Various experts explain and assess the program, both in theory and practice.

781 Harris, Maria. *The D.R.E. Book.* New York: Paulist Press, 1976.

Addressed to professional parish religious educators. While tackling questions of the task of the professional religious educator and how to think about it and carry it on effectively, the book goes deeper in helping to examine the nature of religious education, the person of the professional religious educator, and the use of imagination to conceive of new and creative alternatives to what is now being done.

782 Harris, Maria, ed. *The D.R.E. Reader: A Sourcebook in Education and Ministry.* Winona, MN: St. Mary's Press, 1980.

This well coordinated collection of essays goes a long way toward focusing the issues that the director of religious education faces, toward providing the director with a sense of identity and collegiality, and toward supplying the information and tools that are required by the profession.

783 Harris, Maria, ed. *Parish Religious Education.* New York: Paulist Press, 1978.

The editor appears to have developed a structure for the book (the people, the place, the profession involved in parish religious education), selected outstandingly resourceful authors, and turned them loose. The result is anything but a pedantic symposium. Rather, it is fourteen articles, all of which are of rich quality and depth, and definitely not limited or hampered by the original concept of the book. Requires (and rewards) slow, concentrated reading.

784 Hartman, Warren J. *Five Audiences: Identifying Groups in Your Church.* Nashville: Abingdon Press, 1987.

A popular report of a research that established that the expectations of persons in the church about Christian education vary, and fall into five major groups: those who seek fellowship, the traditional Sunday school, serious study, a base for social action, and those who combine two or more of these concerns. Guidance is given on self-study to determine the situation in particular congregations.

785 Hartman, Warren J., ed. *A Study of the Church School in the United Methodist Church*. Nashville: Board of Education of the United Methodist Church, 1972.

A research study based on a broad sample of United Methodist clergy and laity, including laity active in both church school and church, church alone, and now inactive, to determine influences on declining church and church school participation. Indicates that the church is much more serious in its intent than before, uses more complex methods, and engages in controversy. The recommendations generally hold that it is important to bolster up the institution and support its aims.

786 Heimbrock, Hans-Günter, ed. *Religionslehrer—Person und Beruf.* Göttingen: Vandenhoeck and Ruprecht, 1982.

An examination of the person and work of the professional teacher of religion. Five biographies are studied for the insights they offer and the issues they raise. The professional field is defined in terms of teacher role and student expectations. Contributions are sought from the fields of socialization theory, "theme-oriented interaction," depth psychology, self-identity, and the role of reference persons in a tradition-oriented religious education.

787 Hope, Ann, and Sally Timmel. *Training for Transformation: A Handbook for Community Workers* (3 vols.). Gweru, Zimbabwe: Mambo Press, 1984.

Clear explanations of education for liberation based on Freire's *Pedagogy of the Oppressed*, followed by excellent methods, clearly explained. Written for the use of African leaders. (David Ng)

788 Hopewell, James F. *Congregation: Stories and Structures*. Philadelphia: Fortress Press, 1987.

With all the emphasis on the community of faith as the focus of Christian nurture, there is need for concrete help in getting at the character and dynamics of the congregations in which we actually live, work, and worship. This book, rich in detail and perhaps a bit too complex in theory, provides clues on how to determine the "culture of a congregation."

789 Howell, John C. *Church and Family Growing Together*. Nashville: Broadman Press, 1984.

Replete with guidance on a number of issues in family ministry and focused on the particular responsibility of the church in relation to helping persons to mature adulthood, the formation of strong family units, and the growth of the family through its own cycles of development.

790 Jahsmann, Allan Hart. *Power Beyond Words*. St. Louis, MO: Concordia Publishing House, 1969.

>   Leadership training that seeks to develop a theology of Christian education rooted in a theology of the Word and the Holy Spirit. Naturally this results in a conception of transmission through re-creation and the espousal of creative methods of religious communication.

791 Janowsky, Oscar, ed. *The Education of American Jewish Teachers*. Boston: Beacon Press, 1967.

>   A survey-evaluation of American Jewish teacher education and Hebrew teachers colleges. Mainly a matter of intragroup improvement in separate institutions.

792 Johnson, Douglas W. *The Care and Feeding of Volunteers*. Nashville: Abingdon Press, 1978.

>   A realistic and effective approach to the development and maintenance of a group of volunteers in the church. Reviews research showing that the number and motivation of volunteers has not diminished. Practical sections on identifying and recruiting, giving assignments, helping volunteers plan, running meetings, and training. See also 261, 295, 854, 956, and 1167.

793 Johnson, Douglas W. *Finance in Your Church*. Nashville: Abingdon Press, 1986.

>   Includes an excellent section on stewardship education. One chapter deals with the types of education that are needed, and another with a year-round stewardship program.

794 Judy, Marvin T. *The Multiple Staff Ministry*. Nashville: Abingdon Press, 1969.

>   A much needed research-based analysis of functions and relationships in large church staffs. Presents data on the church educator, among others. Realistic, rational, and detailed, this book should go far to establish a base for effectiveness and creativity for church workers. Singularly and healthily lacking in the mystique that usually surrounds discussion of this situation.

795 Kerr, Horace L. *How to Minister to Senior Adults in Your Church*. Nashville: Broadman Press, 1980.

>   A practical handbook for the development of the church's program with older persons. Built out of the experience of the author, it covers the reasons for the program, the process of planning, ways to achieve a balanced program, and means for program evaluation and expansion. See also 741, 762, 770, 798, and 811.

796 Klopfenstein, David E. "Research in Leadership." *Christian Education Journal* 9, no. 2 (Winter 1989):41-54.

Klopfenstein reviews theories of leadership, organizing his survey around trait theories, leader behavior theories, leading process theories, positional leadership theories, and empathy and social insight theories. He ends the discussion of each theoretical approach by evaluating that approach's understanding of leadership in relation to the central tenets of evangelical Christianity. This survey introduces readers to the significant literature on leadership.

797 Knowles, Malcolm S. *The Modern Practice of Adult Education.* New York: Association Press, 1970.

A comprehensive guide to theory and practice in adult education by the dean of American adult educators. A wealth of sound material is here, based on years of experience.

798 Koch, Günter, Michael Müchtern, and Kalman Yaron. *Lernen in Bildungshäusern und Akademien.* Munich: Kösel-Verlag, 1983.

Brings together three authors, two from Germany and one from Israel, in a discussion of adult education in settings like the lay academy. The Catholic contribution centers on the work at the cathedral in Wurzburg; the Protestant, on the aims and theological character of the evangelical academies; the Jewish, on a "meet-dialogue-learn" model (inspired by Buber) in use in Israel. See also 741, 762, 770, 795, and 811.

799 Lambert, Norman M. *Managing Church Groups.* Dayton, OH: Pflaum Publishing Company, 1975.

A guidebook for church leaders in the use of insights from organization development, an attempt to strike a balance in administration between mechanistic management and human relations management. The model used is Church Management by Objectives and Results (CMOR). This is developed in step-by-step fashion, with appropriate exercises and materials.

800 Lebacqz, Karen. *Professional Ethics: Power and Paradox.* Nashville: Abingdon Press, 1985.

A wonderful book that gives real guidance to the professional religious worker who is forced to make difficult ethical decisions. Using a real case, the author takes us through a step-by-step process, in which the complexities of such decision making are faced in a sequence and carefully reasoned principles established, leading to a decision-making paradigm that has general applicability to a variety of ethical dilemmas.

801   LeFeber, Larry A. *Building a Young Adult Ministry*. Valley Forge, PA: Judson Press, 1980.

> A comprehensive practical handbook, providing the rationale and the "how to" for a rich, appropriate, and effective young adult ministry. Contains a voluminous section on resources.

802 Lewis, G. Douglass. *Resolving Church Conflicts: A Case Study Approach for Local Congregations*. San Francisco: Harper and Row, 1981.

> Presents a theory of conflict, and of creative conflict management in the church, by looking at the nature of conflict itself, examining the differences a faith perspective makes, presenting specific operative principles, and affirming different conflict management styles. Theory then translates into action with full case studies of conflict in foundations of ministry, ministry to the church and to the world, and the management of ministry.

803 Limbert, Paul M. *New Perspectives for the Y.M.C.A.* New York: Association Press, 1964.

> "Can the Y.M.C.A. in America be significantly Christian?" The question is examined against the background of the Y.M.C.A.'s historical policy of being "inclusively Christian, broadly religious, socially neutral, and character building." The new perspectives to be coped with are aspects of secularity, personal work, social action, church relationships, pluralism, world relationships, policy, character education, and leadership development. In each case new light has become available and new problems have arisen. With deep wisdom, Christian commitment, and practicality, the author shows how the Y.M.C.A. may work out its calling to "be loyal...to a Person in whom God was manifest supremely."

804 Lindner, Eileen W., Mary C. Mattis, and June R. Rogers. *When Churches Mind the Children: A Study of Day Care in Local Parishes*. Ypsilanti, MI: High/Scope Press, 1983.

> Provides badly needed information on the status of church-housed day care in fifteen denominations connected with the National Council of Churches. Based on over 25,000 questionnaires received, 14,500 programs were reported. Motives include Christian education, pastoral care, evangelism, stewardship, community service, and social justice. Statistics and anecdotes provide a clear picture. Ends with commentary from the perspectives of both the church and day care.

805 Lines, Timothy Arthur. *Functional Images of the Religious Educator*. Birmingham, AL: Religious Education Press, 1992.

> Parent, coach, scientist, critic, storyteller, artist, visionary, revolutionary, therapist, and minister are ten roles of the religious educator explored in part 2, the major section of this book. Part 1 examines the environmental context, differentiative typologies, and diagnostic categories of the religious educator, and part 3 offers a holistic perspective into which the ten functional roles or images are integrated.

806 Longardt, Wolfgang, and Wolfgang Gerts. *Kinderbibeltage—Kinderbibelwochen.* Gütersloher Verlagshaus Gerd Mohn, 1985.

An intriguing introduction to a series of innovative opportunities for the religious education of children and youth: the children's Bible week, the play week for children, and the children's Bible weekend. Detailed plans, methods, and materials are included.

807 Lynn, Edwin Charles. *Tired Dragons: Adapting Church Architecture to Changing Needs.* Boston: Beacon Press, 1972.

A thorough and technical treatment of what it takes to turn an old church building into "a full-functioning environment of seven-days-a-week religious life." Educational needs are stressed.

808 Madsen, Erik C. *Youth Ministry and Wilderness Camping.* Valley Forge, PA: Judson Press, 1982.

A thorough guide to a form of education ministry in which there is considerable interest. Concentrates on the ways wilderness camping may be a setting for a more specific religious education.

809 Manternach, Janaan, and Carl J. Pfeifer. *Creative Catechist.* Mystic, CT: Twenty-Third Publications, 1983.

Lives up to its subtitle as "a comprehensive, illustrated guide for training religion teachers." Contains three main sections: (1) The what, where, and why of catechesis, (2) an analysis of content (life and culture, Bible, liturgy, doctrine, and witness), and (3) basic processes (creative experience, knowing the learner, and using resources) and specific methods. Combines the fundamentals, a light (but not frivolous) touch, and practical directives. A useful chart analyzes five periods in catechetical theory and practice.

810 McCarter, Neely, and Bert Tippit. "New Styles of Church Leadership." *Spectrum* 45, no. 5 (September-October 1969):4-7, 20.

Styles of leadership are changing in response to changing realities in the world around. Dehumanization is forcing us into larger educational contexts and religious education is expanding its boundaries. The authors see a pattern of study/action emerging, with widespread use of action research in assisting with decision making in the church.

811 McKenzie, Leon. *Adult Religious Education: The 20th Century Challenge.* West Mystic, CT: Twenty-Third Publications, 1975.

One of the key figures in the Indiana Plan for adult education here provides a complete manual for the use of the plan's ideas and techniques in adult religious education. Includes the best of group process, cooperative program planning, and integral evaluation. See also 741, 762, 770, 795, and 798.

812 McMichael, Betty. *The Library and Resource Center in Christian Education: The Complete Guide*. Chicago: Moody Press, 1977.

A large and practical treatment of how to set up, staff, and use the church library that has become a complete resource center for Christian education. Pictures, line drawings, cataloging lists, and the like signify that nothing is left to the imagination.

813 Meyer, Johannes. *Das Berufsbild des Religionslehrers*. Zürich: Einsiedeln, Köln: Benziger Verlag, 1984.

In light of increasing pluralism (cultural, philosophical, and theological) on the German scene, religious education in the schools has been forced to reorient itself. In consequence, the task of the religion teacher has changed, with new implications for teacher training. This book is a close examination of trends in the literature dealing with the vocation of religion teachers, and with their training, during the last century.

814 Mickey, Paul A., and Robert L. Wilson. *Conflict and Resolution: A Case-Study Approach to Handling Parish Situations*. Nashville: Abingdon Press, 1973.

Case studies are used to show how conflict situations in the church may be understood and dealt with—staff conflicts, conflicts over program goals, etc.

815 Mitchell, Grace L. *Fundamentals of Day Camping*. New York: Association Press, 1961.

Guidance on the basic questions of day camp administration and program.

816 Mitchell, Kenneth R. *Psychological and Theological Relationships in the Multiple Staff Ministry*. Philadelphia: Westminster Press, 1966.

A record of a grass-roots investigation of the difficult problem of relationships among ministers in multiple staff situations. The concept of "pastoral authority" is made central. When pastoral authority is exercised, grace is expressed, a faith-response is possible, and the "two or more persons that are involved exemplify the essence of the church fellowship, even if only momentarily."

817 Moore, Joseph, and James P. *Handbook for Peer Ministry*. New York: Paulist Press, 1982.

Since the concepts of ministry with youth and youth ministry began to be used, the possibility of youth ministry with youth has been suggested. Here is a detailed guide for training youth for mutual ministry, together with practical suggestions on how this ministry may be carried on, supported, and evaluated.

818 Mosher, Ralph L., and David E. Purpel. *Supervision: The Reluctant Profession*. Boston: Houghton Mifflin Company, 1972.

A useful and balanced book on supervision, proposing an eclectic approach in which clinical supervision (classroom observation and critique), supervision rooted in techniques of counseling and therapy, and group supervision each has its place.

819 Murphy, Elly, Marisa Guerin, John Roberto, and Margaret Wilson Brown. *Hope for the Decade: A Look at the Issues Facing Catholic Youth Ministry*. Washington, DC: National Catholic Youth Organization Federation, 1980.

Surveys the situation in Catholic youth ministry in a brief, overall way, and more deeply in terms of social factors anticipated in the 1980s, the church's whole concept of ministries, and new directions for catechesis and confirmation. Priorities (eight of them) are sifted out, and promising models and methods are explored. Includes a large section of readings and resources. A basic policy-setting book.

820 Nathans, Alan A. *Maintenance for Camps and Other Outdoor Recreation Facilities*. New York: Association Press, 1968.

Complete criteria and methods for keeping up camps and other similar properties. Combines informative detail with a year-round schedule for maintenance of the property and facilities.

821 Ober, Richard L., Ernest L. Bentley, and Edith Miller. *Systematic Observation of Teaching: An Interaction Analysis-Instructional Strategy Approach*. Englewood Cliffs, NJ: Prentice-Hall, 1971.

Good teaching is a matter of teachers knowing themselves and developing approaches that are authentic and effective in terms of who they are, who their students are, what their situation is, and the objectives of the transaction. The keys are awareness and control. Awareness takes account of the above factors. Control is accomplished through systematic observation and planning. The book details the processes for this.

822 Olson, Richard A., ed. *The Pastor's Role in Educational Ministry*. Philadelphia: Fortress Press, 1974.

Designed to serve as a resource in helping the pastor to reconceive the Christian education task so that it may be done more effectively. Starting with vignettes from local pastors, it moves on to the technical use of theology, human development, teaching-learning, organization, and communication. Based in practice, scholarship, and research.

823 Palmer, Parker J. *Leading from Within: Reflections on Spirituality and Leadership*. Indianapolis: Indiana Office for Campus Ministries, 1990.

> "A leader," states Palmer, "is a person who has an unusual degree of power to project on other people his or her shadow, or his or her light." In this address for the 1990 annual celebration dinner of the Indiana Office for Campus Ministries, Palmer explores five shadows—insecurity, a perception that the world is a hostile rather than friendly place; "functional atheism," fear of life's natural chaos; and denial of death—often found in leaders. He concludes his address with practical suggestions for the "inner work" of leaders.

824 Penha, James, and John Azrak. *The Learning Community*. New York: Paulist Press, 1975.

> For those who want to know about a "learning community" (a relatively unstructured school within a school), this book gives the candid personal story of how one came into being and developed. The assumptions and procedures are delineated clearly and with enthusiasm.

825 Powers, Bruce P., ed. *Christian Education Handbook*. Nashville: Broadman Press, 1981.

> A substantial resource piece on administering the overall educational ministry in the local church. Five authors, professors in Southern Baptist seminaries, have combined their efforts to define the task of educational ministry, to discuss its theological bases, and to deal with the practicalities, from planning and evaluation to leadership education.

826 Powers, Bruce P. *Christian Leadership*. Nashville: Broadman Press, 1979.

> One of the more useful books on leadership. Well-informed in leadership theory, and written clearly and incisively. Thesis: The key to being an effective Christian leader is not so much in knowing a formula or acting in a particular way, as it is in adopting a life-style based on certain process oriented principles.

827 Powers, Bruce P., ed. *Church Administration Handbook*. Nashville: Broadman Press, 1985.

> Southern Baptist professors of church administration and Christian education team up to produce a comprehensive manual on church administration for ministers—including the specifics that Christian educators need in order to function well on a staff. Relating to organizations and people, performing administrative functions, and relating to self and colleagues are the organizing concerns. The mammoth program (e.g., there are job descriptions for ministers of education, of youth, of education and music, and of activities/recreation) is balanced by a concern for the small church.

828 Richards, Lawrence O. *Youth Ministry: Its Renewal in the Local Church.* Grand Rapids, MI: Zondervan Publishing House, 1972.

Conservative in theological outlook, thoroughly grounded in behavioral science research and theory, and extremely detailed in its practicality, this book cannot be neglected by anyone concerned with the church's ministry with youth. In format it is what a useful textbook ought to be.

829 Ross, Richard, and G. Wade Rowatt, Jr. *Ministry with Youth and Their Parents.* Nashville: Convention Press, 1986.

An introduction to the idea and practice of a coordinated youth-parent ministry, in which parents are involved and serve in ways integral to a full ministry with youth.

830 Rudavsky, David. "The Status of the Jewish Secondary School." *Religious Education* 56 (1961):98-108.

A detailed stuuy of the history and situation of the Jewish high school, combined with a plea for participation of larger numbers of young people and for restudy and reform of curriculum.

831 Ryan, Mary Perkins, and Russell J. Neighbor. *There's More than One Way to Teach Religion.* New York: Paulist Press, 1970.

With rising criticism of the parochial school, the challenge to the critics has been to suggest appropriate alternatives. This exciting compilation of grassroots experience does just that, with sections devoted to new ideas in teacher training, adult and parent education, work with other age groups, and community programs.

832 Sawicki, Marianne. *Faith and Sexism: Guidelines for Religious Educators.* New York: Seabury Press, 1979.

Detailed guidance for religious educators (from local teachers to publishers) on ways to use language to carry new insights on male-female equality and relationships—most of it wise, humane, and practicable; some, awkward and unusable. The prologue is one of the best theological statements on the matter.

833 Schiff, Alvin I. "The Synagogue and the Jewish Supplementary School." *Jewish Education*, Spring 1978, pp. 13-21.

The Jewish supplementary school is an "after-school" institution, serving the religious educational needs of the greater number of Jewish children. Schiff, seeing the responsibility as that of the synagogue, chronicles the history of the relationship of synagogue and school, delineates the serious problems facing the supplementary school, and challenges the synagogue to deal with the problem effectively.

834 Schilling, Johannes. *Der Jugendclub: Impulse für die offene Jugendarbeit*. Munich: Kösel-Verlag, 1982.

> A proposal for an openly structured youth work-the self-initiated youth club—in place of the closed youth group. Very practical problems of organizing and beginning a youth club, helping to establish its purposes, and setting its program and activities are covered. Suggestions are made on such matters as smoking, drugs, and alcohol.

835 Shelp, Earl E., and Ronald H. Sunderland, eds. *The Pastor as Teacher*. New York: Pilgrim Press, 1989.

> Contributors to this volume in the Pastoral Ministry Series include Walter Brueggemann, Maria Harris, and James Wall. Protestant, Jewish, Roman Catholic, and Orthodox traditions are reflected in the book's six chapters. Written primarily for the benefit of pastors.

836 Sisemore, John T. *Church Growth Through the Sunday School*. Nashville: Broadman Press, 1983.

> The church growth movement pinpoints the Sunday school as a key agency in the process. But, as Sisemore insists, it has to be more than a pragmatic interest. The key concepts have to be biblical and theological. Within that context, the dynamics and strategies of the Sunday school in contributing to church growth are outlined in detail.

837 Smith, Ruth S. *Running a Library: Managing the Congregation's Library with Care, Confidence, and Common Sense*. New York: Seabury Press, 1982.

> Written in cooperation with the Church and Synagogue Library Association, this book provides detailed guidance on the organization, support, housing, staffing, stocking, and use of the library in the parish.

838 Smith, Sid. *10 Super Sunday Schools in the Black Community*. Nashville: Broadman Press, 1986.

> Informal case studies of large urban and suburban black Sunday schools. Concludes with a short chapter of principles for growth drawn from the studies. See also 726, 760, and 857.

839 Sondermann, Wilfried. *Kirchliche Jugendarbeit in der Krise?* Munich: Kösel-Verlag, 1983.

> German youth work in the midst of a crisis. The League of German Catholic Youth stems from a time of persecution—1947. Since then it has experienced the professionalization of group leadership, methodological change toward more functional operations, a movement toward political relevance, adoption of a situational stance in place of induction into the faith community, and bureaucratization. What now can it mean for it to be authentically Christian?

840 Sweet, Herman J. *The Multiple Staff in the Local Church*. Philadelphia: Westminster Press, 1963.

> Written out of the wisdom of experience, and very helpful if read with that in mind. Sound concepts of the local church and its ministry are used as guides in dealing with task orientation and staff relationships. Basic suggestion: Regular group study by the staff. Heavy reliance is placed on a personal Christian will, a loving spirit, and a deep meeting of minds.

841 Taylor, Bob R., ed. *The Work of the Minister of Youth*. Nashville: Convention Press, 1982.

> A brief, useful guide to the various aspects of the task of the professional minister of youth. Includes helpful job descriptions.

842 Tidwell, Charles A. *Educational Ministry of a Church: An Introduction to Educational Administration*. Nashville: Broadman Press, 1982.

> The basic text on educational administration for the Seminary Extension Department of the Southern Baptist Convention, covering in depth and in detail the grounding, components, leadership, and processes in planning, organizing, and running the Christian education program of the local parish. Assumes the parish program as it is and seeks to understand, undergird, and enrich it.

843 Todd, Wayne E. *The Media Center Serving a Church*. Nashville: Convention Press, 1975.

> The media center is an important resource for the educational operations of many churches. This book shows how it may be organized, equipped, and used effectively. The "media tree" that begins the book shows twenty-six different types of materials to be included. From there on, the task is to select the most useful, make them readily available and known, get them distributed and used, and evaluate their use.

844 Towns, Elmer L. *The Successful Sunday School and Teachers Guidebook*. Carol Stream, IL: Creation House, 1976.

> A huge compendium of information and suggestions on Sunday school operation: the status of the Sunday school, organization, facilities, bus ministry, personnel, promotion and outreach, methods and materials, history, and evaluation. Each section is divided into a number of meaty chapters, reflecting the research and experience of the author and others whose work he has included.

845 Towns, Elmer L., John N. Vaughan, and David J. Seifert. *The Complete Book of Church Growth*. Wheaton, IL: Tyndale House Publishers, 1981.

A compendium of success stories in church growth, together with an analysis of the factors and methods involved. A valuable feature is articles on the matter by nine recognized authorities. Throughout the book a great deal of attention is given to the situation of the Sunday school and the growth factors that pertain to it.

846 Voight, Ralph Claude. *Invitation to Learning: The Learning Center Handbook*. Washington, DC: Acropolis Books, 1971.

The learning center approach has been introduced into the religious education programs of various churches and has been enthusiastically received. Here is a simple, graphic, and detailed guide to this approach, designed for public schools.

847 Vollmer, Howard M., and Donald L. Mills, ed. *Professionalization*. Englewood Cliffs, NJ: Prentice-Hall, 1966.

A comprehensive reader that provides religious educators with the basis for understandings and criteria in their attempt to develop a genuinely professional approach to the field. Ranges broadly through historical, theoretical, and practical aspects of the problem, with primary data from a wide variety of professions.

848 Walsh, Kevin, and Milly Cowles. *Developmental Discipline*. Birmingham, AL: Religious Education Press, 1982.

"Discipline is the process of goal-directed, purposive, channeled, energetic learning." This book deals with both the theory and practice of discipline in terms of basic educational, religious, and moral principles, providing specific guidelines for parents, teachers, school administrators, and religious educators.

849 Walters, Thomas P., ed. *Handbook for Parish Evaluation*. New York: Paulist Press, 1984.

A down-to-earth plan for thorough assessment of parish education, developed by a task force of the Archdiocese of Detroit. Criteria are those of recent definitive statements of the Roman Catholic church on religious education. Covers parish structures, leadership, sacramental program (Eucharist, reconciliation, and confirmation), catechists, parishioners, and learning outcomes. Each section consists of a clear introduction and a set of detailed evaluative instruments. See also 856.

850 Wentzel, Fred D., ed. *Site Selection and Development: Camps—Conferences—Retreats*. Philadelphia: United Church Press, 1965.

A beautifully designed guide to the essentials in planning the physical setting for camps, conferences, and retreats. After a brief treatment of objectives, program, and grouping, it proceeds to how to develop site plans, financing, and providing facilities for administration, maintenance and storage, health, sanitation, utilities, food services, housing, meeting places, and waterfront layout and aquatic facilities.

851 White, Edward A. "The Educational Crisis for the Urban Church." *Religious Education* 62 (1967):5-17.

Painting a bleak picture of public powerlessness, ineffective education, and Protestant retreat in America's cities, White sees the church as "a witness on the margin of the total educational enterprise." Nevertheless, the church has potential to meet the need for religious education that is experimental and innovative, providing a critique of its surrounding pluralistic and secular culture, with deep respect for the powerless people it serves. Several promising religious education programs are cited.

852 Widber, Mildred C., and Scott T. Ritenour. *Focus: Building for Christian Education.* Philadelphia: Pilgrim Press, 1969.

A complete and definitive guide to the project of housing the Christian education program of the local church. Each function is carefully delineated and integrated with the others: that of the architect, church building committee, educator, administrator, and participant. Goes a long way toward solving the problem of how much we are justified in investing in buildings. Beautifully and usefully produced.

853 Wilke, Harold H. *Creating the Caring Congregation: Guidelines for Ministering with the Handicapped.* Nashville: Abingdon Press, 1980.

Probably no one in America is better able to speak to the question of the church and the handicapped than the author of this book. In the simplest way he helps readers see both problems and possibilities clearly and motivates them to appropriate action. No sentimentality here, but warmth, good sense, and urgency.

854 Wilson, Marlene. *How to Mobilize Church Volunteers.* Minneapolis: Augsburg Publishing House, 1983.

Brings together theology and a philosophy of management in a basic understanding of who the volunteer is and why volunteering is of the very nature of the church. The practicalities move from careful planning, through the questions and problems, to "the scattered church" at work in outreach. See also 261, 295, 792, 956, and 1167.

855 Wissmann, E., *et al. Der evangelische Religionsunterricht in der Sonderschule für Lernbehinderte.* Berlin-Charlottenburg: Carl Marhold, 1968.

One of the distinctions of German religious education is its penetration into every level and sort of education. This volume deals thoroughly and sensitively with the problems and possibilities of religious education in the school for children with learning disabilities.

200

856   Wyckoff, D. Campbell. *How to Evaluate Your Christian Education Program*. Philadelphia: Westminster Press, 1962.

>   Theory and procedures for analyzing and evaluating the religious education program in the local parish. Provides a step-by-step plan, together with survey forms. See also 849.

857   Wyckoff, D. Campbell, ed. *Renewing the Sunday School and the CCD*. Birmingham, AL: Religious Education Press, 1986.

>   A critical and constructive look at the Sunday school and its Roman Catholic counterpart, the Confraternity of Christian Doctrine. Contributors provide historical insight, empirical data, and practical analyses of the situation of the general Protestant Sunday school, the evangelical Sunday school, the CCD, the black Sunday school, and the Sunday school in the armed forces. Summary chapters assess the data and point direction for reform and renewal. See also 212, 220, 239, 242, 251, and 760.

858   Zaltmann, Gerald, and Robert Duncan. *Strategies for Planned Change*. New York: John Wiley and Sons, 1977.

>   The discipline of planned change has developed to the point where it is valuable to take stock of what has been discovered and established, what can be discarded, and what issues still need exploration. Careful reading of this book provides this information for the religious educator. Of special interest are findings on strategies for change and on the change agent. Among "neglected topics" is noted the area of ethics in social change. Principles of planned change are gathered in a substantial appendix.

Program, Curriculum, and Method

859 Adams, Doug, and Diane Apostolos-Cappadona. *Art as Religious Studies*. New York: Crossroad, 1987.

> A reviewer comments: "Works of art are 'primary documents' in their own right, a mode of human expression that can and does generate theological reflection and interpretation. Such interpretation, however, needs to be guided by its own hermeneutic, the 'discipline of seeing.'" This discipline of seeing involves the viewer's total engagement with the work of art, and the viewer's transformation within that experience. Practical suggestions are made for classroom process. See also 202, 425, 490, 495, 878, and 967.

860 Adams, Douglas E. *Children, Divorce and the Church*. Nashville: Abingdon Press, 1992.

> This perceptive little book invites pastors to see divorce from a child's perspective and offers pastoral advice for caring for children whose lives are affected by separation and divorce. "Children Don't Get Divorced!," "Helping Children Through Divorce," "Lingering Side Effects," "The Divorce Is Never Over," and "Stepfamilies" are among the chapter titles. Guidelines for support groups for children of divorced parents and a list of helpful resources are included.

861 Agnew, Marie. *Future Shapes of Adult Religious Education*. New York: Paulist Press, 1976.

> Adult education has leapt into importance in the Roman Catholic church. This research uses a Delphi technique to explore its future possibilities. What results is a picture of adult education in the parish being pluralistic, somewhat clinically oriented, with greatly increased lay leadership, but including an intensified continuing education of the clergy. Major themes will be peace and justice in a context of social change.

862 Aleshire, Daniel. *Faithcare: Ministering to All God's People Through the Ages of Life*. Philadelphia: Westminster Press, 1988.

> *Faithcare* is the first in a trilogy, which includes Maria Harris's *Fashion Me a People* (1989) and *Gathered for Learning* (forthcoming) by Freda Gardner and Craig Dykstra. Aleshire introduces the concept of "attending" and shows its importance for ministry with adults, youth, and children.

863 Allstrom, Elizabeth. *You Can Teach Creatively*. Nashville: Abingdon Press, 1970.

> Written out of long experience as a creative teacher of children (at the Riverside Church, New York City), and as a teacher of teachers, this important and inspiring little book pleads for depth, time, and personal give-and-take between adult and child in religious education. After reading it, you feel that you can do it, and that it is important to do it.

864 Apostolos-Cappadona, Diane, ed. *The Sacred Play of Children*. New York: Seabury Press, 1983.

> The interest in children's religious education oriented to liturgy is here elaborated both theoretically and practically. Children's worship is thoroughly explored, with consideration of the participation of children in the sacraments and the use of drama and other means. Most of the writers are Roman Catholic, with contributors who are Eastern Orthodox, Episcopalian, and Presbyterian as well.

865 Apps, Jerold W. *Mastering the Teaching of Adults*. Malabar, FL: Krieger Publishing Company, 1991.

> Introductory chapters deal with myths about teaching adults, teaching style, and development of a working philosophy of teaching. Chapters 8 through 10 describe various teaching tools for presenting information, skills training, developing understanding, and creating a learning environment, while chapter 11 tells how to select the appropriate teaching tool. Remaining chapters cover topics ranging from teaching critical thinking to evaluating teaching.

866 Archibald, Helen. "The Prospects for an Ecumenically Conceived, Socially Aware Curriculum." *Risk* 2, no. 1 (1966):93-108.

> Deals with the challenge to curriculum in the radical social changes taking place in the life and circumstances of urban America. Tells the story of the "Good News Curriculum," a project of the Chicago City Mission Society, ecumenically developed and socially aware. The curriculum, in its content, timing, and educational approach, takes full account of the disruptions to family and neighborhood life characteristic of American urban life.

867 Babin, Pierre. *Adolescents in Search of a New Church*. New York: Herder and Herder, 1969.

> Forthrightly addressing youth's malaise about the church and the fact that society is no longer traditional but pluralistic, Babin develops a concept of education for the "new church" that calls for education for norms of choice and for voluntary community, for the experience of love, for dialogue and solidary with all, and for a sense of mission.

868 Banks, James A. *Teaching Strategies for Ethnic Studies*. Boston: Allyn and Bacon, 1979.

> A useful technical guide to multiethnic curriculum development. Specific help in getting into work with Native Americans, European Americans, Jewish Americans, Afro-Americans, Mexican Americans, Asian Americans, Puerto Rican Americans, and Cuban and Hawaiian Americans.

869 Bannerman, Glenn, and Robert Fakkema. *Guide for Recreation Leaders*. Atlanta: John Knox Press, 1975.

> Introduced with a short section on principles and planning for recreation, the major part of the book consists of specific games and activities that may be used by churches.

870 Barreirro, Alvaro. *Basic Ecclesial Communities: The Evangelization of the Poor*. Maryknoll, NY: Orbis Books, 1982.

> Tells the story of "basic ecclesial communities" in Brazil, a grass roots movement among the poor not unlike the "house church." Neighbors come together to study the Bible, to pray, to discuss their mutual concerns, to clarify their needs, and to act together to meet those needs. Seen as a fundamental context of evangelization and liberation. See also 10 and 35.

871 Bauer, Arthur O.F. *Making Mission Happen*. New York: Friendship Press, 1974.

> A brief guide to mission education, set up for local church study and action. Covers (1) mission imperative, theology, and strategy, (2) the place and process of mission education in the local church, and (3) the practicalities and resources involved. Telling quotations from an international group of mission leaders are used throughout.

872 Bausch, William J. *Storytelling: Imagination and Faith*. Mystic, CT: Twenty-Third Publications, 1984.

> With the use of countless stories, the author explores "the power of stories to capture and pass on from one generation to the next the wisdom, imagination, and faith of a people." Narrative theology filtered through the rich experience of a pastor and educator.

873 Berryman, Jerome W. "Being in Parables with Children." *Religious Education* 74 (1979):271-85.

> Ronald Goldman, biblical scholarship, James Fowler, and Maria Montessori are brought into focus in order to try to deal with the question of using parables with children. Berryman's conclusion is that the adult (the teacher) and the child, while they are at different developmental and faith stages, may be comediators of meaning with the use of a "parable box," a box containing objects representing the elements in the parable. As the box is literally unpacked, the story develops at different levels of meaning.

874 Bienemann, George, and Heinz Withake, eds. *Glaubenentfalten, Leben ermöglichen*. Munich: Kösel-Verlag, 1982.

> Example after example, from German youth work, of how the church's approach to youth may be deepened and enriched, under the theme of faith development and the enabling of life fulfillment.

875 Bingham, Robert E. *New Ways of Teaching the Old Story*. Nashville: Broadman Press, 1970.

> Suggests new concepts for religious education and innovations that are possible for most churches: the use of television, team teaching, and individualized instruction.

876 Bissonier, Henri. *The Pedagogy of Resurrection: The Religious Formation and Christian Education of the Handicapped and the Maladjusted*. New York: Paulist Press, 1979.

> Moves slowly through theological and educational considerations as well as understanding the handicapped, in effect providing a theology of education for the handicapped. Then it gets down to the setting and the leadership team, as well as to special methods. Insists unflinchingly on a real Christian education, not watered-down, for the handicapped.

877 Blazer, Doris, ed. *Faith Development in Early Childhood*. Kansas City, MO: Sheed and Ward, 1989.

> Presents key essays from the 1987 Kanuga National Symposium on Faith Development in Early Childhood. The role of caregivers is the theme of Alice Honig's essay, "The Roots of Faith," and attitude education is Lucie Barber's focus. In "Strength for the Journey," Jim Fowler underlines the importance of providing "holding environments" of language, love, and story. Bettye Caldwell, Kevin Swick, Bob and Patricia Boone are also contributors to this collection. See also 312, 357, 372, 374, 621, and 1152.

878 Boucher, Therese. *Becoming a Sensuous Catechist: Using the Arts in Religion Classes*. Mystic, CT: Twenty-Third Publications, 1983.

> Explores the arts as media for "knowing God through image, hand, and body." Dealing with a theology of art, the person as artist (or klutz!), how art fosters growth, how the teacher uses the arts, and the arts as corporate church activities, the author's approach is personal, clear, practical, and encouraging. The chapters are enriched with many fascinating exercises for expanding the imagination. See also 202, 425, 490, 495, 859, and 967.

879 Boys, Mary C., ed. *Education for Citizenship and Discipleship*. New York: Pilgrim Press, 1989.

> One of two volumes stimulated by the National Faculty Seminar which met between 1983 and 1986. Six essays challenge readers to explore what it means to educate Christians in light of Jesus' summary of the law in terms of loving God and neighbor. Practical moral thinking and action are the focus of these essays on discipleship and citizenship.

880 Brady, E. Michael. "Redeemed from Time: Learning Through Autobiography." *Adult Education Quarterly* 41 (1991):43-52.

> The thesis of this article is that "autobiography, the act of drawing a self-portrait with words, is a vitally important method of facilitating and enhancing the process of adult learning." Autobiography uses both memory and imagination to help adults learn in three ways: the remembered self, the ordered self, and the imagined self.

881 Braunius, Burt D. "Orientations to Curriculum Development for Church Education." *Christian Education Journal* 10, no. 3 (Spring 1990):52-61.

> Analyzes approaches to curriculum as preservative (passing on a stock of knowledge), productive (learning in order to meet social needs), and participative (stressing the value of learners as responsible participants in the planning process). An excellent review of the history, theory, and process of curriculum development, concluding that the participative approach is a vital way of dealing with issues in religious education.

882 Braxton, Edward K. *The Wisdom Community*. New York: Paulist Press, 1980.

> Presents a program for the church to think and study together in depth as a "wisdom community." Encompassing a variety of well-chosen and fruitful educational methods and going to the heart of the church's need for clear communication on its most basic faith and issues, there is promise here of rekindling theology as a parish reality.

883 Brookfield, Stephen D. *The Skillful Teacher: On Technique, Trust, and Responsiveness in the Classroom*. San Francisco: Jossey-Bass Publishers, 1990.

"Teaching is the educational equivalent of white-water rafting," writes Brookfield, and his book serves as a guide for traversing turbulent rivers. Chapter titles include "Teaching Responsively," "Adjusting to the Rhythms of Learning," "Lecturing Creatively," "Giving Helpful Evaluations," and "Overcoming Resistance to Learning."

884 Brookfield, Stephen D. *Understanding and Facilitating Adult Learning*. San Francisco: Jossey-Bass Publishers, 1986.

An important work for understanding the complexity of facilitating adult learning. Brookfield rejects the view that equates facilitation with nondirective teaching in which learners are in charge of their learning activities. Instead, he takes a more transactional view in which the values, aspirations, and goals of both learners and teachers are taken into consideration.

885 Brown, Marion E., and R. Harold Hipps, eds. *Confrontation Curriculum*. Nashville: The Christian Educators Fellowship of the United Methodist Church, 1982.

A set of six papers that were part of a study of United Methodist curriculum. Analytical and critical (and often contradictory), they deal with the history of that church's curriculum development, loci of authority and responsibility, tensions that have grown over the years, and future prospects. While it is not quite clear who is confronting whom with what, the study does provide many critical and constructive insights for the church and those concerned with curriculum—fewer for those working with curriculum in the parish. See also 184, 219, 889, 892, 932, 941, 951, 1010, 1020, 1034, and 1046.

886 Browning, Robert L. *Communicating with Junior Highs*. Nashville: Graded Press, 1968.

A comprehensive guide to the "new junior high work" within the concept of youth ministry. Theologically oriented, specific, and rich in suggestions on methods and approaches for revitalizing this aspect of religious education.

887 Carlson, Bernice Wells, and David R. Ginglend. *Recreation for Retarded Teenagers and Young Adults*. Nashville: Abingdon Press, 1968.

Stresses the need of the mentally retarded for social group experience and provides practical and detailed help for play and party activities that various agencies, including the church, may use. Begins with the basic theory; presents ideas for organized programs, group activities, and special interests; concludes with help on family approaches and activities.

888 Christensen, C. Roland, David A. Garvin, and Ann Sweet eds. *Education for Judgment: The Artistry of Discussion Leadership*. Boston: Harvard Business School Press, 1991.

> Seventeen chapters are organized into five parts: "Learning and Teaching," which provides a general introduction; "Personal Odysseys," in which four teachers share their experiences; "Building Blocks," which deals with teaching/learning contracts, listening, and questioning; "Critical Challenges," in which five specific challenges, such as participation, classroom observation, and independent thinking, are addressed; and "Education for Judgment," which offers a more reflective perspective on discussion as a means of educating for judgment.

889 *The Church's Educational Ministry: A Curriculum Plan*. St. Louis, MO: Bethany Press, 1965.

> The published work of the Cooperative Curriculum Project of the National Council of Churches, comprising a total curriculum plan from which denominations, and conceivably local parishes, might build specific educational plans. Consists of a thorough analysis of curriculum design in theoretical terms (covering objective, scope, context, learning tasks, and organizing principle), followed by a delineation of existential "areas," each involving experience of all the elements of the scope. The areas are broken down by themes, which are developed in detail for four age groups in terms of essential experiences, readiness, learning tasks, and possible achievements. Guidance is provided on administration and on the development of specific teaching-learning units. See also 184, 219, 885, 889, 892, 932, 941, 951, 1010, 1020, 1034, and 1046.

890 Clements, William M., ed. *Ministry with the Aging: Design, Challenges, Foundations*. San Francisco: Harper and Row, 1981.

> An exceptionally well edited volume that will be of special value to religious educators who design and carry out programs with the aging. The articles that come to the point of educational implications are by Allen J. Moore, Melvin A. Kimble, Donald E. Miller, and Elbert C. Cole.

891 Clemmons, William P. *Discovering the Depths*. Nashville: Broadman Press, 1987.

> Rooted in the oldest traditions of spiritual formation and informed by contemporary research in the area, each chapter of this book "examines an element of an ever-deepening life in Christ." Intended not just as a book to be read, but rather as a book to be used as a manual for growth in the Spirit.

892 Colson, Howard P., and Raymond M. Rigdon. *Understanding Your Church's Curriculum*. Nashville: Broadman Press, 1981.

> Provides a general introduction to Protestant curriculum, including broad theoretical and comparative material on the Cooperative Curriculum Project, United Methodist curriculum, Lutheran curriculum, and the work of the Southern Baptist Convention. Sustained attention is given to the work of Joint Educational Development (CE:SA). Strategic high-level help for local churches is provided. See also 184, 219, 885, 889, 892, 932, 941, 951, 1010, 1015, 1020, 1034, and 1046.

893 Cross, K. Patricia. *Adults as Learners*. San Francisco: Jossey-Bass Publishers, 1981.

> Develops a model for understanding adult participation in education. The Chain-of-Response (COR) model takes into account factors such as self-evaluation, attitudes about education, life transitions, goals, opportunities, and barriers.

894 "Culture-Specific Curriculum." *Interlit* 24:3-14.

> Articles on the Arabic Bible Curriculum for the Middle East (Larry Brook), rules for respecting culture in curriculum development, developing curriculum in another culture (Jim and Carol Plueddemann), the use of graphics in Africa (Marita Root), and developing indigenous, integrated curriculum (James R. West).

895 Daloz, Laurent A. *Effective Teaching and Mentoring: Realizing the Transformational Power of Adult Learning Experiences*. San Francisco: Jossey-Bass Publishers, 1986.

> "Education is something we neither 'give' nor 'do' to our students. Rather, *it is a way in which we stand in relation to them*. The nature of that relationship is best grasped through the metaphor of a journey in which the teacher serves as a guide." Daloz draws on developmental theory—including that of William Perry—and his own experience working with nontraditional adult learners in Vermont to offer practical guidance for mentoring.

896 *Dare to Live: The Taizé Youth Experience*. New York: Seabury Press, 1973.

> A compilation of material that explains what young people going to Taizé have experienced. Taizé itself becomes clearer, and there is substantive presentation of the process used there (especially work, meditation, and worship) by young people. Transferable in part to other settings.

897 Davis, Billie. *The Dynamic Classroom*. Springfield, MO: Gospel Publishing House, 1987.

A short but very useful treatment of fundamental method in religious education, based on the conviction that the productive classroom is one in which both teacher and learners are interacting creatively. The dynamics of this interaction are analyzed, as are special problems that arise. Differences at various age levels are pointed out. Special attention is given to the fact of pluralism in church and community.

898 Dean, Joan. *Religious Education for Children*. London: Ward Lock Educational, 1971.

An examination of the British situation. "If we think of religious education as aiming at helping children to become sensitive and balanced people who have formed for themselves a framework of meaning, we see that all education has a religious dimension in that it is concerned with the search for meaning in some way, and all of school life is concerned with personality development." This aim and focus is followed into its implications for knowledge of self, others, and the world; religious knowledge, language, and concept formation; worship and prayer; and moral education.

899 DeSola, Carla. *Learning Through Dance*. New York: Paulist Press, 1974.

Carla DeSola, one of the great practitioners of religious education through dance, here shares her methods and insights in lavish detail. Plunging immediately into the basic educational themes of communication, freedom, love, life, peace, and happiness, she shows how the learner may enter into the theme both in mind and body, and how the learning may grow and be expressed through improvisation and set dances. Reading the book and pondering the illustrations is a religious learning experience in itself.

900 DeWolf, L. Harold. *Teaching Our Faith in God*. Nashville: Abingdon Press, 1963.

A carefully wrought consideration of the role of theology in Christian education. Grows out of DeWolf's work with the National Council of Churches and the United Methodist church on curriculum matters. Enters fully into the give-and-take of sharpening issues and developing positions in curriculum. Particularly strong in its treatment of the content of Christian education and the way that content is to be used at the various levels of instruction.

901 Dixon, Dorothy. *World Religions for the Classroom*. Mystic, CT: Twenty-Third Publications, 1975.

Specific methods and materials for introducing children, youth, and adults to the great religions in school, church, and elsewhere. Contains a useful round-up of programs on teaching about religion in the schools.

902 Doherty, M. Michael. *Spiritual Dimensions in Teaching High School Religion.* New York: Alba House, 1976.

> An exceptionally well-conceived treatment of methods for teaching youth, set in the broad context of personal faith, the community of faith, and effective discipleship. Specifically seeks to implement Roman Catholic directives on religious education. Includes concern for training religion teachers.

903 Dotts, M. Franklin, and Maryann J. Dotts. *Clues to Creativity.* New York: Friendship Press, 1974, 1975.

> A three-volume encyclopedia of creative activities for children, arranged by types of activities. The directions are clear and simple and supplemented by drawings, so that there should be no difficulty in using the ideas. The age range is generally kindergarten through junior high.

904 DuBois, Rachel Davis, and Mew-Soong Li. *The Art of Group Conversation.* New York: Association Press, 1963.

> Rachel DuBois developed a most impressive approach to relieving intergroup tensions and promoting understanding of self and others through group conversation that helps persons share their most cherished memories in search for universals in human experience. This book is the fruit of her work and beautifully expresses both spirit and technique.

905 Duckert, Mary. *New Kid in the Pew: Shared Ministry with Children.* Louisville, KY: Westminster/John Knox Press, 1991.

> Six chapters make up this little book. Chapter 1 deals with space for children to be in shared ministry, while chapter 2 explores ways scripture and shared ministry intersect. The third and fourth chapters both focus on worship. Children in the congregation's worship is the focus of chapter 3. Festivals from Advent to Pentecost are the focus of the next chapter. Chapter 5 is about disciple work and the importance of adult role models for children. The final chapter looks to the future, emphasizing the importance of planning so that shared ministry will continue to be a reality in the twenty-first century. Each chapter ends with a concise summary of the main points.

906 Eastman, Frances. "A Model of Innovation in the Church School: The Learning Center Approach." *Spectrum* 49, no. 1 (Spring 1973):4-7.

> The learning center approach is individualized learning in which students are encouraged and enabled to make their own discoveries of what the faith is all about. At the same time it involves them in the life of the whole church community. It requires rich interest and resource centers for exploration and discovery, resource people to help learners in decisions about aims and procedures, and experiences of sharing and common worship.

907 Egan, Kieran. *Teaching as Story Telling: An Alternative Approach to Teaching and Curriculum in the Elementary School*. Chicago: University of Chicago Press, 1986.

> Argues that the dominant curriculum planning model of identifying objectives, selecting content, choosing methods, and determining evaluation procedures can result in a mechanistic approach to teaching, and that the research on learning has emphasized logical thinking skills. Proposes an alternative planning model which builds on children's imagination. "A continuing theme of this book," Egan writes, "is that children's imaginations are the most powerful and energetic learning tools."

908 Ehrensperger, Harold. *Religious Drama: Ends and Means*. Nashville: Abingdon Press, 1962.

> One of the authorities on religious drama gives us a solid book covering the theory and practice of drama in the church. A helpful chapter attempts a definition of religious drama. Details of choice and production are covered.

909 Eisner, Elliot W. *The Educational Imagination: On the Design and Evaluation of School Programs*. New York: Macmillan Publishing Company, 1985.

> A critical review and assessment of the curriculum situation, encompassing both curriculum theory and curriculum practice. Sees teaching as an art, not amenable to the thoroughgoing scientific treatment that has dominated American curriculum work. At the same time, not persuaded that the cure lies entirely with the reconceptualists, the author demonstrates both what he considers to be adequate curriculum planning and the art of curriculum criticism.

910 Eisner, Elliot W. *The Enlightened Eye: Qualitative Inquiry and the Enhancement of Educational Practice*. New York: Macmillan Publishing Company, 1991.

> In this book, Eisner develops the concept of educational criticism first presented in *The Educational Imagination* (909). He offers a thorough argument for the importance of qualitative research for educational practice. Religious educators will find helpful guidance for conducting qualitative research.

911 Eliason, Claudia, and Loa Jenkins. *A Practical Guide to Early Childhood Curriculum*. 4th ed. New York: Macmillan Publishing Company, 1990.

> A comprehensive guide to early childhood curriculum. Part 1 introduces readers to early childhood education, the developmental and learning characteristics of two- to six-year-old children, play and the physical environment, and curriculum planning. The remaining seven parts of the book address topics such as language and literacy development, socioemotional skills, sensory experiences, aesthetic development, science and critical thinking skills, and math and problem-solving skills.

912 Everist, Norma J. *Education Ministry in the Congregation.* Minneapolis: Augsburg Publishing House, 1983.

> A wise and practical book that quickly emphasizes the theological context of congregational Christian education, and then gets right down to business with the "how to": presentation, worshiping community, discussion, inductive study, individualized learning, confrontation and clarification, experiential learning, and the journal.

913 Fitzpatrick, Jean Grasso. *Something More: Nurturing Your Child's Spiritual Growth.* New York: Viking, 1991.

> The author uses the word "spiritual" to refer to an "awareness of our sacred connection with all of life." Spiritual nurture thus has more to do with ordinary, everyday life than with unusual or dramatic events and "false certainties" or "abstract doctrines." The first part of the book focuses on parents as spiritual nurturers and the second part on the nature of children's spiritual growth.

914 Fletcher, Kenneth R., Ardyth Norem-Hebelson, David W. Johnson, and Ralph C. Underwager. *Extend: Youth Reaching Youth.* Minneapolis: Augsburg Publishing House, 1974.

> The Youth Research Center developed a series of four experimental training programs for youth. This book reports on the fourth--a program for training youth in extending friendship to other youth. The extensive research behind this program and the pilot project in which it was tested are now reflected in a practical step-by-step guide that may be used by youth leaders in local situations. The instruments that are needed are included.

915 Foltz, Nancy T., ed. *Religious Education in the Small Membership Church.* Birmingham, AL: Religious Education Press, 1990.

> Research trends, sociological perspective, Sunday school and CCD, worship, administration, planning, curriculum, and conflict are topics covered by contributors to this important book on small membership churches. The overarching message is that the pastor has a significant role as a religious educator in the small membership church.

916 Ford, LeRoy. *A Curriculum Design Manual for Theological Education: A Learning Outcomes Focus.* Nashville Broadman Press, 1991.

> The author is an outstanding authority on the use of a taxonomical approach to curriculum design in Christian education, and has tested its use in the redesign of the curriculum for the training of professional Christian educators at the School of Christian Education, Southwestern Baptist Theological Seminary, as well as in the global context of Theological Education by Extension. He has managed in this volume to present the process in such a way that it satisfies the curriculum theoretician as to its value and authenticity, and at the same time

provides the practitioner with the steps involved, with clear and adequate examples of setting purposes, goals, and objectives, determining course structures, and developing detailed course descriptions.

917 Ford, LeRoy. *Design for Teaching and Training*. Nashville: Broadman Press, 1978.

Ford, a leading exemplar of rational lesson and curriculum planning, uses as a base the *Taxonomy of Educational Objectives: Cognitive Domain* (Bloom). In this book (a self-study guide to lesson planning), the processes of rational lesson planning are presented in exhaustive detail, and in a format that follows directly from his theory of learning.

918 Frakes, Margaret. *Bridges to Understanding*. Philadelphia: Muhlenberg Press, 1960.

A treatment of the "academy movement" and other significant developments in adult education and the education of the laity.

919 *Free to Know, Free to Choose: An Alcohol and Drug Education Program for Religious Education*. San Francisco: A Harper/Hazelden Book, 1983.

A curricular resource for four one-hour sessions, complete with scriptural references, paper and pencil exercises, a narrative or recommended film designed to trigger discussion, and suggested closing prayer.

920 *Fundamentals and Programs of a New Catechesis*. Pittsburgh, PA: Duquesne University Press, 1966.

Describes the program of catechesis for school-age children and youth of The Higher Institute of Catechetics of Nijmegen, The Netherlands. The need for a new educational approach is outlined; pastoral work and the school's responsibility for it are discussed. The pupil, catechist, purpose, and method are related in principle, followed by detailed grade-by-grade descriptions of the program. The necessary renewal of catechesis involves "an authentic religious education in the faith, rather than instruction...."

921 Furnish, Dorothy Jean. *Experiencing the Bible with Children*. Nashville: Abingdon Press, 1990.

This book is a revision of two earlier books by the author: *Exploring the Bible with Children* (1975) and *Living the Bible with Children* (1979). For Furnish, "The goal of Bible study with children is to open the Bible for them in such a way that they are able to experience the Bible content and discover the meaning for their present lives, while keeping open the possibility of future learning and meanings."

922 Furnish, Dorothy Jean. *Exploring the Bible with Children*. Nashville: Abingdon Press, 1975.

> Both the Bible and the child are to be taken seriously. "The goal of Bible study with children is to help them deal with the 'meaning' questions of their lives as they discover meanings in the Bible." The practicalities (group/team teaching, learning centers, intergenerational teaching) are treated integrally and not just as methodological addenda.

923 Furnish, Dorothy Jean. *Living the Bible with Children*. Nashville: Abingdon Press, 1979.

> The Bible is to be "felt into" using creative drama, "met with" in story-telling, and "responded out of" with dance and in ideas and acts. It adds up to a "total-environment way of teaching."

924 Galbraith, Michael W. ed. *Facilitating Adult Learning: A Transactional Process*. Malabar, FL: Krieger Publishing Company, 1991.

> Contributors explore teaching, individualization, critical reflection, teaching methods and techniques, technology, and evaluation from the perspective of a transactional understanding of the teaching and learning process. Galbraith defines this transactional process as "a democratic and collaborative endeavor whereby facilitators and learners are engaged in a mutual act of challenge, critical reflection, sharing, support, and risk-taking."

925 Getz, Gene A. *Audio-Visual Media in Christian Education*. Chicago: Moody Press, 1972.

> Detailed treatment of audiovisual methods and resources, set in the context of Christian education theory. Vividly illustrated throughout. There is nothing esoteric about this book; it provides basic and practical help on the kind of audiovisual use that is practical for the church.

926 Gillispie, Philip H. *Learning Through Simulation Games*. New York: Paulist Press, 1973.

> Plans for specific games are grouped under the themes of freedom, life, peace, love, happiness, and communication.

927 Gobbel, A. Roger, and Gertrude G. Gobbel. *The Bible—A Child's Playground*. Philadelphia: Fortress Press, 1986.

> The authors want to change the limiting concept of the Bible as an exclusively adult book. Fully aware of misuses of the Bible with children, they show in concrete ways how children are capable of responding to it. Goldman's research has tended to make children's religious educators hesitant; this book frees them to use the Bible in appropriate ways.

928 Gobbel, A. Roger, Gertrude G. Gobbel, and Thomas E. Ridenhour, Sr. *Helping Youth Interpret the Bible*. Atlanta: John Knox Press, 1984.

> Provides a new identification and analysis of the developmental tasks of youth. Develops and illustrates in detail a method of Bible study that addresses itself to assisting in accomplishing those tasks in a way that leads toward Christian formation. Five chapters of interpretation and six chapters of practice (showing how the Bible may engage each developmental task).

929 Gobbel, A. Roger, and Phillip C. Huber. *Creative Designs with Children at Worship*. Atlanta: John Knox Press, 1981.

> Basically a set of practical strategies for children's worship and training in worship, organized around the church year and life in the church. Introductory material provides the rationale for the strategies and guidance in implementing them.

930 Goodwin, Carole. *Quicksilvers: Ministering with Junior High Youth*. Mystic, CT: Twenty-Third Publications, 1992.

> Goodwin organizes her book on junior highs around five questions: "Who Are Quicksilvers?" "How Should We Minister with Them?" "What Stresses and Pressures Are on Quicksilvers?" "What Critical Issues Do Quicksilvers Face?" and "How Do Quicksilvers Grow in Faith?" A helpful resource for church youth group sponsors and junior high Sunday school teachers. See also 298 and 946.

931 Grad, Eli, ed. *The Teenager and Jewish Education*. New York: Educators Assembly of United Synagogues of America, 1968.

> The proceedings of the 1967 assembly of those involved in education in Conservative Judaism. Gives a splendid substantive overview of the movement, its educational problems, and the variety of practical steps being taken to deal with them at the adolescent level.

932 Gress, James R., ed., with David E. Purpel. *Curriculum: An Introduction to the Field*. Berkeley, CA: McCutchan Publishing Corporation, 1988.

> The major sections treat the most important issues in curriculum theory and design. Within each section the readings are the right ones to give necessary information on technical curriculum matters, and most of them serve as summary introductions from which one may go intelligently to the sources where the concerns are treated more fully. The readings are tied together with running analysis and critique, which gives the book a unity that other books of readings lack. See also 184, 219, 885, 889, 892, 941, 951, 1010, 1020, 1034, and 1046.

933   Habermas, Ronald T. "An Examination of Teaching Paradigms: Three Dialogical Approaches Which Strengthen Traditional Andragogical Practice." *Christian Education Journal* 10, no. 2 (Winter 1990):47-54.

> Habermas weaves four biblical metaphors—architecture (1 Corinthians 3:9b-15); apprenticeship (Acts 18:24-28); adventure (Hebrews 11:8-9); and agriculture (1 Corinthians 3:6,9a)—with references from the work of Reuel Howe to explore how three dialogical approaches (apprenticeship, adventure, and agriculture) strengthen traditional andragogy (architecture). He uses a musical analogy to distinguish between the three dialogical approaches: apprenticeship/prelude; adventure/interlude; and agriculture/postlude.

934   Hammet, Edward H. "Updating Adult Christian Education in Today's Southern Baptist Convention Church." *Christian Education Journal* 13, no. 2 (Winter 1993):9-27.

> After identifying five problem areas in adult Christian education in Southern Baptist Convention churches, the author offers practical suggestions in four areas: (1) program evaluation; (2) learning readiness; (3) curriculum design; and (4) content relevance. The analysis is informed by a wide range of sources within the literature of adult education as well as more familiar resources from the field of religious education.

935   Hardt, A., E. Schmitz, and A. Thome. *Dichter und Propheten: Moderne Dichtung im Religionsunterricht*. Trier: Spee-Verlag, 1973.

> American religious education has claimed to take the arts seriously, but no guide for religious educators like this German one has appeared in English. About seventy-five superb twentieth century pieces are introduced and analyzed for their religious education values. Böll, Borchert, Brecht, Buber, to name only a few, indicate the quality. A few non-Germans have crept in: Schau heimwärts, Engel!

936   Hargrove, Barbara, and Stephen D. Jones. *Reaching Youth Today: Heirs to the Whirlwind*. Valley Forge, PA: Judson Press, 1981.

> Barbara Hargrove, sociologist of religion, places today's youth in the context of a dynamic youth culture with specific roots and definite stages of historical development. She relates that youth culture to the world of work, to self-identity, and to public responsibility. Stephen Jones, pastor, faces the question of evangelism—"reaching" these youth, nurturing them, enabling them to experience conversion, and relating that evangelism to the realities of their culture.

937 Harrell, John. *Teaching Is Communicating: An Audio-Visual Handbook for Church Use*. New York: Seabury Press, 1965.

> An audiovisual handbook for the church, but one that is done with deep artistic sensitivity, theological integrity, a profound knowledge of communications, and a feel for the practicalities of the church situation. Features a wide variety of media and materials, far beyond the usual projected audiovisuals.

938 Harrell, John, and Mary Harrell, with Kathleen Summitt, Giles Asbury, and Thom Tyson. *To Tell of Gideon*. Berkeley, CA: John and Mary Harrell, 1975.

> A fine, graphic book on storytelling in the church. Includes theoretical, explanatory, and practical sections on every aspect of storytelling, a recording of three storytellers at work, and picture sections of the same people telling stories to various groups. The book itself is a work of art and an invitation to readers to try out storytelling themselves.

939 Harris, Maria. *Dance of the Spirit: The Seven Steps of Women's Spirituality*. New York: Bantam Books, 1989.

> The seven steps (as in dance steps) could be understood as basic steps in teaching/learning. The book includes exercises for each step. The exercises are suggestive of teaching strategies for both men and women.

940 Harris, Maria. *The Faith of Parents: As Your Child Begins Formal Religious Education*. New York: Paulist Press, 1991.

> Written as a hands-on resource for parents of children about to begin their formal religious instruction. Includes commentary, reflection questions, and suggestions for further exploration and action to help parents develop their own faith. The book is organized around the themes of remembering, roles, and resources.

941 Harris, Maria. *Fashion Me a People: Curriculum in the Church*. Louisville, KY: Westminster/John Knox Press, 1989.

> Harris divides this book into three parts: context, vocation, and planning. Part 1 examines the pastoral and educational vocation of God's people and views curriculum as the course of a congregation's life. *Koinonia, Leiturgia, Didache, Kerygma,* and *Diakonia* are presented in part 2 as the five curricula required for the fashioning of a people. Planning is the focus of part 3, and is understood in terms of contemplation, engagement, formgiving, emergence, and release. See also 184, 219, 885, 889, 892, 932, 951, 1010, 1020, 1034, and 1046.

942 Harris, Maria. *Women and Teaching: Themes for a Spirituality of Pedagogy.* Mahwah, NJ: Paulist Press, 1988.

> The 1988 Madeleva Lecture in Spirituality at the Center for Spirituality, St. Mary's College, at Notre Dame, *Women and Teaching* addresses the issues of women, spirituality, and pedagogy. The five dance steps—silence, remembering, ritual mourning, artistry, and birthing—Harris explores should be understood as generative themes (Freire).

943 Hebeisen, Ardyth. *PEER Program for Youth.* Minneapolis: Augsburg Publishing House, 1973.

> "A group intersection plan to develop self-esteem, self-understanding and communication skills." PEER means "positive education experiences in relationships," and centers on the kind of positive reinforcement featured in Parent Effectiveness Training and in *I'm OK-You're OK.* A ten-session program for church (and other) youth, developed by the Youth Research Center.

944 Heck, Glenn, and Marshall Shelley. *How Children Learn.* Elgin, IL: David C. Cook Publishing Company, 1979.

> A direct application of Benjamin Bloom's "mastery learning" concept to Christian education. The learner is guided through the stages of planning, informing, doing, encouraging, and assessing, with the overall assumption that what is to be learned may be really mastered by virtually every learner.

945 Hestenes, Roberta. *Using the Bible in Groups.* Philadelphia: Westminster Press, 1983.

> Roberta Hestenes, who designed and developed the field of Christian formation at Fuller Seminary, here explores twenty methods for Bible study in small groups. Thorough and discriminating guidance is given, from which groups may select appropriate approaches and know how to proceed effectively.

946 Holderness, Ginny Ward. *The Exuberant Years: A Guide for Junior High Leaders.* Atlanta: John Knox Press, 1976.

> Probably the most thorough and practical guide to junior high work in the church. Frankly pragmatic, the author's approach avoids gimmicks and stresses careful programming. The structure of the book itself reinforces this approach, with its development of leader-participant relationships, planning process, program structures, and program elements in sequential order. The concluding section is a rich collection of "mini-courses"—units—on the basic concerns of the religious education of youth. See also 298 and 930.

947 Holmes, Urban T., III. *Young Children and the Eucharist*. New York: Seabury Press, 1982.

> The case for including children in the sacraments and corporate worship, based on theology, history, and Erikson's understanding of psychosocial development. (David Ng)

948 Howell, John C. *Church and Family Growing Together*. Nashville: Broadman Press, 1984.

> Centering on the church's responsibility for life in the context of partnership, this popular treatment considers such matters as maturing adulthood, marriage strength, and healthy family growth. In addition, it is specifically programmatic, laying out designs for organizing family ministry.

949 Hull, John M. *God-Talk with Young Children: Notes for Parents and Teachers*. Philadelphia: Trinity Press International, 1991.

> In this little book, English religious educator John Hull clarifies for parents and teachers certain misconceptions about nurturing faith in young children. Thinking concretely and in images, moral growth, prayer and the Bible, and religious conversation are among the topics covered. Typical questions and concerns are answered with helpful examples and clear explanations.

950 Hunter, Edith F. *Conversations with Children*. Boston: Beacon Press, 1961.

> An unusual book explaining the significance and use of conversation in the religious education of children and providing fifty conversations with suggestions for using them meaningfully.

951 Hyman, Ronald T., ed. *Approaches in Curriculum*. Englewood Cliffs, NJ: Prentice-Hall, 1973.

> Provides representative selections of eleven different approaches to the curriculum, from Dewey to the humanistic emphasis. For the person trying to see what the curriculum alternatives are, this is a good place to start. See also 184, 219, 885, 889, 892, 932, 941, 1010, 1020, 1034, and 1046.

952 Irving, Roy G., and Roy B. Zuck, eds. *Youth and the Church*. Chicago: Moody Press, 1968.

> A large, practical guidebook for youth ministry. There is logic and comprehensiveness in the way it is organized, and it is pitched at a very practical level with a great deal of detail.

953 Issler, Klaus. "Designing Supportive Patterns for Partners and Parents: An Exercise in Curriculum Innovation." *Christian Education Journal* 10, no. 3 (Spring 1990):81-90.

> "To turn the tide of weakening habits in the home, a comprehensive strategy for building stronger Christian marriages and families is essential. The cumulative effect of 1) seizing the teachable moments, 2) modeling the truth, and 3) encouraging corrective action when practice departs from Christian norms can provide a facilitative context in which continued marital and parental growth can be nurtured."

954 Jendorff, Bernhard. *Kirchengeschichte—wieder gefragt!* Munich: Kösel-Verlag, 1982.

> Church history produces special and perennial problems for religious educators. Here its aims and content are analyzed in detail, and a host of practical suggestions are made for vitalizing it in the classroom through methods that involve learner participation and enriched learning materials.

955 Johnson, Douglas W. *The Challenge of Single Adult Ministry.* Valley Forge, PA: Judson Press, 1982.

> With a reminder that one-third of the adult population is single, and that singleness covers a variety of situations, the author uses his experience and research to provide a practical handbook on the bare bones of planning and programming for work with singles. He maintains that it is a very specialized ministry, that it requires a conscious commitment on the part of the church, that leadership is crucial, and that it does not conform to conventional church programming.

956 Johnson, Douglas W. *Empowering Lay Volunteers.* Nashville: Abingdon Press, 1991.

> Practical guidance for recruiting, training, and affirming lay volunteers for the church's ministries in the context of the new demographics which point to a shrinking pool of potential volunteers in the under thirty and over fifty age groups. Johnson recommends that churches with more than 200 members have a paid coordinator of volunteers. See also 23, 33, 96, 261, 295, 792, 854, and 1167.

957 Johnson, Evelyn M.R., and Bobbie Bower. *Building a Great Children's Ministry.* Nashville: Abingdon Press, 1992.

> Chapter 1 examines children's vulnerability of size, age, innocence, dependency, potential, and relationship. Chapter 2 shifts focus from the characteristics of children to influential adults in their lives. Chapters 3 through 7 address the church's ministry with children, the teaching-learning process, curriculum materials, the learning environment, and staffing. "Becoming a Family Resource Center" (chap. 8) offers a vision for the church's ministry

with children and their families. Each chapter provides a helpful checklist, sample questionnaire, or set of guidelines.

958 Jones, Nathan. *Sharing the Old, Old Story: Educational Ministry in the Black Community.* Winona, MN: St. Mary's Press, 1982.

Beautifully produced, rich in background material, and clear in its educational process, this book is "grounded in the conviction that catechists should be exposed to the very soul of black religious experience as the starting point for their ministry." Roman Catholic in context, and ecumenical in spirit, tone, and usefulness.

959 Jones, Stephen D. *Faith Shaping: Nurturing the Faith Journey of Youth.* Valley Forge, PA: Judson Press, 1980.

A popular but profound treatment of growth in faith in adolescence. Realistic about social change, the author insists that the nurture of youth in faith must today be very intentional. A wealth of practical suggestions is backed up with psychological and theological understandings. Most valuable is the clarification of adult roles in the process.

960 Judson, Stephanie, ed. *A Manual on Nonviolence and Children.* Philadelphia: Friends Peace Committee, 1977.

Parents and teachers concerned about helping children learn nonviolent attitudes and behavior have long been baffled on how to proceed, what approaches and activities to use, and actually how to think about the matter. This manual, a product of the Nonviolence and Children Program of the Quakers, will go far in helping them. Theory and practice are convincingly interwoven, activities are described in detail, and many sources of additional help are cited.

961 Kelsey, Morton T. *The Other Side of Silence.* New York: Paulist Press, 1976.

Concerned that, in the interest in meditation stemming from Eastern sources, the distinctive resources of Christian meditation be lost, the author has written a long but very clear and simple guide to the tradition and practice of Christian prayer and the meditative process. Comparative and critical, as well as constructive, with many examples and practical details.

962 Kirchhoff, Hermann, ed. *Ursymbole und Ihre Bedeutung für die Religiöse Erziehung.* Munich: Kösel-Verlag, 1982.

Maintains that basic symbols are essential to religious education, since they deal with the underlying components of human existence, relate life experience and faith experience, have a therapeutic function, and are germane to biblical and Christian speech. The symbols "way, wilderness, tree, water, mountain, and light" are explored in art, text, and experience.

963 Klink, Johanna. *Teaching Children to Pray*. Philadelphia: Westminster Press, 1975.

Pithy, practical guidance on how to help children develop a meaningful experience of prayer, and at the same time to deepen our own adult experience of prayer. Prayers with, by, and for children, as well as rephrased prayers from the Bible, are included.

964 Kohler, Mary Conway. *Young People Learning to Care: Making a Difference Through Youth Participation*. New York: Seabury Press, 1983.

With case after case, the author explains "youth participation," a program that "means the involvement of young people in responsible, challenging action that meets a genuine need, with young people having the opportunity for planning and decision making that affects others in an activity that has an impact on others (people or community), but definitely beyond the young people themselves." A key is adult leadership, with chapters devoted to finding adults and preparing them.

965 Layman, James E. *Using Case Studies in Church Education*. Scottsdale, AZ: National Teacher Education Project, 1977.

Here the case study method is skillfully applied to Christian education, fully explained, with simple cases and suggestions for writing your own cases. Special attention is given to the use of the method in church school classes, in teacher education, and with church committees.

966 LeFever, Marlene D. *Creative Teaching Methods*. Elgin, IL: David C. Cook Publishing Company, 1985.

The creative process and creative methods are vividly and invitingly explored for their potential to deepen the spiritual life through ways of hearing the Word of God that involve aesthetic experience, and of using heretofore untapped resources in responding to it. Old methods that have become hackneyed are revitalized. Methods not usually classed as creative are handled in new ways. New methods are introduced in practical detail. Teaching is treated as a creative experience for both teacher and learner.

967 Legential, Renée Dubeau, and Marcel Doyon. *L'Enfant et le Dessin au Catéchisme*. Quebec: Les Presses de l'Universtité Laval, 1966.

Constitutes a plea for substitution of creative for authoritarian methods in religious instruction, holding that the children's response to God must be in terms of their own nature and resources. Emphasis is placed on discussion and on the children's own art work as they are guided in religious experience. The psychological and methodological bases for religious education are extensively developed. See also 202, 425, 490, 495, 859, and 878.

968 Lema, Anza A. *Child Development and Planning*. Geneva: Lutheran World Federation, 1981.

Faces the question of cultural specificity in curriculum development by reporting on a multicultural research on age level characteristics, undertaken by the Office of Christian Education of the Lutheran World Federation, and by interpreting the results of the research cross-culturally. The research embraced children and youth in the United States, India, Liberia, the Middle East, South Africa, and Tanzania.

969 Maas, Robin. *Church Bible Study Handbook*. Nashville: Abingdon Press, 1982.

A plan for lay Bible study that puts the actual tools and methods of biblical exegesis in the hands of lay students. A serious book on preparing people systematically, step-by-step, to study the Bible for themselves.

970 Malone, Antonia. *Spreading Light: Religious Education for Special Children*. New York: Paulist Press, 1986.

Antonia Malone is a mother and a professional religious educator who has focused her work as a practitioner on the religious education of the handicapped. This book grows out of her rich experience and shows how the program is conceived, set up, and managed, and how the curriculum is designed to minister to the very special needs of the handicapped.

971 McCarroll, Tolbert. *Guiding God's Children: A Foundation for Spiritual Growth in the Home*. New York: Paulist Press, 1983.

Drawing from an unusually broad ecumenical background (including Native American and Eastern religious experience) and concerned for a Christian education that is in reality "spirituality in the world," the author proposes a very practical twelve-step program for spiritual growth and insists that the focus be on parents or parent substitutes.

972 McConnell, Taylor, and June McConnell. *Family Ministry Through Cross-Cultural Education*. Evanston, IL: The Leiffer Bureau of Social and Religion Research, Garrett-Evangelical Theological Seminary, 1990.

The report of a cross-cultural research in "culture bridging" involving Anglo, Pueblo, and Spanish-American families in northern New Mexico, working through cultural barriers for the sake of family life. Objectives like these guided the study: to gain insight into the role of families within the three cultures; to determine styles of ministry appropriate in multicultural settings; to find effective means for gaining access to the inner workings of other cultures; to respond to the need to train both clergy and laity in the skills, attitudes, and knowledge needed for cross-cultural ministry.

973 McGinnis, James, *et al. Educating for Peace and Justice*. St. Louis, MO: The
Institute for Peace and Justice, 1984, 1985.

> This manual now consists of three volumes: National Dimensions, Global
> Dimensions, and Religious Dimensions. Additional teachers' helps are
> provided.

974 McManis, Lester W. *Handbook on Christian Education in the Inner City*. New
York: Seabury Press, 1966.

> The first of its kind. A complete guide to setting up and conducting a
> functional Christian education program in the inner city church, rooted in
> sound concepts of social psychology, urban education, and the educational
> mission of the church. Covers youth and adult work, work with children, and
> methods, activities, and resources, with a broad plan of through-the-week and
> year-round responsibility. Special attention is paid to the situation of the
> Spanish-speaking.

975 Mezirow, Jack, *et al. Fostering Critical Reflection in Adulthood: A Guide to
Transformative and Emancipatory Learning*. San Francisco: Jossey-Bass Publishers,
1990.

> The focus of part 1 is precipitating critical self-reflection. Victoria Marsick,
> William Bean Kennedy, and Roger L. Gould are among the contributors. In
> part 2, Maxine Greene and Joseph Lukinsky and others describe six approaches
> to helping learners become critically reflective, ranging from critical incidents
> to life histories. In part 3, repertory grids, metaphor analysis,
> action-reason-thematic technique, and conceptual mapping are presented as
> ways of uncovering and mapping learner perspectives. Mezirow's work in
> perspective transformation and emancipatory learning provides the organizing
> theme.

976 Moore, Alan J. *The Young Adult Generation*. Nashville: Abingdon Press, 1969.

> A careful review of research on young adulthood, intended to correct
> impressionistic views. Concludes that the major phenomenon is not a
> generation gap, but a fundamental social change initiated by the previous
> generation but only being realized in this generation of young adults.

977 Moore, Jane B. *Movement Education for Young Children*. Nashville: Broadman
Press, 1979.

> A manual on the church's use of creative movement with children. Discusses
> the meaning and use of movement, how to structure a program, and the
> facilities and equipment that are needed. Myriads of activities are clearly
> explained. Photographs and drawings enhance the manual's usefulness.

978 Müller-Fahrenholtz, Geiko, ed. *Partners in Life: The Handicapped and the Church*. Geneva: World Council of Churches, 1979.

> The emphasis is on the wholeness of the Christian community, and the consequent need for the community to include the handicapped, as well as for them to feel welcome within it. Solid theological and practical sections are included, together with special contributions from East Germany, Kenya, and the United States.

979 Myers, Barbara Kimes, and William R. Myers. *Engaging in Transcendence: The Church's Ministry and Covenant with Young Children*. Cleveland, OH: Pilgrim Press, 1992.

> In this inspiring book on ministry with young children and their experiences of transcendence, Barbara and Bill Myers identify four core conditions for a covenantal ministry with children: (1) the practice of *hospitality*, (2) the *presence* of caring and challenging adults, (3) the recognition and affirmation of the dynamics of *transcendence*, and (4) the affirmation and acceptance of the reality of children's *experience*. The authors' examples of how these core conditions have been met in various covenantal ministries with children offer inspiration for those who seek to deepen and enrich their own ministry with children.

980 Neff, Herbert B. *Meaningful Religious Experiences for the Bright or Gifted Child*. New York: Association Press, 1968.

> Charges the church with complete neglect and loss of its gifted children and youth and urgently advocates special attention and training for them. Research based and detailed in both theory and practice.

981 Nelson, C. Ellis. *Helping Teenagers Grow Morally: A Guide for Adults*. Louisville, KY: Westminster/John Knox Press, 1992.

> Nelson distinguishes between conventional morals which reflect society's beliefs and values and Christian morals which reflect the church's beliefs and values. Since persons can be influenced by society or by their belief in God, the concern is to help adult church members create the kind of congregation where the moral growth of teenagers is more shaped by a vision and practice of Christian morality than by conventional morals. Nelson does this by helping adults understand the nature of morality, the formative power of a congregation in shaping morals, and the dynamics of adolescent growth. In later chapters, he offers practical help for applying these significant learnings.

982 Nelson, Gertrude Mueller. *To Dance with God: Family Ritual and Community Celebration*. New York: Paulist Press, 1986.

> Resources and inspiration for the enrichment of the family's faith through a creative approach to the rituals of the church year. Drawn from the author's own experience, appealing possibilities are opened up and presented in such a

way (although the book is not a set of recipes) that they are easy to emulate and expand.

983 Newbury, Josephine. *Nursery-Kindergarten Weekday Education in the Church*. Richmond, VA: John Knox Press, 1960.

Clear and detailed picture of the purposes, setting, activities, and leadership of the weekday church nursery and kindergarten.

984 Ng, David. *Youth in the Community of Disciples*. Valley Forge, PA: Judson Press, 1984.

Advocating a theologically informed approach to youth ministry with emphasis on discipleship and community, rather than the "fun and games" approach. Makes use of Dietrich Bonhoeffer's *Cost of Discipleship* and *Life Together*. DN

985 Ng, David, and Virginia Thomas. *Children in the Worshiping Community*. Atlanta: John Knox Press, 1981.

A substantial treatment of the inclusion of children in corporate worship and the life of the congregation, providing theological and educational rationale. Avoids the children's sermon and other gimmicks. DN

986 Olsen, Charles M. *Cultivating Religious Growth Groups*. Philadelphia: Westminster Press, 1984.

Describes the "life cycle" of small groups in the church (the initiating stage, the formative stage, the functioning stage, and the terminating stage) in order to provide the pastor (or the educator, as the case may be) with a framework within which to understand and guide such groups as the "base community" and the house church. Contains an informative history of the ups and downs of the house church movement.

987 O'Reilley, Mary Rose. "The Centered Classroom: Meditations on Teaching and Learning" *Weavings* 4, no. 5 (September-October 1989):21-31.

Recognizing the power teachers can exert in the classroom, O'Reilley presents a utopian vision of the classroom as a community of "reflection, acceptance, and useful work" inspired by Edward Hicks's painting, *The Peaceable Kingdom*. She sees the classroom as a place for interplay between community and interiority. Seeing kinship between teaching and spiritual guidance, she draws on contemplative practices, such as reading a text aloud and silent contemplation, for teaching in the centered classroom.

988 Osmer, Richard Robert. *Teaching for Faith: A Guide for Teachers of Adult Classes*. Louisville, KY: Westminster/John Knox Press, 1992.

> Osmer reminds teachers that "the basic purpose of their teaching is to create a context in which faith can be reawakened, supported, and challenged." Keying off the thought of H. Richard Niebuhr, he introduces the concept of faith as a "many sided cube" involving beliefs, relationship, commitment, and mystery. Each side of the faith cube is then related to a specific teaching method (lecture, discussion, reinterpretation of life stories, and paradox).

989 Paul, James L., ed. *The Exceptional Child: A Guidebook for Churches and Community Agencies*. Syracuse, NY: Syracuse University Press, 1983.

> Faces the question of working with handicapped children in ordinary church and community settings—everything from the Sunday school class to the scout troop. Four background chapters provide the nonprofessional with information about the handicapped in home and community. Three practical chapters discuss programming, community services, and pastoral care.

990 Perry, David W., ed. *Homegrown Christian Education: Planning and Programming for Christian Education in the Local Congregation*. New York: Seabury Press, 1979.

> Essays recounting situations in which Christian education has been developed on a grass roots basis. Illustrative of the wide variety of forms that develop when local needs, resources, character, and mission are taken seriously.

991 Peterson, Gilbert A., ed. *The Christian Education of Adults*. Chicago: Moody Press, 1984.

> A detailed historical and functional orientation to adult religious education (Peterson); educational theory, method, and curriculum (Perry G. Downs); the varieties and practicalities of adult educational ministries (Peterson and Bruce R. McCracken); and the various aspects of family ministry (William L. O'Byrne).

992 Pinar, William, ed. *Curriculum Theorizing: The Reconceptualists*. Berkeley, CA: McCutchan Publishing Company, 1975.

> Raises the whole question of the context for rebuilding the curriculum by examining the work of critics in the historical field, educational research, and the humanities. Huebner and MacDonald are cited as the most important reconceptualists, Huebner bringing existentialist, phenomenological, and theological insights to bear on understanding the educational experience. Phenix is included in order to gain the perspective of transcendence in educational theory. Essential for anyone who sees all of education as having religious dimensions.

993 Proctor, Frank. *Growing through an Effective Church School*. St. Louis, MO: CBP Press, 1990.

The author views Christian education in relationship to church growth, inviting religious educators to think about evangelism and education as partners rather than as separate and unrelated congregational activities. Barriers to church growth to be found in the congregation's education program are identified and suggestions offered for enhancing church growth through church education.

994 Reed, Elizabeth L. *Helping Children with the Mystery of Death*. Nashville: Abingdon Press, 1970.

This excellent little book is carefully wrought from a lifetime's experience in working with children and their parents. Dealing adequately and sensitively with its topic, perhaps its most valuable asset is the inclusion of many vignettes from parents and others who have helped children with situations involving death. Includes a long section of valuable resources—Bible passages, poems, stories, and the like.

995 Reimer, Sandy, and Larry Reimer. *The Retreat Handbook*. Wilton, CT: Morehouse-Barlow, 1986.

A manual for planning and conducting four kinds of retreats: the all-church retreat, youth group retreats, the small group adult retreat, and the planning retreat. Specific, detailed, and resourceful. Step-by-step guidance helps those planning such retreats to visualize the possibilities and to become comfortable with unfamiliar techniques.

996 Richards, Lawrence O. *Creative Bible Teaching*. Chicago: Moody Press, 1970.

A vigorous exposition and critique of "the contemporary view of the Bible" (referring to Little, DeWolf, Iris Cully, and others) is followed by a defense of literalism. This position is then worked out in terms of methods that promise results both in terms of understanding and faith. Age-level treatments follow.

997 Rogers, Donald B., ed. *Urban Church Education*. Birmingham, AL: Religious Education Press, 1989.

Sixteen chapters are included. Two chapters by Rogers provide an introduction and theoretical orientation; C. Renee Rust discusses "Christian Religious Education and Urban Church Education;" Bill Myers looks at models for urban youth ministry; Bill Gambrell relates adult religious education to urban church growth. Two appendices provide access to the "Results of the Urban Ministries Religious Education Needs Assessment and List of the Issues in Urban Religious Education Survey of the United Methodist Church."

998 Rusbuldt, Richard E. *Basic Teacher Skills: Handbook for Church School Teachers.* Valley Forge, PA: Judson Press, 1981.

> A very personal and graphic orientation to the task of teaching. The teacher's roles are clarified, and a systematic step-by-step plan for getting ready to teach is laid out and illustrated by citing and explaining a variety of teaching activities and their uses. Substantive attention is paid to the questions that come up in the volunteer teacher's career.

999 Russell, Ken, and Joan Tooke. *Learning to Give as Part of Religious Education.* New York: Pergamon Press, 1967.

> Oriented to religious education in British schools, this book "takes as its starting point a sure ground of adolescent concern: the compassion for human suffering which is normally awakened and keenly felt in the middle teens." It then proceeds to inform this compassion. Finally, it goes on to biblical and other statements about the human situation that set these specific agonizing points of suffering against the vast problem of evil, viewed in the light of a belief in a God who cares.

1000 Santa-Maria, Maria L. *Growth Through Meditation and Journal Writing: A Jungian Perspective on Christian Spirituality.* New York: Paulist Press, 1983.

> Presents a "Covenant Life Program" involving three background studies and guidance through a seven-dimensional process of spiritual growth. The background studies are on the search for meaning and for God, adult development and the receptive (Jung's feminine) mode, and contemporary spirituality. The seven-dimensional process starts with conversion and proceeds to a living ministry, with Bible study, prayer, mature love and relationships, reconciliation, and celebration and community along the way. Beautifully worked out and very appealing.

1001 Sarno, Ronald A. *Using Media in Religious Education.* Birmingham, AL: Religious Education Press, 1987.

> Builds on a searching examination of religious education theory and practice, with critical treatments of leaders in these fields. After an exhaustive look at the technical aspects of the constructive use of the media in religious education, the concluding section of the book deals with the development of media literacy and with applications in the areas of motion pictures and television, with focus on values for the religious educator and the religious learner.

1002 Sawin, Margaret M. *Family Enrichment with Family Clusters.* Valley Forge, PA: Judson Press, 1979.

> Great interest has developed in the "family cluster" idea as a possibility for intergenerational religious education. This is a definitive manual for its use, providing the theoretical rationale for it, its basic structure and operation, and a rich set of examples and illustrations of its use.

1003 Schaefer, James R. *Program Planning for Adult Christian Education.* New
York: Newman Press, 1972.

A theory of religious education worked out with breadth and precision,
comparing a number of Protestant and Catholic approaches. The practical
focus is on building a sound basis for adult work.

1004 Schaller, Lyle E. *44 Ways to Expand the Teaching Ministry of Your Church.*
Nashville: Abingdon Press, 1992.

Schaller describes practical ways congregations can strengthen and expand their
teaching ministries and illustrates important ideas with stories of everyday
experiences and conversations drawn from a broad range of congregations. He
also presents lists of practical suggestions and provides summaries of major
learnings. Chapters 1 and 2 focus on priorities and criteria. Together, they set
the stage for the thirteen chapters that follow. Chapters 3, 4, and 8 examine
some important factors which influence the teaching ministry of a congregation.
Criteria for evaluation can be found in chapter 5. Several chapters focus on
various groups of people who might be considered "clients" of the
congregation's teaching ministry, and chapters 9 and 12 focus on two of the
congregation's educational programs: the Sunday school and the vacation Bible
school.

1005 Scheihing, Theresa O'Callaghan, and Louis M. Savary. *Our Treasured
Heritage: Teaching Christian Meditation to Children.* New York: Crossroad, 1981.

A "how to do it" book on introducing and deepening the meditative life of
children. Part 1 faces the developmental, and some of the theological, issues
involved. Part 2 consists of guides for parents and teachers in the educational
processes to be used. Part 3 relates the whole thing to the church year.

1006 Schilling, Johannes. *Kirchliche Jugendarbeit in der Gemeinde.* Munich:
Kösel-Verlag, 1979.

A clear indication of the international interchange of ideas and programs in the
realm of church youth work. The concept here is that of a freely structured
program including such elements as youth club, discotheque, coffee house, and
youth council.

1007 Sell, Charles M. *Family Ministry.* Grand Rapids, MI: Zondervan Publishing
House, 1981.

A forthright analysis of the situation and condition of the family, set against a
theological understanding of the family in the Christian faith. On the basis of
this theological and situational analysis, and long and scholarly work in the
field, carefully considered suggestions are made for the church's understanding
and practice of its mission to families.

1008 Sinclair, Donna and Yvonne Stewart. *Christian Parenting: Raising Children in the Real World.* Louisville, KY: Westminster/John Knox Press, 1992.

> John Westerhoff writes the foreword to this little book, whose six chapters address the tough realities children and youth face growing up in today's world: consumerism, competition, sexuality, conflict, crisis, and diversity. An appendix offers suggested questions for group or individual discussion and study of each chapter.

1009 Skinner, Craig. *The Teaching Ministry of the Pulpit.* Grand Rapids, MI: Baker Book House, 1973.

> An unusually valuable book dealing with the educational nature and dynamics of preaching, within the broad context of ministry. In this context, preaching is seen to have a key nurturing aspect. This insight is explored historically, educationally, theologically, and functionally.

1010 Skolnick, Irving H. *A Guide to Curriculum Construction in the Religious School.* Chicago: College of Jewish Studies Press, 1969.

> Systematically employs Ralph Tyler's approach to curriculum construction in exploring the sources of learning experiences, arriving at objectives, and organizing learning experiences. Can serve as a model for similar enterprises in other religious communities. See also 184, 219, 885, 889, 892, 932, 941, 951, 1020, 1034, and 1046.

1011 Smith, Glenn C., ed. *What Christians Can Learn from One Another About Evangelizing Youth.* Washington, DC, and Wheaton, IL: Paulist National Catholic Evangelization Association and Tyndale House Publishers, 1985.

> An intriguing volume in which Catholics and Evangelicals find common ground on youth evangelism, sharing ideas, experiences, and expertise. Organized around outstanding evangelizers, outstanding churches in youth evangelization, outstanding evangelizing organizations, and agencies where help is available.

1012 Smith, W. Alan. *Children Belong in Worship: A Guide to the Children's Sermon.* St. Louis, MO: CBP Press, 1984.

> Tackles difficult aspects of the pastoral role—including children in the congregation's worship and preaching to them. The author draws on his own pastoral experiences and experimentation in preparing the whole church to assist children in worship.

1013 Snyder, Ross. *Contemporary Celebration.* Nashville: Abingdon Press, 1971.

> "Celebration" is an interest of religious educators. Snyder gives it his particular interpretation, couched in his "existential-phenomenological" style.

1014 Snyder, Ross. *Young People and Their Culture*. Nashville: Abingdon Press, 1969.

A heady starter for youth and their leaders, built around the concepts of the individual human consciousness, "the lived moment," and "that corporate humanness which is a culture." Youth are advised: "Create a world culture—and thus culture yourself....Be 'poetry to the present.' Break out into being....Move into a life style of celebration."

1015 *Specialized Resources for National Curriculum Developers in the Church's Educational Ministry*. New York: National Council of Churches, 1967.

This massive volume completes the published work of the Cooperative Curriculum Project and Cooperative Curriculum Development. (This is the third and final volume published, and is in multilithed, loose-leaf form.) Contains the detail of the "correlations" upon which curriculum developers may base their selective and constructive operations in dealing with the organization of learning experiences. Part 2, "Guidelines to Developing Curriculum Plans," will probably prove most useful. See also 892, 1020.

1016 Spotts, Dwight, and David Veerman. *Reaching out to Troubled Youth: How to Touch the Lives of Young People with Critical Needs*. Wheaton, IL: Victor Books, 1987.

Two skilled and experienced counselors connected with Youth Guidance, sponsored by Youth for Christ/USA, provide a rich professional discussion of the context and methods for religious work with troubled, disturbed, and delinquent youth. Their evangelical orientation enables them to be particularly insightful on communicating the gospel, teaching the Bible, and helping troubled youth into the church.

1017 Stewart, Sonja M., and Jerome W. Berryman. *Young Children and Worship*. Louisville, KY: Westminster/John Knox Press, 1989.

Three parts make up this book. The first part orients the reader to the rationale behind this approach. This introductory section is followed by a series of four preparatory sessions with directions and text for the leader. The third part consists of forty presentations, complete with an outline for the presentation, a list of materials, and sample patterns. See also 297.

1018 "Symposium: Curriculum in Religious Education." *Religious Education* 75 (1980):507-605.

Articles include: "From Curriculum Research to Foundational Theorizing" (William L. Roberts), "Curriculum Thinking from a Roman Catholic Perspective" (Mary C. Boys), "The Two Hundred Year Struggle for Protestant Religious Education Curriculum Theory" (Mary Jo Osterman), "Evangelical Curriculum Development" (Joseph Bayly), "Towards an Integrated Curriculum for the Jewish School" (Barry W. Holtz), "Jewish Education—An Opportunity

Model" (David Zisenwine), "Generative Words in Six Cultures" (Douglas E. Wingeier), "Fashion Me a People: A New Ecumenical Caribbean Curriculum" (Joyce H.E. Bailey), and "Developing a Handbook for Christian Education in Appalachia" (John J. Spangler).

1019 Taylor, Margaret Fisk. *A Time to Dance*. Philadelphia: United Church Press, 1967.

"Symbolic movement in worship" treated both in terms of practice and in terms of its historical context. The author has a knack for writing in such a way that the reader is both interested and motivated. Profusely illustrated with a mixture of traditional art and photographs, showing the continuities in symbolic movement in the Christian tradition—and illustrating how it is done.

1020 *Tools of Curriculum Development for the Church's Educational Ministry*. Anderson, IN: Warner Press, 1967.

The major product of Cooperative Curriculum Development (successor to the Cooperative Curriculum Project) of sixteen denominations working through the National Council of Churches. Contains four curriculum building aids: analysis (taxonomies) of motivations, methods, and appropriate outcomes; implications for leader development in the five curriculum areas; an outline of the teacher's character and role; detailed suggestions of biblical material basic to each area and theme. See also 184, 219, 885, 889, 892, 932, and 941.

1021 Topp, Dale. *Music in the Christian Community*. Grand Rapids, MI: William B. Eerdmans Publishing Company, 1976.

Practically every aspect of music in the life of the church is dealt with, including congregational music, special music, music for evangelistic purposes, music in the home, music with children and youth, and music in the Christian school. Criteria for the choice and use of music are carefully discussed, and in remarkably positive terms.

1022 Toton, Suzanne C. *World Hunger: The Responsibility of Christian Education*. Maryknoll, NY: Orbis Books, 1982.

Taking seriously the idea that religious education is education for justice, the author centers on the problem of world hunger. The problem is described and analyzed, lines of effective action are suggested, and methods of education for critical consciousness are delineated and related to this particular situation.

1023 Towns, Elmer L., and Roberta L. Groff. *Successful Ministry to the Retarded*. Chicago: Moody Press, 1972.

The result of wide study and experience in ministry with the retarded, this book presents bases and possibilities for such ministry. Particularly striking because it deals forthrightly and compassionately with the Anabaptist anguish at this problem. Thoroughly documented, with a splendid bibliography.

1024 Valenzuela, Dorothy, and Raymond Valenzuela. "Audio-Visual Communication in the 'New Life in Christ Course' in Latin America." *International Journal of Religious Education* 44, no. 6 (February 1968):12-13, 39-40.

> At the time of writing, eighty percent of Latin Americans were either totally or functionally illiterate. The curriculum, "New Life in Christ," was designed specifically to meet their needs. In the curriculum, pictures were used as simple illustrations, as "impact pictures" (forcefully depicting a dramatic situation and provoking an emotional as well as reflective reaction), and as symbolical representations of theological truths.

1025 Vanier, Jean, ed. *Vivre une Alliance dans les foyers de l'Arche.* Paris: Editions Fleurus, 1981.

> The first Community of the Ark was founded by Jean Vanier in France in 1964, when he took a house and brought two mentally handicapped men to live with him. Catholic in origin and ecumenical in scope, Communities of the Ark have the character that the Christian associates with the care of God's sheep. This book recounts the experience of persons from many lands who have founded or worked in some of the fifty-five communities then in existence (seventeen in Canada and five in the United States).

1026 Van Ness, Patricia W. *Transforming Bible Study with Children: A Guide for Learning Together.* Nashville: Abingdon Press, 1991.

> Walter Wink (1980, 1990) developed a distinctive approach to Bible study for adults, known as "transforming Bible study" in contrast to Bible study based on more traditional historical and critical scholarship. In this book, Van Ness adapts Wink's approach for use with children. The first chapter argues for a new paradigm for Christian education; chapter two offers help with developing lesson plans based on Wink's new paradigm; the third chapter deals with practical problems like adapting curricula; the last chapter suggests ways to involve children in worship using transforming Bible study. See also 1041 and 1042.

1027 Vieth, Paul H. *Worship in Christian Education.* Philadelphia: United Church Press, 1965.

> A thorough guide to principles and practice in church school worship, attuned to the needs and experience of children and youth.

1028 Vogel, Linda J. *Teaching and Learning in Communities of Faith: Empowering Adults Through Religious Education.* San Francisco: Jossey-Bass Publishers, 1991.

> The metaphor of pilgrimage or journey is one of the threads woven through this book. Vogel writes: "Adult religious education invites teachers and learners to journey together toward knowing, loving, and serving the living God. It is a journey toward wholeness." Chapter 1 explores "How People of Faith Journey Through Life." Vogel turns to the work of Walter Brueggemann

to offer readers words for the journey and looks to Robert McAfee Brown, Tad Guzie, and Thomas Groome for ways of knowing for the journey. Pilgrimage is one of four metaphors (schooling, household of faith, and new earth are the others) Vogel introduces in chapter 4 to describe the four ways adults experience religious education. The metaphor of pilgrimage or journey also appears as the focus of chapters 6 and 10. Guide and companion are offered as another way of thinking about the role of the teacher (chap. 6). Chapter 10 offers suggestions for "Supporting Journeys of Learning Within and Across Communities of Faith."

1029 Walrath, Douglas Alan. *Counterpoints: The Dynamics of Believing*. New York: Pilgrim Press, 1991.

Written for Christians living in the critical climate of a culture where compartmentalized believing is no longer an option. Walrath distinguishes between faith and believing; he understands the former as a gift from God and the latter a human activity. This could serve as a resource for an adult study group.

1030 Warren, Michael. *A Future for Youth Catechesis*. New York: Paulist Press, 1975.

Basic rethinking of the why and how of teaching religion with adolescents. Suggests a variety of settings including retreat-type weekend programs in which "core truths of Christian faith are presented, discussed, role-played, prayed over, and rejoiced over in worship."

1031 Warren, Michael. *Youth and the Future of the Church: Ministry with Youth and Young Adults*. New York: Seabury Press, 1982.

Summarizes and brings up to date much that Warren has previously written on youth work, indicates its theoretical grounding and its basis in his own professional experience, and projects a new concern for ministry with young adults. Differentiates among, and develops theory and practice for, youth ministry, youth catechesis, and youth spirituality.

1032 Warren, Michael. *Youth, Gospel, Liberation*. San Francisco: Harper and Row, 1987.

Characterizing contemporary youth as "silent," Warren calls for an approach to youth ministry that involves the raising of youth's social consciousness for identification with the needy and the oppressed, for liberation that involves a deeper encounter with Jesus, and for empowerment. The result is a theology of youth ministry of the first order, developed out of years of experience in youth ministry and serious scholarly research.

1033 Weber, Hans-Ruedi. *Experiments with Bible Study*. Geneva: World Council of Churches, 1981.

> "Listening, analyzing, and reading, students of the Bible meet a living reality which begins to challenge them. This divine presence starts to question, judge, and guide us. Perhaps gradually, perhaps quite suddenly, the book which was the object of our reading and study becomes a subject which reads us." Part 1 discusses the bases for such Bible study and the ways it may be conducted. Part 2 consists of twenty-five accounts of such Bible study experiences.

1034 Wegenast, Klaus. *Curriculumtheorie und Religionsunterricht*. Gütersloh: Gütersloher Verlag Gerd Mohn, 1972.

> Summarizes the profound changes in curriculum thinking in German religious education. The sources for the new ideas include many American curriculum theorists (Bloom, Krathwohl, Taba, Phenix, and others). It is clear that curriculum development in Germany has an educational, international, and interconfessional basis. See also 184, 219, 885, 889, 892, 932, 941, 951, 1010, 1020, and 1046.

1035 White, James W. *Intergenerational Religious Education: Models, Theory, and Prescription for Interage Life and Learning in the Faith Community*. Birmingham, AL: Religious Education Press, 1988.

> The book is divided into "Models," "Theory," and "Prescription." "Models" provides the reader with an introduction and orientation to the intergenerational approach. Faith resources, social science, developmental theory, and religious education are utilized in "Theory." "Prescription" includes such practical matters as goals and objectives, curriculum, and evaluation.

1036 White, William R. *Speaking in Stories: Resources for Christian Storytellers*. Minneapolis: Augsburg Publishing House, 1982.

> A simple, excellent guide to storytelling for religious educators. Enough is said about the "why" and the "how" to provide the help that is needed. The bulk of the book opens up the varieties of stories available: Bible, Christmas, folktales, fables and legends, great lives, and modern stories and parables.

1037 Wilbert, Warren W. *Strategies for Teaching Christian Adults*. Grand Rapids, MI: Baker Book House, 1984.

> A careful look at the theory and practice of an adult education that is both biblically and experientially based. Beginning with a summary of fundamental principles, the bulk of the book consists of examples of lecture-discussion, skill mastery (equipping), and case studies. Readers are led through discriminating use of each of these methods to the point of ability to design them themselves.

1038 Wilhoit, Jim, and Leland Ryken. *Effective Bible Teaching*. Grand Rapids, MI: Baker Book House, 1988.

> The teacher, teaching methods, and the nature of the Bible are the topics. The authors' aim is to improve the Bible teaching currently taking place in the church. Inductive Bible teaching is introduced and special attention is given to the qualities of an effective teacher.

1039 Williams, Herman, and Ella Greene. *Attitude Education: A Research Curriculum*. Schenectady, NY: Character Research Press, 1975.

> An outline of the history and theory of the Union College Character Research Project's Research Curriculum (the long-famous Ligon Plan), with an overview of its six units (Christian Social Potential, Growth in Magnanimity, Vicarious Sacrifice, Vocational Adjustment, Adjustment to the Universe, and Vision), and guidance for their use in the settings of church and home.

1040 Wingeier, Douglas E. *Working out Your Own Beliefs: A Guide for Doing Your Own Theology*. Nashville: Abingdon Press, 1980.

> The author takes the four approaches to religious truth that are characteristic of the United Methodist church—experience, reason, Scripture, and tradition—and shows how each may be implemented in specific ways by persons concerned with deepening their theological understandings and their faith.

1041 Wink, Walter. *The Bible in Human Transformation: Toward a New Paradigm for Biblical Study*. Philadelphia: Fortress Press, 1973.

> Proposing to go beyond the historical-critical approach to Bible study, the author uses both sociology of knowledge and a psychoanalytical approach to overcome the "subject-object dichotomy" in dealing with the Bible and replace it with a "subject-object relationship." "Subjects and objects remain, each as object of the other, each as subject to the other. Together they become copartners in the quest of life. Having begun (fusion) as the object of a subject (the heritage), I revolt (distance) and establish myself as a subject with an object (the text), only to find myself in the end (communion) as both the subject and the object of the text and the subject and object of my own self-reflection."

1042 Wink, Walter. *Transforming Bible Study*. 2nd ed. Nashville: Abingdon Press, 1989.

> A revised and expanded edition of the 1980 Bible study resource, which in turn builds on Wink's previous book, *The Bible in Human Transformation*. Wink's holistic approach to Bible study takes into account the affective domain, right/left brain research, and experiential learning. Written as a guide for Bible study leaders. See also 1026.

1043 Wren, Brian. *Education for Justice: Pedagogical Principles*. Maryknoll, NY: Orbis Books, 1977.

A distillation of investigations of and experiences with the processes by which people are educated in sensitivity to and effective action in the realm of social justice. While the assumption is that this is mainly a matter of adult relearning, there are some implications for early and lifelong learning.

1044 Wright, Kathryn S. *Let the Children Paint*. New York: Seabury Press, 1966.

Written out of considered and mature experience, this handbook on painting (correlated with the other arts) in Christian education is substantive (half of the book is devoted to the rationale), practical (details on procedures and resources are fully given), and inviting (the author's enthusiasm is contagious).

1045 Wright, Kathryn S. *Let the Children Sing*. New York: Seabury Press, 1975.

Gathers together experience and resources in the arts (especially music) for religious educators. The book has a fine sensitivity to aesthetic and religious values, traditional and new, and the experiences through which children grow and learn.

1046 Wyckoff, D. Campbell. *Theory and Design of Christian Education Curriculum*. Philadelphia: Westminster Press, 1961.

Sets forth historical perspectives, basic principles, and practical suggestions for Protestant curriculum, reflecting the curriculum studies of the Cooperative Curriculum Project of the National Council of Churches. See also 184, 219, 885, 889, 892, 932, 941, 951, 1010, 1020, and 1034.

1047 Yates, John W., III. *For the Life of the Family*. Wilton, CT: Morehouse-Barlow, 1986.

In light of the problems demoralizing and destroying families, this is a tested program for a church to use in building strong groups for mutual support, involving families as a whole. There is special emphasis on the need to involve single-parent families.

1048 Yount, William R. *Be Opened! An Introduction to Ministry with the Deaf*. Nashville: Broadman Press, 1976.

A compendium of theoretical and practical information for those planning or conducting ministry with the deaf. The author writes from long experience and study in the field and has provided wide bibliographical help throughout the book. Special chapters treat education and teaching the deaf.

1049 Zuck, Roy B., and Warren S. Benson, eds. *Youth Education in the Church*. Chicago: Moody Press, 1978.

A voluminous treatment of foundations, principles, practice, and possibilities for youth work. Outstanding are Benson on "adolescents in an age of acceleration and crisis," Pugh and Skoglund on the history of youth work and on parachurch youth movements, Joy on sociopsychological perspectives, and LeFever on creative methods. See also 686, 717, 867, 896, 930, 981, 1014, and 1032.

1050 Zuck, Roy B., and Robert E. Clark, eds. *Childhood Education in the Church*. Chicago: Moody Press, 1975.

A broad-gauged and well-documented treatment of theory and practice in the religious education of children. The roster of contributors is a "who's who" of scholars and leading authorities and practitioners in the field among evangelicals. The topics are inclusive, as are the bibliographies.

1051 Zuck, Roy B., and Gene A. Getz, eds. *Adult Education in the Church*. Chicago: Moody Press, 1970.

An impressive and comprehensive book on the problem of approaching adults responsibly in and through the church. Part 1 deals with adults in the church and community. Part 2 deals with parents in the family. The writers are well equipped by training and experience.

Religion and the School

1052 Ackerman, James S., with Jane Stouder Hawley. *On Teaching the Bible as Literature*. Bloomington, IN: Indiana University Press, 1967.

Prepared to be used by public school teachers of English literature, this manual presents background material for teaching thirty-one selected biblical narratives, from "The Two Stories of Creation" through "David and Goliath." The authors advise teachers, "If you have any qualms about doing this—don't!"

1053 Ackerman, James S., Alan Wilkin Jenks, Edward B. Jenkinson, with Jane Blough. *Teaching the Old Testament in English Classes*. Bloomington, IN: Indiana University Press, 1973.

A contribution to the slowly growing literature on teaching religion in the public school. This large volume (almost 500 pages) is the result of years of work with English teachers and takes the Old Testament sequentially, providing introductory material and commentary, questions for discussion, and suggested activities.

1054 Adesina, Segun. "Christian Missions Versus State Governments in Nigeria: The Battle for the Nation's Schools." *Religious Education* 68 (1973):483-96.

A historical and political study of the crisis in Nigerian education at the time of independence in 1960. At that time eighty percent of pupils were in church-sponsored schools, yet the new government tended to see this as threatening to perpetuate colonialism. Concluded: "Perhaps the Christian missions in Nigeria, rather than press for retention of their control, which they are almost certain to lose in the face of popular anticlericalism, should work toward a system which will make them independent of future government interference."

1055 Bartel, Roland, ed., with James S. Ackerman, and Thayer S. Warshaw. *Biblical Issues in Literature*. Nashville: Abingdon Press, 1975.

> Another splendid volume from the Indiana University Bible in Literature Project. This one, with analyses of specific works, deals with biblical allusions, biblical structuring, and biblical interpretations in fiction, poetry, and drama.

1056 Biemer, Günter, and Albert Biesinger, eds. *Theologie im Religionsunterricht*. Munich: Kösel-Verlag, 1976.

> A carefully developed grid for determining both content and experience in the curriculum of religious education at the secondary level in Germany. The elements are theological content itself (biblical theology, church history, dogmatics, ethics, and practical theology), the existential elements in being human (work, power, sexuality, death, and play), and the demands of Jesus Christ for meaning, love, and hope.

1057 Borowski, Karol. "Secular and Religious Education in Poland." *Religious Education* 70 (1975):70-76.

> The clash of church and state in Poland during the Marxist years was grounded in the conflict between the traditional Christian culture of a thousand years and the Marxist counterculture. The Marxists tried to create new cultural patterns and to wipe out the old patterns so strongly connected with the Christian tradition of the country. The church wanted to preserve not only what was Christian, but also what was "old and familiar." There was a gradual convergence of these two cultures, and a growing mutual influence and relationship between them.

1058 Brown, William E., and Andrew M. Greeley. *Can Catholic Schools Survive?* New York: Sheed and Ward, 1970.

> Consists of two parts: (1) A penetrating look at the educational theory of the Catholic schools, and (2) a candid assessment of their organizational and financial situation. Essential for an intelligent assessment of the state of the enterprise and informed planning for its future.

1059 Carper, James C., and Thomas C. Hunt. *Religious Schooling in America*. Birmingham, AL: Religious Education Press, 1984.

> A singular contribution to the literature on American religious education, providing essential information on the following systems: Roman Catholic, Lutheran, Calvinist, Seventh-Day Adventist, Christian day schools, and Jewish day schools. A second section on concerns deals with the history and status of the common school in relation to religious matters, tuition tax credits and educational vouchers, and state regulation of private schools.

1060 Coleman, James S., and Thomas Hoffer. *Public and Private High Schools: The Impact of Communities*. New York: Basic Books, 1987.

A follow-up of an earlier study of public and private (in most cases Catholic) high schools and their students. This study followed students from the sophomore through the senior years. Findings showed higher achievement, fewer dropouts, more likelihood of going to college, and greater achievement gains for socially disadvantaged students in private schools.

1061 de Grandpré, Marcel. *L'enseignement Catholique dans un Système Scolaire National*. Montreal: Fédération des Collèges Classiques, 1964.

A comparative education study, in which policy and practice in European education are brought to bear upon the church-state problem in Quebec as it affects education. Gives evidence of renewal in Canadian Catholic educational thought and planning.

1062 Farrelly, T.M. "A New Generation Seeks a Faith to Live by: Religious Education in Kenya." *Religious Education* 70 (1975):54-69.

"The young people of Kenya are growing up in a new nation which is becoming increasingly involved in world affairs....In common with other subjects, religious education is attempting to help the young people of Kenya to face the future with confidence. It does not attempt to answer all their problems, but it does aim to give them an attitude to life and a set of values which will sustain them in a rapidly changing world. It also aims at equipping them to evaluate their problems and to attempt to solve them in the light of these values."

1063 *The Fourth R: The Report of the Commission of Religious Education in Schools*. London: SPCK, 1970.

One of the most important recent documents in religious education, a survey of history, theory, and practice in Great Britain, leading to recommendations for the future of religious education in the British system.

1064 Freund, Paul A., and Robert Ulich. *Religion and the Public Schools: The Legal Issue; The Educational Issue*. Cambridge, MA: Harvard University Press, 1965.

Terse treatments, by legal and educational experts, of the historical and recent American problem of religion in education. Presses the issue of whether or not education can be complete without teaching about religion, moral education, and the development of religious qualities in experience.

1065 Frigger, Manfred. *Religiöse Erfahrung im Schulalltag*. Munich: Verlag J. Pfeiffer, 1983.

In light of social and cultural change, the author considers the place of religious experience in the school, not only in the religion classroom, but also in the school's daily life. Taking the expectations of pupil, parent, and community into account, his focus is on values as the connecting point between pupil experience and Christian faith, on counseling as the key process, and on anthropological and theological guidelines to fundamental method. Many appropriate and intriguing methods are outlined.

1066 Gaffney, Edward McGlynn, Jr., ed. *Private Schools and the Public Good: Policy Alternatives for the Eighties*. Notre Dame, IN: University of Notre Dame Press, 1981.

A hard look at the services that nonpublic schools are rendering to the inner city, the handicapped, and racial and ethnic minorities, and the legal and political roadblocks that make it difficult for them to expand these services. The various plans for correcting the situation are evaluated, together with the political and legal factors involved.

1067 Goldman, Ronald. *Readiness for Religion*. London: Routledge and Kegan Paul, 1965.

A proposal for radical revision of the program of religious education in British schools, away from Bible-centered syllabi (for which children are not ready, and in which they are not interested), toward a curriculum based upon their needs and their readiness for religious learning. Carefully analytical in terms of pre-religious, sub-religious, and personal religion phases of growth. Introduces the author's "Readiness for Religion" curriculum.

1068 Gros Louis, Kenneth R.R., ed., with James S. Ackerman, and Thayer S. Warshaw. *Literary Interpretations of Biblical Narratives*. Nashville: Abingdon Press, 1974.

The third volume to appear in connection with Indiana University's studies on the use of the Bible as literature in the public schools. This one, after two chapters on biblical interpretation, deals in detail with the interpretation of fifteen key books, passages, and characters in the Old and New Testaments.

1069 Gros Louis, Kenneth R.R., ed. *Literary Interpretations of Biblical Narratives*. Vol. 2. Nashville: Abingdon Press, 1982.

Designed for the guidance of public school teachers in the use of the Bible as literature, the bulk of this book consists of literary analyses of a variety of biblical passages, mostly from the Old Testament, but one from the Apocrypha and three from the New Testament. The first two chapters are critical approaches to the methods of literary analysis and to the troublesome pedagogical problems that come up in handling the Bible in a secular setting.

1070 Gross, Engelbert. *Religion als akutes Problem der Schule*. Kevelaer: Verlag Butzon & Berker, 1974.

> An inquiry into religious education and prayer in the school setting. Evaluates the claim for religious education in the school in terms of the questions of meaning, religion, and health. Analyzes the pros and cons of the relation of religious education to science, to the church, and to the school.

1071 Hauerwas, Stanley, and John H. Westerhoff, eds. *Schooling Christians: "Holy Experiments" in American Education*. Grand Rapids, MI: Wm. B. Eerdmans Publishing Company, 1992.

> The common school, higher education, and the school of the church are the focus of this collection of papers presented at a consultation on the schooling of Christians in modern liberal society. Authors wrestle with the implications of liberalism's assumptions about respect and tolerance of differences and include Nicholas Wolterstorff, Stanley Hauerwas, Michael Warren, Patricia Beattie Jung, and Jean Beth Elshtain.

1072 Hill, Brian. *Faith at the Blackboard: Issues Facing the Christian Teacher*. Grand Rapids, MI: William B. Eerdmans Publishing Company, 1982.

> A philosopher of education who has previously addressed himself to questions of religious education here gathers articles that deal with issues pertinent to the Christian teacher (in the secular or Christian school): de-schooling, curriculum orientation, teaching religion itself, the Christian school, community involvement, sharing one's faith in the classroom and elsewhere, and teaching style. An introduction provides an integrating context for thinking about such issues.

1073 Holm, Jean L. *Teaching Religion in School*. London: Oxford University Press, 1975.

> A very practical book on religious education in a pluralistic setting, growing out of the British experience. Taking Phenix's "realms of meaning" as the key, religious education's task is seen as synoptic. Thus it must be broadly informative (inclusive of the world's religions), religious (partaking of the nature of religious experience itself), and decisive (helping the learner to know what it means to take a particular religion seriously). Curriculum scope and sequence are developed, and sample units are provided.

1074 Hull, John M. "From Christian Nurture to Religious Education: The British Experience." *Religious Education* 73 (1978):124-43.

> Traces the movement in British religious education in the schools in which fostering of faith and explicit nurture in Christian discipleship are being abandoned in favor of a religious education that contributes to community life in a plural society, develops a critical understanding of religion, and enables

pupils to formulate their own personal philosophies and outlooks as a result of their encounter with the world religions.

1075 Hulmes, Edward. *Commitment and Neutrality in Religious Education*. London: Geoffrey Chapman, 1979.

When religious education is a function of the school, what is the place of the teacher's religious commitment, and what is to be done about religious commitment on the part of the learner? This book takes the British discussion a significant step forward by insisting that commitment is not only appropriate but essential in such religious education.

1076 Jendorff, Bernhard. *Religionspädagogik—aber wie?* Munich: Kösel-Verlag, 1992.

Tackles the emerging problem of religious education with students who have little or no background in religion and religious experience—no contact with the church, and no religious observances in the home. Practical suggestions are made as to the reorientation of religious education to this situation, ranging from curriculum and method to the training of teachers.

1077 Jordheim, Anne. "Religious Education in East Germany." *International Journal of Religious Education* 46, no. 10 (June 1967):12-13.

A largely positive study of the religious education situation in East Germany, done in 1967. The status of the church had been changed from state to private support, but the systems of religious education, from children to adults, remained largely functional, though carefully watched by the state. Christian music, literature, and art remained important elements in the culture, and in religious education as well. Concludes that the church through religious education infiltrated the lives of Christians in East Germany and, perhaps, the lives of many nominal or non-Christians as well.

1078 Juel, Donald, *et al. An Introduction to New Testament Literature*. Nashville: Abingdon Press, 1978.

A textbook for teachers of literature in the public schools, prepared as one of the publications of the Indiana University Institute on Teaching the Bible in English Classes. Historical and critical background are provided, and the traditions of the New Testament are carefully analyzed, with particular emphasis on their major themes. Concrete evidence that biblical scholars and educators can work together with integrity.

1079 Kathan, Boardman W. "Prayer and the Public Schools: The Issue in Historical Perspective and Implications for Religious Education Today." *Religious Education* 84 (1989):232-48.

> Recognizing the persistent issue of school prayer, Kathan provides a historical perspective. He offers six reasons for the persistence of this issue and traces its history through six periods, from the colonial period to the second half of the twentieth century and the Supreme Court decisions of the sixties. The conclusion offers three implications for religious education.

1080 Kienel, Paul A., ed. *The Philosophy of Christian School Education.* Whittier, CA: Association of Christian Schools, International, 1978.

> A forthright statement of a position on Christian education that rejects any secular influence in favor of a Bible-based educational theory. This is followed through in detail, with attention not only to its theological, philosophical, and historical explication, but also in terms of objectives, methods, and curriculum.

1081 Koob, C. Albert, and Russell Shaw. *S.O.S. for Catholic Schools.* New York: Holt, Rinehart and Winston, 1970.

> One of the most considered analyses available of the Catholic school system. After a description of the present situation, there are chapters dealing systematically with policy-making, control, finance, personnel, rationale, and the future outlook of the schools. The hope is in special services and educational innovation.

1082 Krause, Victor C., ed. *Lutheran Elementary Schools in Action.* St. Louis, MO: Concordia Publishing House, 1963.

> An official and detailed symposium describing policy and practice in the elementary schools conducted by the congregations of the Lutheran church (Missouri Synod). Indicates significant developments in the growth, acceptance, and professionalization of these schools, and at the same time (between the lines) inadequacies in educational and theological approaches. Topics covered include school purposes, personnel, and pupils; the school and its home, church, and community relations; school instruction and services; school facilities and finances; the school and its future. "In addition to direct instruction in religion, all content and skill subjects are given an integrated, Christian religious dimension."

1083 Lockerbie, D. Bruce. *The Way They Should Go.* New York: Oxford University Press, 1972.

> The story of the Stony Brook School on Long Island is used as the background for the consideration of the most fundamental questions in American education, together with the question of the definition, character, and conduct of a secondary school that claims to be Christian.

1084 Mayer, Rainer. *Von der Evangelischen Unterweisung
zurgesellschafts-politischen Ethik: Religionsunterricht an berufsbildenen Schulen.*
Stuttgart: Calwer Verlag, 1980.

> Religious education in German vocational schools presents somewhat different
> opportunities and problems from religious education in more academic settings.
> This book reviews the options that have been proposed and used since 1949:
> clarification of God's social orders (Müller), confrontation of social reality by
> the Word of God (Nordmann), an existential interpretation of reality (Otto),
> metaphysical inquiry as a method for the clarification of existence (Gloy), and
> the search for a social-political ethic (Lott).

1085 McCarthy, Rockne M., James W. Skillen, and William A. Harper.
Disestablishment a Second Time: Genuine Pluralism for American Schools. Grand
Rapids, MI: Christian University Press (William B. Eerdmans Publishing Company),
1982.

> Calls for a recognition that the nation is not so much a unity as a plurality, and
> that consequently parental (and corresponding "founding organizations and
> cooperating institutions") rather than bureaucratic governmental authority is
> called for in education. The argument is built historically, sociologically, and
> legally. Martin Marty provides a critical introduction. An interesting chapter
> deals with education in Europe's "consociational democracies."

1086 McLaren, Ian A. *Education in a Small Democracy: New Zealand.* London:
Routledge and Kegan Paul, 1974.

> In addition to a review of education in New Zealand, this book contains a
> chapter on church and state in education there, telling the story of the
> secular-religious tensions of the last century in the schools, particularly with
> regard to religious instruction, worship practices, and state aid to church
> schools.

1087 Mommsen, F.J. *Erziehung, Bildung, Religion.* Frankfurt: Verlag Moritz
Diesterweg, 1969.

> How far may religious education go in a state-supported system? The author
> examines the various positions of German theorists and finds the clue to his
> proposals in anthropology and its view of building a world of meaning.
> Specific recommendations are set forth for Protestant religious education in
> Germany.

1088 Neuwien, Reginald A., ed. *Catholic Schools in Action.* Notre Dame, IN:
University of Notre Dame Press, 1966.

> The report of a nationwide study of Roman Catholic elementary and secondary
> education (92% of all elementary schools cooperated, and 84% of all secondary
> schools; thirteen dioceses were also studied more intensively). Delves into
> enrollment, staffing and teacher preparation, outcomes in terms of religious

understandings and student attitudes and opinions, and parents' options. A model of objective educational and sociological research.

1089 Otto, Gert. *"Religion" contra "Ethik"?* Neukirchen-Vluyn: Neukirchener Verlag, 1986.

In a careful examination of alternatives proposed to deal with the problems inherent in religious education when it is a mandated subject in the schools, the author concludes that education in ethics best meets the problem.

1090 Phenix, Philip H. *Education and the Worship of God.* Philadelphia: Westminster Press, 1966.

A volume on the religious aspects of public education. "Its central thesis is that the concerns of faith are chiefly manifest in the regular subjects of study....Deals specifically with the religious perspectives implicit in the study of several of the standard academic disciplines": language, science, art, ethics, and history. Discusses the basic stance of the religious person in the secular school.

1091 Piediscalzi, Nicholas, and William E. Collie, eds. *Teaching About Religion in Public Schools.* Niles, IL: Argus Communications, 1977.

Outstanding practitioners of the teaching of religion in public schools have contributed their experience and wisdom to this symposium, centering on religious studies in two clusters: (1) The humanities and the fine arts, and (2) social studies. Five exemplary courses and units of study are included. The concluding chapter deals with religious studies in programs with values clarification and moral education.

1092 Power, F. Clark, and Daniel K. Lapsley, eds. *The Challenge of Pluralism, Education, Politics and Values.* Notre Dame, IN, and London: University of Notre Dame Press, 1992.

The volume contains ten papers which grew out of a symposium, "Moral Education in a Pluralist Society" held at Notre Dame. Writers include educators like Michael Apple ("Ideology, Equality, and the New Right") and Ann Diller ("What Happens When an Ethics of Care Faces Pluralism?"), and theologians like James W. Fowler ("Character, Conscience, and the Education of the Public") and Michael J. Himes ("Catholicism as Integral Humanism: Christian Participation in Pluralistic Moral Education").

1093 *Religious Information and Moral Development: The Report of the Committee on Religious Education in the Public Schools of the Province of Ontario.* Toronto: Ontario Department of Education, 1969.

The so-called Mackay Report, which recommended that the Ontario schools discontinue their traditional approach to religious education in favor of one that, while teaching about religion, stressed moral education—"the ideals, attitudes, and values derived from our heritage." The new approach to moral education, and the training of professionals to handle it, are developed in detail. See also 1102.

1094 Rossiter, Graham M. *Religious Education in Australian Schools.* Canberra, Australia: Curriculum Development Centre, 1981.

Described as "an overview of developments and issues in religious education in Australian schools with descriptions of practices in different school types," this large and informative volume is based on a vast survey of the Australian situation. It also contains a helpful section of "resource articles" that deal with religious education theory, foundations (including the role of aboriginal religion), the use of the Bible, moral education, values clarification, and faith development.

1095 Ryan, Mary Perkins. *Are Parochial Schools the Answer?* New York: Holt, Rinehart and Winston, 1963.

A Roman Catholic view of the parochial school issue. "The essential mission [is] to build up the body of Christ, to form hearers and doers of the Word, worshipers of the Father in Spirit and in truth." The author advocates a policy of disengagement from parochial schools, as diverting energies from this mission, and "increasing engagement in the work of providing religious formation for all Catholics" by other means.

1096 Sealey, John. *Religious Education: Philosophical Perspectives.* London: George Allen and Unwin, 1985.

Religious education in British schools is in the process of changing, due in part to attention to hitherto ignored segments of an increasingly pluralistic citizenry, and in part to questions of the very nature of religion itself. This serious, but modest, book is an attempt to understand these changes and the direction they are taking, using the disciplines of philosophy of education as the investigative instrument.

1097 Simon, Werner. *Inhaltsstrukturen des Religionsunterrichts.* Zürich: Benziger Verlag, 1983.

What constitutes the proper content of religious education in the schools? The question lies at the heart of the structure of religious teaching and learning. The author's exhaustive analysis leads him to conclude that the clue lies in the symbols of faith experience, the symbols that testify to the experience, that partake of it, and that enable new experience.

1098 Sjögren, John. "Religious Education in Sweden." *Religious Education* 58 (1963):298-301, 328.

Written in 1963, this article reports that "at present every Swedish child with few exceptions gets compulsory religious instruction in the public schools. To this knowledge is added the instruction given by the Christian churches and what can be acquired from reading Christian literature." But it also reports serious misgivings about the future of religious instruction.

1099 Smart, Ninian, and Donald Horder, eds. *New Movements in Religious Education*. London: Temple Smith Ltd., 1975.

A review and assessment of religion in British schools by a large panel of leaders of thought and practice in the field. Many of the chapters (the one on curriculum is a good example) are exceptionally informative, even though brief.

1100 Stearns, Harry L. "Shared Time, A Proposal for the Education of Children." *Religious Education* 57 (1962):5-36.

"Shared time" was a proposal that involved "a sharing of the school time of children between state supported schools, which provide general education in a denominationally neutral context, and church supported schools which proceed with a specific denominational religious emphasis." Here the superintendent of the Englewood, New Jersey, schools (a proponent of the plan) describes the proposal and how it worked. Appended are nineteen comments and reports from public educators, critics, and from an interfaith panel of religious educators.

1101 Stravinskas, Peter M. *Catholic Education: A New Dawn?* Canfield, OH: Alba House Communications, 1977.

An appreciative, careful, and scholarly defense of the parochial school, with specific suggestions for its improvement in such areas as supervision and organization.

1102 Sullivan, Edmund V. *Moral Learning*. New York: Paulist Press, 1975.

Based on Piaget and Kohlberg and reflecting the report of the Mackay Commission in Canada, this book reviews the theory and practice of moral education in the public schools (suggesting that it be explicit and inductive), subjects it to research, and recommends methods for elementary and secondary schools and for teacher education. See also 1093.

1103 Warshaw, Thayer S. *Handbook for Teaching the Bible in Literature Classes.*
Nashville: Abingdon Press, 1978.

>   Confronts the practical questions of what to teach about the Bible in secondary
>   school or college literature courses, and how to teach. From the Indiana
>   University Institute on Teaching the Bible in Literature Courses. Part 1 treats
>   classroom approaches and emphases in dealing with the Bible. Part 2 is a
>   fascinating compendium of problems of religious sensibilities and how to deal
>   with them. Parts 3-5 consist of teaching aids, study questions and quizzes, and
>   a glossary.

1104 Warshaw, Thayer S. *Religion, Education, and the Supreme Court.* Nashville:
Abingdon Press, 1979.

>   A straight, thorough account of the legal situation regarding religious education
>   in the schools of the United States. Annotates pertinent cases and contains
>   valuable reference materials.

1105 Weeren, Donald J. *Educating Religiously in the Multi-faith School.* Calgary,
Alberta: Detseling, 1986.

>   A Canadian view of the ways in which religion may be included in the school
>   curriculum. Based on practical experience, three suggestions are made: (1)
>   Include religion in the "secular" curriculum (the Bible as literature, the world's
>   religions in social studies); (2) design specific courses to further knowledge,
>   understanding, and tolerance of religious traditions (rather than to nurture,
>   impose, or indoctrinate); and (3) design observances to assist personal
>   meditation.

1106 Will, Paul J., ed. *Public Education Religion Studies: An Overview.* Chico, CA:
Scholars Press, 1981.

>   The research group most concerned with religion studies in the public school
>   here surveys the field "after more than a decade of unprecedented growth." A
>   theoretical work, a practical guide, and a resource volume all in one. The
>   legitimate motivation for religion studies in the schools is that "it is impossible
>   to conduct a complete study of world history, American history, literature, art,
>   music, and a host of other subjects without including a consideration of the
>   religious factors at work in these areas."

1107 Wilson, Douglas. *Recovering the Lost Tools of Learning: an Approach to
Distinctively Christian Education.* Wheaton, IL: Crossway Books, 1991.

>   A manifesto on behalf of a Christ-centered classical curriculum for the
>   Christian school. Taking his cue from Dorothy Sayers's essay, "The Lost
>   Tools of Learning," the author's proposal is that the curriculum be organized
>   around the medieval *trivium*—grammar, logic, and rhetoric, enriched by
>   mathematics, Bible, English, history, geography, science, and Latin. The
>   family has the basic responsibility, and the child is provided with the essential

tools for understanding and living in the culture basic to Western civilization. The book is based on the author's experience in designing and conducting such a school.

1108 Wood, James E., ed. *Religion, the State, and Education.* Waco, TX: Baylor University Press, 1984.

A reconsideration of the perennial issues in religion and the schools in America, published on the thirty-fifth anniversary of the McCollum (1940) decision on religious instruction in the public schools and the twentieth anniversary of the Schempp-Murray (1963) decision on prayer and Bible reading in the public schools. Consideration is given to public education, church schools, and religion in state universities. Especially valuable are the studies of experimental programs in Florida and in Minnesota.

1109 Young, Carl, ed. *The Identity of Christian Schools in Melanesia.* Port Moresby, Papua: The United Church, 1974.

Mainly a report of a gathering on the future of Christian education in Papua New Guinea, when the question of the kind and degree of participation by the churches in general education was yet to be decided. Substantive material is provided in transcripts of lectures by Theo Mathias, the Indian Jesuit educator, who spoke with critical balance from a Third World perspective. Interesting guides for independent and group study of the situation are provided.

Religion and Higher Education

1110 Averill, Lloyd J., and William W. Jellema, eds. *Colleges and Commitments*. Philadelphia: Westminster Press, 1971.

> A series of "frankly partisan pieces" supporting the position that "value commitments are integral, indispensable, and indeed inescapable, in higher education, and most particularly within the tradition of the liberal arts and sciences." The articles have been collected from such persons as Kenneth Kenniston, Huston Smith, Albert C. Outler, William G. Pollard, Michael Novak, Will Herberg, and Waldo Beach.

1111 Betz, Hans Dieter, ed. *The Bible as a Document for the University*. Chico, CA: Scholars Press, 1981.

> "The function of the Bible in the university seems to be two-fold. First, the Bible is recognized as a piece of world literature with a wide range of references to many disciplines. Second, the Bible is recognized sociologically as the holy scripture of living religious communities and traditions which exercise great influence in the contemporary society." Gerhard Ebeling addresses himself to the first, James Barr to the second, and Paul Ricoeur to "The Bible and the Imagination."

1112 Cantelon, John E. *A Protestant Approach to the Campus Ministry*. Philadelphia: Westminster Press, 1964.

> "The trend has been away from conservation of the church's youth in a nurture experience toward involving them in a responsible witness in the university seen as a microcosm of the culture. [The ministry] is directed to the university's principal academic task. The stress is placed upon responsible studentship. The Christian in the university is called upon to learn to love God with the mind."

1113 Carpenter, Joel A., and Kenneth S. Shipps, eds. *Making Higher Education Christian: The History and Mission of Evangelical Colleges in America*. Grand Rapids, MI: William B. Eerdmans Publishing Company, 1987.

A clear-headed look at the variety of types of higher education that go under the name "evangelical." Seven interesting and informative chapters trace the history of the movement (and its predecessors). Curricular and social challenges are analyzed in a section called "Refining the Vision." Finally, under the heading, "Advancing the Mission," needed emphases are put forward, including those of an inclusive curriculum and attention to minorities.

1114 Chamberlin, J. Gordon. *Churches and the Campus*. Philadelphia: Westminster Press, 1963.

A contribution to the phenomenology and the theory of religion in American higher education. In part 1 the author reports his visits to five representative campuses where he interviewed students, administrators, faculty, pastors, and laity. He found little active relationship between the church and higher education and little articulate understanding of what the relationship might be. "The Christian church and the modern college have little need of each other." Part 2 suggests that the parish church help students, teachers, and administrators see their vocations in Christian terms; that it perform the analytical, constructive, illuminative, and integrative functions of theology; and that it engage in a personal pastoral ministry to the college community.

1115 *Christian Liberal Arts Education: Report of the Calvin College Curriculum Study Committee*. Grand Rapids, MI: William B. Eerdmans Publishing Company, 1970.

A study by the faculty of Calvin College, Grand Rapids, this volume goes into the history and nature of Christian education before exploring three approaches to Christian liberal arts education: pragmatist, classicist, and disciplinary. Opting for the last, the report presents a curriculum plan, candidly acknowledging that it has been somewhat modified in light of subsequent experience.

1116 De Jong, Arthur J. *Reclaiming a Mission: New Direction for the Church-Related College*. Grand Rapids: Wm. B. Eerdmans Publishing Company, 1990.

This treatise by a Christian college president begins with an analysis of post-World War II American society, mainline Protestantism, and higher education and then turns to the place of Christian tenets in the church-related college, the postmodern paradigm in science, and the influence of secularism in modern American culture. Arguing that church-related colleges need to redefine their mission every ten years, De Jong argues for a new mission based on an integrative and holistic approach to faith and learning.

1117 Farley, Edward. *The Fragility of Knowledge: Theological Education in the Church and the University*. Philadelphia: Fortress Press, 1988.

> Farley argues that church education should be theological education. The concept of "ordered learning" is central to his argument. Ordered learning refers to learning that is cumulative, sequential, disciplined, and rigorous, in contrast to the random, psychologically oriented Bible study Farley finds passing for Christian education in many churches.

1118 Gribbon, R.T. *Students, Churches, and Higher Education: Congregational Ministry in a Learning Society*. Valley Forge, PA: Judson Press, 1981.

> Tackles the difficult question of the ministry of the local congregation to college students, but not just those in the traditional residential college. The challenge is to deal with both young and older students in the community college and in nearby commuter colleges. All phases of the problem, and many possibilities, are dealt with, including partnership in mission and with campus ministries.

1119 Hall, Charles A.M. *The Common Quest*. Philadelphia: Westminster Press, 1965.

> A serious attempt to relate theology and the academic disciplines in "a common quest." Theology is seen as having functions as a convictional discipline correlating with the functions of the sciences, the social studies, and the arts. What is proposed is "an internal dialogue of theology about its own convictions in academic language and in Academy....This dialogue may, in the process of internal unfolding, assume external dimensions as well."

1120 Hammond, Phillip E. *The Campus Clergyman*. New York: Basic Books, 1966.

> A sociological investigation of the campus ministry (based on a questionnaire study of the entire profession), highlighting its social structural patterns and occasioned by its "nascent and immature form" as an institution after half a century. (The campus ministry is ambiguously defined, lacks professionalization, has high personnel turnover, etc.) Professionalization, the author finds, is impeded by lack of shared expectations (the style of ministry) and lack of shared commitment (career expectations). Self-organization on an ecumenical basis is advocated.

1121 Hassenger, Robert, ed. *The Shape of Catholic Higher Education*. Chicago: University of Chicago Press, 1967.

> A group of young teachers in Catholic colleges provides a straightforward study of the situation in Catholic higher education in America, with an emphasis on gathering and interpreting existing research on the subject. Includes case studies, assessment of educational results, the existence and handling of controversy, and future perspectives. The major contribution of the book is to explain the situation forthrightly and comprehensively. A

valuable by-product will be to influence the direction of future research and study.

1122 Heie, Harold, and David L. Wolfe, eds. *The Reality of Christian Learning: Strategies for Faith-Discipline Integration*. Grand Rapids, MI: Christian University Press, 1987.

Noted scholars in Christian higher education examine the way the Christian faith deals with, and is dealt with by, the major areas of knowledge (the humanities, the social sciences, the natural sciences, and mathematics), to the end of clarifying the role of religion in Christian higher education. Various general approaches are suggested: dealing with presuppositions of the disciplines, their value commitments, and the ways in which they are systematized.

1123 Hessel, David J. *City of Wisdom: A Christian Vision of the American University*. Chicago: Loyola University Press, 1983.

A global yet personal treatment of the relationships of church, faith, and education at the university level. It is global in seeking to deal with all the problems of the university's orientation and task, and personal in seeing the guidance of philosophy and theology caught up in a "vision" like Teilhard's. Down to earth in handling the question of the university and its "religious founding groups."

1124 Holbrook, Clyde A. *Religion, A Humanistic Field*. Englewood Cliffs, NJ: Prentice-Hall, 1963.

A discussion of the function and structure of the study of religion in the college (and in the seminary). The book is a history, survey, phenomenology, and evaluation of the study of religion at the college and university level. Pains are taken to show the legitimacy of religion as a field in the humanities and its harmony with all but the extreme theologies of "religionless Christianity." Helpful discussions of curricular and administrative problems, together with emphasis on the furtherance of scholarship.

1125 Holmes, Arthur F. *The Idea of a Christian College*. Grand Rapids, MI: William B. Eerdmans Publishing Company, 1987.

A revision of the book first published in 1975. A thought-provoking treatment of liberal arts education in Christian perspective. Differentiates between integration, interaction, and disjunction of faith and learning, searching for possibilities of integration and candidly admitting that interaction is more likely to be the situation. Interesting chapters on academic freedom, the college as a community, and the uses of Christian liberal arts education. There are two new chapters on "the liberal arts as career preparation" and "the marks of an educated person."

1126 Holmes, Arthur F. *Shaping Character: Moral Education in the Christian College*. Grand Rapids, MI: Wm. B. Eerdmans Publishing Company, 1991.

Holmes decries the view which relegates ethics to a course in the philosophy department and calls for a broader appreciation for the important integrating role of ethics across the college curriculum. He recalls the 19th century tradition in which the college president taught an integrative moral philosophy course designed to shape students' social consciences. Arguing that ethics is everyone's business, Holmes offers eleven objectives for moral education in the Christian college. See also 1136.

1127 Hough, Joseph C. Jr., and Barbara G. Wheeler, eds. *Beyond Clericalism: The Congregation as a Focus for Theological Education*. Atlanta: Scholars Press, 1988.

Responding to James Hopewell's work, essays in part 1 by David Kelsey, John B. Cobb, Jr., Letty Russell, and Marjorie Hewitt Suchocki examine the congregational paradigm for theological education. In part 2, Jane Dempsey Douglass, Carl Holladay, E. Brooks Holifield, Don Browning, Stanley Hauerwas, and Beverly Harrison explore the implications of the congregational paradigm for historical and practical studies.

1128 Kelsey, David H. *To Understand God Truly: What's Theological About a Theological School*. Louisville, KY: Westminster/John Knox Press, 1992.

Shifts the discussion from theological education to the theological school. Notes the place of theological schools in the overall scheme of higher education, likening them to crossroads hamlets. Subjects, understandings, and communities are used to help reframe the discussion. Charts key aspects of theological schools in part 1 and offers a proposal for reforming theological schooling in part 2.

1129 Marsden, George M., and Bradley J. Longfield, eds. *The Secularization of the Academy*. New York: Oxford University Press, 1992.

While British and Canadian higher education is the subject of two chapters, the majority of the chapters are written from the perspective of American higher education, primarily in relation to Protestantism. Marsden provides a historical overview in the first chapter. Longfield writes about midwestern public universities in relation to evangelicalism and liberalism and about religion at Yale between the world wars. Other contributors include James Turner, Robert Wood Lynn, D. G. Hart, and Philip Gleason. The collection of essays in this volume offer insights into the dynamic of secularization in higher education.

1130 McBee, Mary Louise, ed. *Rethinking College Responsibilities for Values*. San Francisco: Jossey-Bass Publishers, 1980.

> A variety of essays move into the neglected and confused area of education in values and morality in college in an unusually insightful way. While a relativistic approach is still dominant, there is evidence of a growing concern for normativity and for institutional responsibility for moral education.

1131 McCluskey, Neil G., ed. *The Catholic University: A Modern Appraisal*. Notre Dame, IN: University of Notre Dame Press, 1970.

> Thoughtful and informed essays describing and evaluating the state of Catholic higher education. Among the contributors: Hesburgh, Schillebeeckx, Shuster, Walsh, Reinert, and Ellis. The chapter, "The University and Christian Formation," is particularly stimulating.

1132 Meyer, John R. "Religious Studies and Canadian Universities." *Religious Education* 66 (1971):274-79.

> A descriptive analysis of the study of religion in Canadian institutions of higher learning, as of 1971. Characterizes the situation as mature and integral to the university system. Recommends that: (1) at the undergraduate level religion be studied as it pervades the various disciplines, and at the same time as a subject in which one may major; (2) graduate study of religion be more specific as to vocational objectives; (3) the study of religion be given more public exposure; and (4) attention be given to the question of confessionalism and the discipline.

1133 Moore, Leila V. and M. Lee Upcraft. "Theory in Student Affairs: Evolving Perspectives." *Evolving Theoretical Perspectives on Students*. New Directions for Student Services 51 (Fall 1990):3-23.

> Among the current general and specialized theories of student development reviewed in this article is spiritual development, which devotes outlines to Fowler's familiar six stages. See also 312.

1134 Moots, Philip R., and Edward McGlynn Gaffney, Jr. *Church and Campus: Legal Issues in Religiously Affiliated Higher Education*. Notre Dame, IN: University of Notre Dame Press, 1979.

> A study of legal issues that arise when higher education is connected with religious bodies: church, state and education, legal liability of the religious body, employment policies, academic freedom, religious preference in student admissions, disciplinary codes, use of public funds, and ownership of property. A major resource book.

1135 Mundahl, Anne, and Tom Mundahl, eds. *Vision and Revision: Old Roots and New Routes for Lutheran Higher Education.* Minneapolis: The American Lutheran Church, 1977.

> Occasional articles by scholars of the American Lutheran church on Christian higher education, focusing on the Lutheran situation. Explores "old roots" (the biblical and prophetic visions, a theological agenda, vocation and higher education, and the ecology of faith) and miscellaneous "new routes," among them the learning community, the pedagogy of church leadership, Asian feminine perspectives, and Native American perspectives.

1136 Neuhaus, Richard John, ed. *Theological Education and Moral Formation.* Encounter Series, no. 15. Grand Rapids: Wm. B. Eerdmans Publishing Company, 1992.

> Historical and contemporary perspectives on moral formation in theological education by Dennis Campbell (a survey of theological and moral education in seminaries today), Rowan Greer (a look at ordained ministry in the fourth century), E. Brooks Holifield (a survey of moral formation in American Protestant seminaries from 1808 to 1934), John O'Malley, (past and present Roman Catholic traditions of spiritual formation for ministry), and Merle D. Strege (a survey of 1980s efforts to reform theological education). See also 1126.

1137 Novak, Michael. *Ascent of the Mountain, Flight of the Dove.* New York: Harper and Row, 1971.

> A profoundly useful introduction to "religious studies," interpreting them as involved with our ultimate drives in relation to the transcendent, to the self, to our communities, to nature, and to history, a "conversion of one's experience of life," and the articulation of that conversion. The traditional areas of religious studies are easy to discern here, but they are given a new coherence and perspective by being treated integrally and existentially.

1138 Palmer, Parker J., Barbara J. Wheeler, and James W. Fowler. *Caring for the Commonweal: Education for the Religious and Public Life.* Macon, GA: Mercer University Press, 1990.

> This volume of essays honors Robert W. Lynn. Essays are grouped under four headings: "Paideia for Public Life," "Paideia for Religious Education," "Paideia for Higher Education," and "Paideia and Profession." Robert Handy, Sara Little, Robin Lovin, Henri Nouwen, James Fowler, Parker Palmer, and Edward Farley are among the contributors.

1139 Parsonage, Robert Rue, ed. *Church Related Higher Education.* Valley Forge, PA: Judson Press, 1978.

> Anyone grappling with the problem of the role and future of the church college will find that this volume provides essential guidance. Policies and practices are carefully reviewed, categorized, and assessed, with guidelines for study and action. The historical background is also provided.

1140 Pattillo, Manning M., Jr., and Donald M. Mackenzie. *Church-sponsored Higher Education in the United States.* Washington, DC: American Council on Education, 1966.

> The plight and potential of the church-sponsored college and university (Protestant, Catholic, and Jewish) in the United States are discussed with utter realism and candor, based upon a thorough study sponsored by the Danforth Foundation. Basic problems: theological uncertainty, lack of coordinated planning, size (most are too small to provide educational variety), and quality (of 817, only fifty could be rated as of high quality). Imaginative recommendations follow.

1141 Pelikan, Jaroslav. *The Christian Intellectual.* New York: Harper and Row, 1965.

> A free-ranging examination of the meaning of Christian scholarship, religious research, and religious studies in relation to the liberal arts and sciences, with critical and constructive suggestions for the university curriculum, both at the undergraduate and graduate levels, and for theological education.

1142 Ramsey, Paul, and John F. Wilson, eds. *The Study of Religion in Colleges and Universities.* Princeton, NJ: Princeton University Press, 1970.

> The vigorous study of religion at the college and university level is a fairly recent American phenomenon. With interpretative commentary to introduce and conclude the volume, the following fields are treated: biblical studies, history, philosophy of religion, theology, Catholic and Jewish studies, sociology of religion, ethics, history of religions, and religious art and literature.

1143 Rankin, Robert, ed. *The Recovery of Spirit in Higher Education.* New York: Seabury Press, 1980.

> An assessment and projection of the future ingredients of religion in higher education. This is both a tribute to and an outgrowth of the work of Robert Rankin, longtime member of the staff of the Danforth Foundation. Searching for the full range of inquiry and at the same time for balance, David Hubbard analyzes the ingredient of spirit; Parker Palmer, contemplation and action; and Martin Bloy, ministry. Each element is commented on from Roman Catholic, Jewish, evangelical Protestant, and liberal Protestant perspectives.

1144 Ringenberg, William C. *The Christian College: A History of Protestant Higher Education in America*. Grand Rapids, MI: William B. Eerdmans Publishing Company, 1984.

> A full and candid study of the development of the American church college from earliest times. Stress is on the increasing secularization of the schools, and the response in the growth of evangelical schools. Very useful sections on the Bible college as part of the response. Criteria for future developments are carefully assessed.

1145 Schall, James V. *Another Sort of Learning*. Harrison, NY: Ignatius Press, 1988.

> Concerned with the situation in colleges and universities where the ultimate questions of religion and religious experience are neglected (a situation that exists in the best of schools), the author suggests methods and materials for self-education "when ultimate questions remain perplexing." Notable for its book reviews and reading lists.

1146 Schrotenboer, Paul G., ed. "The Church and Higher Education." *Theological Forum* 20, no. 4 (December, 1992).

> This issue of the publication of the Reformed Ecumenical Council Commission for Theological Education and Interchange focuses on the church and higher education. Includes both historical perspectives (from the early Christian era through the Reformation) and regional reports (the Netherlands, Indonesia, Asia, South Africa, Australia, and the USA).

1147 Shook, Lawrence K. *Catholic Post-secondary Education in English-speaking Canada*. Toronto: University of Toronto Press, 1971.

> An exhaustive historical and evaluative study, school by school, of the Roman Catholic colleges and universities in Canada, excluding those that are predominantly French-speaking. Candidly assesses the critical financial situation and the likelihood that radical readjustment will be necessary.

1148 Solberg, Richard W. *Lutheran Higher Education in North America*. Minneapolis: Augsburg Publishing House, 1985.

> A history of Christian higher education under Lutheran auspices. Lutherans have seen higher education as a means of determining and preparing for Christian vocations, thus providing leaders for both church and society. At the same time they have affirmed the centrality of humane values and a curriculum strong in religion, literature, history, and the arts.

1149 Wheeler, Barbara G., and Edward Farley. *Shifting Boundaries: Contextual Approaches to the Structure of Theological Education.* Louisville, KY: Westminster/John Knox Press, 1991.

> Essays examine the basic shifts that have affected the existing pattern or structure of theological education and its presuppositions.   A new conception of the practice of ministry, the prophetic challenge of feminism, the recognition of difference, and the need to overcome alienation are among the themes presented. Contributors include Don S. Browning, Rebecca S. Chopp, John B. Cobb, Jr., Craig Dykstra, and Francis Schüssler Fiorenza.

Reference Works

1150 Adam, Gottfried, and Rainer Lachmann, eds. *Gemeindepädagogisches Kompendium*. Göttingen: Vanderhoeck und Ruprecht, 1987.

In contrast to most German works in religious education, this handbook deals with the concerns of education and nurture in the congregation. The first part deals with urgent questions of a fundamental nature: What is church education? Church education in East Germany. Catholic catechetics. Ecumenical impact. "Guest workers" and church education. The relationship of life stages and religious development. The second part suggests approaches to religious education in the family, the kindergarten, worship, confirmation education, church youth work, adult education, and work with the elderly.

1151 Adelson, Joseph, ed. *Handbook of Adolescent Psychology*. New York: John Wiley and Sons, 1980.

When the religious educator dealing with the question of youth wants to go beyond popular treatments and surveys of the psychology of adolescents, this handbook serves well. It summarizes research and theory on key questions of concern to those dealing with youth, written by the most informed persons in the field. Makes reference back to the research studies themselves easy.

1152 Astley, Jeff, and Leslie Francis, eds. *Christian Perspectives on Faith Development: A Reader*. Herefordshire, England: Gracewing Fowler Wright Books and Grand Rapids, MI: William B. Eerdmans Publishing Company, 1992.

This basic collection of readings on faith development consists of twenty-eight selections from a variety of previously published sources. The readings are organized into eight categories including evaluation of Fowler's work, theology and faith development, philosophy and faith development, pastoral care and faith development, and Christian education and faith development. See also 312, 357, 372, 374, 621, and 877.

1153 Benner, David G., ed. *Baker Encyclopedia of Psychology*. Grand Rapids, MI: Baker Book House, 1985.

> An enormous volume, heavy on psychopathology and therapy. Religious education concerns are represented in articles on Christian growth, culture and cognition, educational psychology, values clarification, and the like. Intersections of psychology and religious education are seen in articles on Coe, Dewey, Kohlberg, Piaget, and others. Religious educators (e.g., Joy and Plueddemann) are among the contributors.

1154 Berelson, Bernard, and Gary A. Steiner. *Human Behavior: An Inventory of Scientific Findings*. New York: Harcourt, Brace and World, 1964.

> A compendium of the social sciences, summarizing their findings and suggesting key sources and readings. May serve as an "organizer" for the fields basic to education.

1155 Bitter, Gottfried, and Gabriele Miller, eds. *Handbuch Religionspädagogischer Grundbegriffe*. Munich: Kösel-Verlag, 1986.

> German handbooks of religious education present detailed overviews of the subject. This two-volume work, with many contributors, concentrates on matters of theory. It canvasses the partners involved, learning processes, places, types, areas, themes, theories per se, methodological concepts, foundations, and basic theological concepts. Thus, it provides the grounds and resources for productive theorizing in the field.

1156 Cully, Iris V., and Kendig Brubaker Cully, eds. *Harper's Encyclopedia of Religious Education*. San Francisco: Harper and Row, 1990.

> Over 600 entries, ranging from "Adult Development and Family Life Education" to "Narrative Theology and Vacation Church School" and contributed by 270 scholars and religious educators, make this an essential reference for religious educators.

1157 Cully, Kendig B., ed. *The Westminster Dictionary of Christian Education*. Philadelphia: Westminster Press, 1963.

> Alphabetically arranged articles provide wide coverage of appropriate theological concepts, important persons, the international scene, the denominational and interdenominational picture, and theoretical, curricular, methodological, and administrative concerns. Over 800 pages, about 400 contributors, and a bibliography of 1,277 items!

1158 Feifel, Erich, Robert Leuenberger, Günter Stachel, and Klaus Wegenast. *Handbuch der Religionspädagogik*. Gütersloh: Gütersloher Verlagshaus Gerd Mohn, 1973, 1974, 1975.

Volume 1 deals with the basic orientation of religious education, the theory of religious education and enculturation, the individual and the sociological context, and the theory of religious instruction. Volume 2 is in two parts. The first is an exhaustive analysis of the theoretical bases for curriculum, objectives, content, textbooks, lesson planning, methods, the media, and grading, together with sections on social psychology and models. The second is a systematic review of the scientific sources for religious education theory and practice, scientific being broadly interpreted to comprehend the theological and behavioral disciplines. Volume 3 has treatments of faith and education as the task of the church, education in the sacraments and in spirituality, the various areas of the church's responsibility for education (elementary, free Christian schools, training schools, youth work, and adult education), and religious education of persons with special needs (the institutionalized, those with learning problems, and those treated through social work).

1159 Foshay, Arthur W., ed. *The Rand McNally Handbook of Education*. Chicago: Rand McNally, 1963.

Comprehensive analyses of the principal facts and trends in American education, supplemented by comparative data on education in England, France, and the U.S.S.R. Deals with organization and administration at federal, state, and local levels, and with curriculum (ways of organizing curriculum, the subject fields, instructional materials, supporting services and programs, and major proposals for change).

1160 Gangel, Kenneth O., and James C. Wilhoit, eds. *The Christian Educator's Handbook on Adult Education*. Wheaton: Victor Books/SP Publications, 1993.

A comprehensive handbook from an evangelical perspective. Twenty-four essays cover topics ranging from biblical and theological foundations to gender differences and ethnic minority communities. Warren Benson, Catherine Stonehouse, and Robert Pazmiño are among the contributors to this second volume in Scripture Press's The Christian Educator's Handbook Series. What distinguishes this book is the careful attention given to the adult education literature by evangelical religious education practitioners and scholars.

1161 Houle, Cyril O. *The Literature of Adult Education: A Bibliographic Essay*. San Francisco: Jossey-Bass Publishers, 1992.

Covering more than 1,200 books, this monumental work seeks to present a comprehensive view of the adult education literature. Chapters are organized around the history of the field and its literature (part 1), the institutions or providers and goals of adult education (part 2), and the practice of adult education (part 3). What the book may lack by being the product of one writer, it makes up for by Houle's immersion in the field and its literature over the course of a long and distinguished career as an adult educator.

1162 Lee, James Michael, ed. *Handbook of Faith*. Birmingham, AL: Religious Education Press, 1990.

Historical, religious, philosophical, and psychological foundations of the concept of faith are presented in part 1. Roman Catholic and Protestant scholars examine biblical and theological perspectives on faith in part 2, while in part 3 contributors focus on facilitating growth in faith through liturgy, social ministry, pastoral counseling, spiritual direction, and religious instruction.

1163 Merriam, Sharan B. and Rosemary S. Caffarella. *Learning in Adulthood*. San Francisco: Jossey-Bass Publishers, 1991.

Provides a convenient synthesis of current thinking and research on the context and environment of adult learning, the adult learner, the learning process, theory, and challenges. Written from a sociocultural perspective, the book offers a much needed counterbalance to the individualism of dominant psychological approaches.

1164 Ratcliff, Donald ed. *Handbook of Children's Religious Education*. Birmingham, AL: Religious Education Press, 1992.

Topics in this handbook include: age-level characteristics, faith development, religious concepts, social contexts, spiritual growth, general and specific teaching procedures, assessment, placement, and evaluation. The book is one of a series of age-level handbooks published by Religious Education Press (770, 1165, 1166).

1165 Ratcliff, Donald ed. *Handbook of Preschool Religious Education*. Birmingham, AL: Religious Education Press, 1988.

Preschoolers' cognitive, physical, linguistic, social, emotional, religious, and moral development are the focus of the first two parts of this handbook. Charlotte Wallinga, Patsy Skeen, Claity P. Massey, Romney Moseley, and Mary Anne Fowlkes are among the contributors to the parts dealing with characteristics and religious development of preschoolers. James Michael Lee and Donald Ratcliff contribute to the third part, which focuses on the processes and procedures of preschool religious education.

1166 Ratcliff, Donald, and James A. Davies, eds. *Handbook of Youth Ministry*. Birmingham, AL: R.E.P. Books, 1991.

This handbook is distinguished by its emphasis on research. Adolescent religion, moral development and sexuality, communication and relationships, thinking and understanding, religious education procedures, and needs analysis and research are among the topics covered by the contributors.

1167 Ratcliff, Donald, and Blake J. Neff. *The Complete Guide to Religious Education Volunteers*. Birmingham, AL: Religious Education Press, 1993.

> Planning, recruiting, supervision and training, administering, and evaluating religious education volunteers are among the themes of this book. In addition to the primary contributions of the authors, Harold William Burgess contributes a chapter entitled, "What Is a Volunteer?" and James Michael Lee writes a chapter on the special character of religious education volunteers. Especially helpful are addresses and resources listed in the appendix. See also 792, 854, and 956.

1168 Sapp, Gary L., ed. *Handbook of Moral Development*. Birmingham, AL: Religious Education Press, 1973.

> As a handbook, this volume is inclusive and comprehensive of the variety of theories, research efforts, processes (cognitive, affective, and life-style), and methodological approaches to fostering moral development. It is held together by a "quest dimension," a concept that accepts and uses complexity, self-criticism, tentativeness, contradiction, and tragedy in the search for direction. See also 482, 583, 599, 682, 692, 1093, 1102, 1126, and 1136.

1169 Strommen, Merton P., ed. *Research on Religious Development: A Comprehensive Handbook*. New York: Hawthorn Books, 1971.

> A massive compendium of research on various aspects of religious development, a project of the Religious Education Association. Summaries by twenty-six authorities in their specialized areas of the behavioral sciences and religion. The twenty-two essays are organized in six categories: religion and research; personal and religious factors in religious development; religion, personality, and psychological health; dimensions of religious development (beliefs, experiences, practices, motivation, and religious behavior); religious development by age grouping; research in religious education. Exhaustive bibliographies are appended to the chapters. See also 334, 341, and 717.

Name Index

(Numbers refer to bibliographical entries in which name appears.)

Abbagnano, Nicola 166
Abelard 209
Ackerman, James S. 1052,
      1053, 1055, 1068
Adam, Gottfried 1150
Adams, Carol Markstrom 284
Adams, Doug 859
Adams, Douglas E. 860
Adamson, William R. 1
Adelson, Joseph 1151
Aden, LeRoy 391
Adesina, Segun 1054
Adler, Mortimer J. 529
Affolderbach, Martin 203
Agnew, Marie 861
Akenson, Donald H. 204
Aleshire, Daniel 621, 862
Alfred the Great 209
Allen, Dwight 745
Allport, Gordon W. 392
Allstrom, Elizabeth 863
Amalorpavadass, D.S. 585
Amos, Pamela T. 393
Anderson, Andy 746
Anderson, Ray S. 2
Anderson, Robert H. 778
Ankoviak, Mary Ann 136
Anthony, Michael J. 586
Apostolos-Cappadona, Diane
      859, 864
Apple, Michael 556, 1092
Apps, Jerold W. 865
Aquinas, Thomas 209
Archibald, Helen 866

Argyle, Michael 285
Argyris, Chris 747
Aritonang, Jan S. 205
Arn, Charles 748
Arn, Win 748
Arnold, Eberhard 587
Asbury, Giles 938
Ashbrook, James B. 477
Astley, Jeff 1152
Aubert, April 301
Augustine 209, 294
Austin, Gilbert R. 394
Ausubel, David P. 395, 551,
      567
Averill, Lloyd J. 1110
Azad 187
Azrak, John 824

Babbitt, Lewis 546
Babin, Pierre 588, 867
Bailey, Joyce H.E. 1018
Baillie, John 3
Banks, James A. 530, 868
Bannerman, Glenn 869
Bar-Tal, Daniel 396, 397
Barber, Lucie 877
Barden, Garrett 4
Barr, David L. 206
Barr, James 1111
Barreirro, Alvaro 870
Barrett, Lois 749
Barrow, Robin 531
Bartel, Leo 765
Bartel, Roland 1055

Gerts, Wolfgang 806
Getz, Gene A. 38, 387, 389,
            925, 1051
Gielen, Uwe 504
Gilbert, W. Kent 491, 632
Gillespie, V. Bailey 317, 318
Gilligan, Carol 311, 427
Gillispie, Philip H. 926
Giltner, Fern M. 633
Ginglend, David R. 887
Glasser, William 551
Gleason, John J., Jr. 319
Gleason, Philip 1129
Glen, J. Stanley 634
Glickman, Carl D. 777
Glock, Charles Y. 371, 428
Gloy 1084
Gmünder, Paul 356
Gobbel, A. Roger 927-29
Gobbel, Gertrude G. 927, 928
Godin, André 320, 321, 605
Goldhammer, Robert 778
Goldman, Ronald 322, 336,
            345, 498, 605,
            655, 873, 927,
            1067
Goleman, Daniel 323
Goodenough, Erwin R. 39
Goodenough, Evelyn W. 39
Goodman, Paul 531, 560
Goodwin, Carole 930
Goodykoontz, Harry G. 492
Gorsuch, Richard L. 369
Gould, Joseph E. 230
Gould, Roger L. 975
Grabner-Haider, Anton 153
Grad, Eli 931
Graendorf, Werner C. 635
Grams, Armin 324
Grassi, Joseph A. 231
Graveline, Roger 301
Greeley, Andrew M. 308,
            325-27, 493,
            1058
Green, Thomas F. 154
Greenberg, Elinor Miller 478
Greene, Ella 1039
Greene, Maxine 975

Greenleaf, Robert K. 779
Greer, Rowan 1136
Gresham, Charles 610
Gress, James R. 932
Gribble, James 155
Gribbon, R.T. 1118
Grierson, Denham 636
Grimes, Howard 40, 261
Groff, Roberta L. 1023
Grom, Bernhard 328, 329
Groome, Thomas H. 19, 41,
            85, 97, 637, 638,
            1028
Gros, Louis 1068, 1069
Gross, Engelbert 1070
Gruber, Frederick C. 156
Guardini, Romano 190, 197,
            198
Guerin, Marisa 773, 819
Gutierrez, Gustavo 694
Guzie, Tad 1028

Habermas, Ronald 639, 933
Hafner, Dudley 765
Hageman, Alice L. 494
Haillie, Philip 618
Halbfas, Hubertus 199, 640
Hall, Brian P. 330
Hall, Charles A.M. 1119
Hall, G. Stanley 366
Hamilton, Neill Q. 42
Hammet, Edward H. 934
Hammond, Phillip E. 1120
Handy, Robert 1138
Hanisch, Helmut 780
Hardt, A. 935
Hardy, Alister 331
Hargrove, Barbara 936
Häring, Bernard 43
Harkness, Georgia 44, 45
Harmin, Merrill 571
Harper, F. Nile 238, 641
Harper, Norman E. 157
Harper, William A. 1085
Harper, William Rainey 230
Harrell, John 937, 938
Harrell, Mary 938
Harrell, Steven 393

Subject Index

(Numbers refer to pages on which subjects appear.)

292

doctrine, 14;
ethics, 7, 9, 10,
14, 24, 27;
feminist, 14;
liberation, 7, 9,
14, 19; narrative,
7; new, 7;
practical, 8, 14;
process, 7, 9, 19;
spirituality, 8, 14,
17, 22, 23;
systematic, 14
Training 6, 8, 11, 15, 16, 20,
25
Transcendence 7
Transformation 8, 15

Unconscious 15
Union College Character Research
Project 23

Union Theological Seminary 11
United Church of Christ 18, 23
University 24-26

Values 3, 5, 11, 17, 19, 24, 25
Vision 8, 15
Volunteer/s 20-22, 26

Waldorf Schools 17
Wisdom 17, 21
Women 9, 13, 15, 19, 22
World hunger 23
World religions 23
Worship 7, 14, 22, 23

Youth 4, 12-14, 21-23
culture, 22;
ministry, 13, 21,
22;
Indo-Hispanic,
14; troubled, 22

Title Index

(Numbers refer to bibliographical entries in which titles appear.)

318

Religious Education